Liam Ryan Studied Law at St Aidan's College, Durham University and completed a LLM at Nottingham University specialising in Commercial law, Criminal law and Human Rights. He was called to the bar in 2007 and is a member of Inner Temple.

Liam has a civil practice specialising complex and high value personal injury actions. He has a noted and recognised specialism in both stress at work and psychiatric injury claims.

A Practical Guide to Psychiatric Claims in Personal Injury

Third Edition

A Practical Guide to Psychiatric Claims in Personal Injury

Third Edition

Liam Ryan

LLB (Dunelm), LLM (Nottingham)

Barrister at Law, 7BR

Law Brief Publishing

Published 2024 by Law Brief Publishing, an imprint of Law Brief Publishing Ltd
30 The Parks
Minehead
Somerset
TA24 8BT

www.lawbriefpublishing.com

Paperback: 978-1-916698-55-0

For my family

PREFACE

There are, in my mind, three main principal reasons why psychiatric injury claims present as a daunting prospect to any legal practitioner who is not familiar with them.

Firstly, the common law principles which govern such claims are not located at a single common source, but are derived from numerous judgments, each building on the ones that came before. These need to be read and understood in turn before the law can be applied to the facts of any claim.

Additionally, previous decisions of the Courts demonstrate that different conclusions are arrived at due to what may appear to be minor, but important factual differences in the claim being decided. Unless the practitioner has as full and complete an understanding of these nuances as possible, then serious issues can arise. In essence, it can be a legal minefield.

Secondly, the diagnosis of a psychiatric disorder can be complex and multifactorial. Unlike an orthopaedic injury, there is no means by which a psychiatric injury can be readily and objectively verified. This in turn, often leads to conflicting expert opinion evidence adding a further layer of complexity to a litigation and at times, more than a little confusion.

Finally, psychiatric injury claims (especially claims arising from stress at work) are factually complicated, require intensive preparatory work and can be attritional and draining for the parties and their legal representatives alike.

Considering the above, any hesitancy on the part of any party dealing which such a claim is understandable.

With these points in mind, this 3rd edition differs somewhat from the previous editions and seeks to build on the feedback received. For example, the textbook now adopts full footnotes on each page where a case is referred to, in order to ensure that the relevant citation is at the readers hands and readily accessible at all times.

This text at its heart though aims to help overcome the hurdles inherent in claims involving psychiatric injury, or at least to provide a starting point for how such claims can be approached.

Firstly, this text collates the relevant legal principles governing each type of claim, and each of the individual subtypes therein into an accessible and understandable framework. It is hoped that this will enable the ready assimilation of, and a confident application of, the legal principles to the facts of any claim.

When dealing with the relevant parts of a Judgment, the textbook has sought to ensure that the reader is provided with the relevant material in a clear format, as opposed just modest selections.

This has been done to arm the reader with the material they may need for any legal argument of discussion in a single source. Be you a Barrister in Court, Solicitor in a complicated conference or Mediator addressing the parties, you will have what you need, when you need it, at your fingertips.

Secondly, the criteria relating to how a psychiatric injury can be diagnosed is considered in some detail, a point which other textbooks appear to move past, or direct the reader to psychiatric literature. This textbook seeks to grapple with the issue in a practical manner, and does so to ensure the reader not only understands the basis on which a recognisable psychiatric disorder may be diagnosed, but to enable expert opinion to be challenged from an informed position.

Thirdly, and very much led by feedback received in previous editions, there is now at the end of the textbook a "*triage checklist*". This is designed to act as a single document to practically direct the reader to the relevant issues, next steps and chapters in this text that they may need to consider, depending on what type of claim they are dealing with.

The law stated in this book is believed to be up to date and accurate as of 1st October 2024.

Liam Ryan
October 2024

CONTENTS

CHAPTER ONE

INTRODUCTION

For over a century psychiatric injury claims have given rise to difficult issues of fact, and contentious legal issues for both legal practitioners and the Courts.

The law which currently governs claims for psychiatric injury has arisen from a series of factual disputes infrequently encountered in general personal injury litigation, which has in turn resulted in an unhurried and measured pace of legal evolution. Notwithstanding this, psychiatric injury claims have consistently proven to be emotive, factually complex and a source of novel issues of law and public policy.

Despite resisting the easy formulation of comprehensive governing common law principles, the Courts of England and Wales have been proactive in dealing with and accommodating such claims. The House of Lords In **McLoughlin v O'Brian** [1983] 1 A.C. 410[1] through Lord Wilberforce made the point eloquently with "*English law, and common understanding, have moved some distance since recognition was given to this symptom as a basis for liability. Whatever is unknown about the mind body relationship … it is now accepted by medical science that recognisable and severe physical damage to the human body and system may be caused by the impact, through the senses, of external events on the mind. There may thus be produced what is as identifiable an illness as any that may be caused by direct physical impact.*"

As inferred above, the law in relation to psychiatric injury claims following **McLoughlin**[2] has developed at a regulated pace, with the

[1] **McLoughlin v O'Brian** [1983] 1 A.C. 410

[2] **McLoughlin v O'Brian** [1983] 1 A.C. 410

Courts remaining ever vigilant of unintended consequences through limiting what types of psychiatric injury claims can be said to be actionable, each with nuanced and at times complicated rules governing the presentation of such a claim.

This text seeks to explore these rules and frameworks but also to serve as a practical starting point for any practitioner dealing with a claim involving psychiatric injury.

Unconventional claims?

Lord Steyn in **Frost v Chief Constable of the South Yorkshire Police** [1999] 2 A.C. 455[3] identified four points of caution that the Courts in his opinion needed to remain mindful of when dealing with psychiatric injury claims. These were;

a. That there is a wide range of complexity and diagnostic uncertainty in defining what is a psychiatric injury;

b. That the actual litigation itself can be the cause of, or at least an aggravating feature in the maintenance of such injuries, and presents an unconscious disincentive of rehabilitation;

c. That relaxation of the restrictions and limitations as to which classes of potential Claimants were able bring claims could, and probably would, result in "*floodgate*" litigation;

d. That the potential scope of a party's liability for injury and loss could become disproportionate to the tortious conduct involved.

3 **Frost v Chief Constable of the South Yorkshire Police** [1999] 2 A.C. 455

Notwithstanding the points raised in **Frost**[4] by Lord Steyn, in my mind there are three further identifiable sources of friction which have emerged in the 25 years following the judgment.

Psychiatric science, floodgates and the common law

First, as identified by Lord Steyn in point (a) above, the science of psychiatry has advanced significantly. DSM-1 first published in January 1952 recognised 106 psychiatric disorders, the current edition of DSM-5 published in May 2013 recognises nearly 300 separate disorders. ICD-6 first recognised mental disorders in 1949, with the current edition 11th (ICD-11) published on the 1st January 2022 recognising 21 groups of psychiatric disorders, with over 900 unique codes for mental, behavioural, and neurodevelopmental disorders contained therein. Underlining psychiatric sciences increased understanding of the numerous forms a recognisable psychiatric injury can take, the World Health Organization on the 8th June 2022 published statistical data demonstrating that 1 in 8 people globally are now estimated to suffer from a recognisable psychiatric disorder, with an estimated 301 million people suffering from anxiety, and 280 million people suffering from depression.

This should not be taken to mean that the diagnostic criteria have become easier to satisfy or any less stringent. It remains the case that for any Claimant's reported psychiatric symptoms to be classed as a recognisable psychiatric disorder, they need to, and must present as a "*clinically significant disturbance in an individual's cognition, emotional regulation, or behaviour*"[5].

The Courts are however required to consider far more than just the issue of causation and diagnosis of injury when dealing with a claim for psychiatric injury, and the development and maintenance of the control

4 **Frost v Chief Constable of the South Yorkshire Police** [1999] 2 A.C. 455

5 World Health Organisation 2024

mechanisms referred to by Lord Steyn at (c) above has been both necessary and sensible. However, the opportunity for the Upper Courts to update and review these control mechanisms doesn't arise with reliable or predicable frequency, since for this to occur, a claim needs to move on appeal up to the Upper Courts. Practically, this takes time, is expensive and carries no small amount of risk to the parties involved. If an appellant doesn't want to follow this route or if their claim is settled, then the common law will remain static and unchanged. In this sense, the development of the common law in claims of psychiatric injury can be seen to be held back by matters entirely unrelated to the important questions it governs.

The way people work, live and interact has changed drastically since the judgment in **Frost**[6] and the common law needs to the opportunity to continue to evolve to reflect this. The means by which a person could potentially suffer psychiatric injury has grown alarmingly in the last 25 years, with the availability and use of the internet, mobile telephones, social media, and artificial intelligence standing out as especially prevalent potential causes of injury.

It's unlikely that Lord Steyn when delivering the Judgment in **Frost**[7] would have foreseen that both ICD-11 and DSM-5 would classify addiction to internet gaming a recognisable psychiatric disorder, nor may he have foreseen that we would now live in a world where harmful and degrading images of a Claimant can be generated by artificial intelligence in seconds, and circulated to their family, employer and friends at the press of a button.

It should be uncontroversial that these control mechanisms need to be reviewed with regularity in order to avoid becoming outdated and archaic. However, the absence of a system through which this can be

6 **Frost v Chief Constable of the South Yorkshire Police** [1999] 2 A.C. 455

7 **Frost v Chief Constable of the South Yorkshire Police** [1999] 2 A.C. 455

achieved outside of litigation, risks that unjust outcomes may, and will occur.

Human nature and QOCS

Secondly, human experience tells us that where any claim for damage or injury cannot be visually verified, it is only natural to approach its reporting with some degree of scepticism.

For example, the Claimant who suffers a serious and obvious physical injury such an amputation, and goes on to develop a severe depressive reaction as a result is more likely to be believed than the Claimant who suffers no physical injury but suffers a severe depressive reaction. Be it done consciously or subconsciously when confronted with the obvious signs of physical injury, we will all ask ourselves "*how would I react?*". There is after all a readily identifiable and relatable source of injury before us which serves to ground the intangible psychiatric reaction in the tangible reality we perceive. Where there is no such tangible connection the same just doesn't seem to apply.

Defendants may well ask themselves (albeit rhetorically) that since Claimants have a commercial interest in presenting their injury to be as serious as possible, how can their truthfulness and reporting be trusted as being both objective and fair? As psychiatric diagnosis is heavily dependent on the oral account given by a Claimant to any Psychiatrist, the danger that a Claimant will take this opportunity to exaggerate or fabricate their symptoms cannot be discounted.

Experience further teaches us that once one a part of a Claimant's account is questioned, we are more naturally inclined to readily question it entire. The other side of the same coin is that an injured Claimant may genuinely believe that any and all misfortunes they experience post suffering a psychiatric injury have been caused by the Defendant. This inevitably seems to result in polarised positions being taken by the parties to a claim when it comes to the quantum of a Claimant's claim

Quantitative One-way Costs Shifting (QOCS) has since the 1st October 2013 prevented Defendants from being able to enforce an orders for costs directly against a unsuccessful Claimant without any further order of the Court (rule 44.14 (1) CPR), subject to a number of exceptions. Rule 44.16 (1) CPR provides that in a costs order can be enforced with the permission of the Court in a case where the Claimant has found to be fundamentally dishonest. Further, by operation of section 57 (2) of the Criminal Justice and Courts Act 2015, unless satisfied that the Claimant would suffer a substantial injustice, the Court must dismiss the whole claim.

Due to this, claims of psychiatric injury can quickly become "*high stake*" and stressful claims for injured Claimants and Defendant insurers alike, only adding to the point made by Lord Steyn at (b) above.

For Claimants who are seriously psychiatrically injured, the negative impact of this can be especially acute. They may feel angered and attacked by a Defendant criticising their truthfulness, but also know that if they are found to be fundamentally dishonest not only will their claim be dismissed, but they are likely to face a costs order, and potential contempt of Court proceedings. A Claimant may well view the accusation of being fundamentally dishonest as yet another cruel and vindictive act by a Defendant, further entrenching and maintaining their psychiatric disorder.

The application of QOCS, and the pressure it can place on seriously psychiatrically injured Claimants can seem at times to be disproportionate to the goal of deterring dishonest claims. It can further lead to a stark commercial imbalance in negotiations between the parties, with threat of the finding of a finding of fundamental dishonesty causing Claimants to withdraw from proceedings, or accept sums demonstrably below what they may recover at trial.

Social trends, how symptoms are reported and why

Thirdly, there is a growing trend amongst litigants to readily describe their subjective reactions to events as causing them (for example) depression. This is not intended by them to denote or convey that they have developed a recognisable psychiatric disorder, but rather it is an example of the common use of such language, with it now having one meaning in the common discourse of today, but quite another in psychiatric circles.

While certain tortious claims do permit Claimants to recover damages for distress and injury to feelings (for example, claims of discrimination or misuse of private information), practically this has led to a muddying of the waters between what are claims for a recognisable psychiatric injury, and claims which are for pure mental distress. Any claim for psychiatric injury must be supported by medical opinion which evidences a that a recognisable psychiatric injury has been caused because of a proven breach. Without this, the claim has no prospect of success.

In the last four decades, our understanding and acceptance of psychiatric injury has hugely advanced, as has our ability to diagnose and treat psychiatric conditions. The most impactful development in the field of psychiatric injury litigation has not been a scientific one or a legal one, but rather the social destigmatisation of psychiatric injury. People affected by psychiatric injuries are now more willing to talk about their difficulties, and listeners more likely to listen and accommodate them.

Following the Covid-19 lockdown in England and Wales we seemed to reach a watershed moment when it came to the visibility and acceptance of issues relating to mental health. The shared experience of the pandemic, and the stressful events it caused created a shared social experience of adversity. People became not only more willing to discuss issues of mental health following the pandemic, but have also shown signs of placing their own wellbeing before concerns that prior to the pandemic, took priority. We need only to consider the World Health Organisations findings which identifies an increase in reported cases of anxiety and depression of some 25% following the pandemic, let alone the fact that remote working is now a norm, as opposed to being an exception.

Whilst acknowledging this social change, in any civil claim for psychiatric injury a Claimant must prove their case and must do so on the balance of probabilities. This, requires evidence, not assertion. As long as this principal remains, there will always be a practical bulwark between the neurotic habitual complainant, and the genuinely injured Claimant. The Courts need to remain vigilant and conservative in how they handle such cases.

In an age where identify and belonging to specific groups and classes of people of has become ever more important, having a psychiatric injury should never be seen as vouge or fashionable. It's troubling that the actions of small, but growing number of people engaged in "*moral grandstanding*" or "*victim signalling*[8]" in relation to an actual or perceived disorder they have, are not raising awareness of psychiatric illness in a positive manner. Their actions at times can be harmful, antagonistic and marginalise the very group they claim to represent.

Historically, disabilities were dealt with in private for reasons of social stigma. Whilst the change in the common psyche towards acceptance and support of psychiatric injury is to be applauded, we need to be mindful that divisive and harmful conduct is not incentivised, nor the potential severity of psychiatric injury trivialised. I am met to meet a Claimant who when asked what they want to achieve from a litigation has not replied with words to the effect of, "*I just wish this had never happened to me*".

Psychiatric injuries can be short lived yes, but in the worst cases, they end lives. It's vital that we don't lose sight of that fact.

---

8 Behaviour in which a person prominently displays their challenges, real or perceived, to gain sympathy, validation, or social status

CHAPTER TWO

CLAIMS IN NEGLIGENCE AND PSYCHIATRIC INJURY

All claims in the Civil Courts which deal with the cause of psychiatric injury are at their core, stories of the factual aetiology of a Claimant's injury.

Whilst the facts underpinning each and every claim are unique, what makes a claim for psychiatric injury different from a patient recanting the history of how they came to develop a psychiatric disorder to a clinician, is that there will be an identifiable and actionable wrong which can be said to have caused, or contributed to the development of their injury. A Claimant's main, if not sole cause of action will as a result of this almost always rest in negligence.

Claims in negligence

The law of negligence has undergone significant developments historically, but one of, if not the most important decision for Claimants seeking to bring claims for psychiatric injuries remains **Caparo Industries plc v Dickman** [1990] UKHL 2[9]. Here the House of Lords established that in order for any claim to be brought in negligence, a Claimant needs to be able to establish four things. These are;

a. The existence of a duty of care owed to a Claimant by a Defendant;

b. A breach of the duty of care by the Defendant;

9 **Caparo Industries plc v Dickman** [1990] UKHL 2

c. A causational connection between the Defendant's careless conduct and the damage;

d. That the damage suffered was not so unforeseeable as to be too remote.

In a case where these four components can be satisfied, a Defendant may be liable to the Claimant in negligence for damages flowing from their specified breach of duty of care. This text will later explore some of the nuances of this, but in essence this can be enough to ground an actionable claim in negligence.

As referred to above, in the majority of personal injury claims, the most relevant cause of action is likely to be found in negligence, where a duty of care owed to the injured Claimant has been breached. Practically, this often arises from facts commonly classed by Claimants as an "*accident*", or something that was caused by the "*recklessness*" or "*carelessness*" on the part of a Defendant, as opposed to being done with any form of intent or malice. The use of these words can lead to some confusion and a loss of focus on what the Courts require a Claimant to prove, with each having a specific meaning in law as opposed to how they are more commonly used in conversation.

By way of example, the duty of care owed by a Defendant to a Claimant who presents a claim for personal injury in negligence is not a duty not to act carelessly. It predominately, if not always is based on the breach of a duty not to inflict damage carelessly. Whilst the nuance of the language may seem pedantic, it is important. In practical terms it is advisable to always be mindful of the following four points;

a. The mere fact that a Claimant is injured by another's action doesn't create a cause of action;

b. There must exist a duty of care;

c. It must be shown that this duty was breached by the Defendant; and

d. That this breach has caused the Claimant injury.

A Defendant who acts negligently in the context of a claim for negligence can be said to have acted without giving proper, or any thought to the consequences of their actions and the risk of harm they posed. Practically, it may can include;

a. The driver of a car who in driving too fast, while not intending to collide with the vehicle in front of themselves does so;

b. The person who throws a stone into a crowd, and whilst not intending to strike anyone in the crowd does;

c. The occupier of a shop who leaves a trip hazard across a walkway, and while not intending to do so causes a visitor to the shop to trip and fall;

d. The employer who requires an employee to work in dangerous conditions, and while not intending any harm to the employee, causes them harm by requiring them to carry out their work in the manner instructed.

Practitioners in the field of psychiatric injury are going to encounter situations where the facts that give rise to a claim intersect and overlap with a number of other potential causes of action. For example, a claim based on serious and sustained workplace bullying may be capable of presentation as both a claim in negligence and under the Protection from Harassment Act 1997.

It's vital however not lose sight of the fact that any claim in negligence is based on the breach of a duty or care owed the Claimant by the Defendant. It is advisable to take time to carefully consider the construction of the duty, along with this scope and range. For example;

a. A Claimant is employed by a Defendant business;

b. The Claimant is owed a non-delegable duty of care by the Defendant to provide them with a safe working environment and to prevent them from suffering from foreseeable injury caused by their work;

c. The Claimant is bullied by a co-worker employed by the Defendant whilst at work, and during the course of their employment with the Defendant;

d. The Claimant due to this develops a recognisable psychiatric injury.

On the basis of the basis of the above, our hypothetical Defendant may (subject to the available evidence), be held vicariously liable for the actions of its employee who bullied the Claimant. This is because it is in breach of its duty of care owed to the Claimant to provide them with a safe working environment. Contrast this with the following scenario;

a. A Claimant is employed by a Defendant business;

b. The Claimant is owed a non-delegable duty of care by the Defendant to provide them with a safe working environment and to prevent them from suffering from foreseeable injury caused by their work;

c. The Claimant is bullied by a coworker employed by the Defendant outside of work and unconnected to the work for which the Claimant is employed;

d. The Claimant develops a recognisable psychiatric injury as a result.

Our hypothetical Defendant in this scenario is unlikely to be in breach of any duty owed to the Claimant, with the actions of its employee occurring outside of work and entirely unconnected to work. The duty owed to the Claimant is to provide a safe working environment and to prevent the risk of the Claimant suffering foreseeable injury in the course of their work. Ergo, it is very unlikely that this hypothetical Claimant can and will establish a claim against their employer based in negligence.

The creation of a duty of care

When deciding if a duty of care exists, **Caparo Industries plc v Dickman** [1990] UKHL 2[10] established a 3 stage test that needs to be applied and satisfied by Claimants. A Court needs to ask itself;

a. Was the harm caused to the Claimant foreseeable?

b. Was there a proximate relationship between the Claimant and Defendant?

c. Is the imposition of a duty would be fair, just and reasonable?

Lord Oliver when setting out this test made 4 points that are often overlooked but if they are borne in mind when addressing the issue of if a duty of care should be imposed, will provide a practical framework to better enable a fuller understanding of the overarching nature of each individual component;

a. Firstly, that "*… it is difficult to resist a conclusion that what have been treated as three separate requirements are, at least in most cases, in fact merely facets of the same thing, for in some cases the degree of foreseeability is such that it is from that alone that the requisite proximity can be deduced, whilst in others the absence of that essential relationship can most rationally be attributed simply to the Court's view that it would not be fair and reasonable to hold the Defendant responsible*".

10 **Caparo Industries plc v Dickman** [1990] UKHL 2

b. Secondly, that whilst "*Proximity is, no doubt, a convenient expression*" it is important for a practitioner not to lose sight of the fact that "*it is no more than a label which embraces not a definable concept but merely a description of circumstances from which, pragmatically, the Courts conclude that a duty of care exists*;

c. Thirdly, that despite this there are "… *cases where, in any ordinary meaning of the words, a relationship of proximity (in the literal sense of 'closeness') exists but where the law… denies a remedy to the injured party on the ground of public policy*"; and

d. Fourthly that "… *the attempt to state some general principle which will determine liability in an infinite variety of circumstances serves not to clarify the law but merely to bedevil its development in a way which corresponds with practicality and common sense*".

The categories of negligence that exist in law have been described by the Courts as "*never closed*", with the common law remaining a flexible cause of action for Claimants who suffer psychiatric injury, and is likely to do so for the foreseeable future. While the circumstances in which duties of care can be created and their form has inspired many a text book, this text doesn't propose to cover the history of the development of the law of negligence, but to provide a practical starting point in dealing with this issue.

Primary or secondary victim?

A Claimant who intends to bring a claim for psychiatric injury needs to be able to identify their potential claim as satisfying 2 factors. Firstly, that the claim is actionable, and secondly, that the Claimant can be identified as either a primary or secondary victim. This legal concept of was identified and set out in the case of **Alcock v Chief Constable of South Yorkshire Police** [1992] 1 A.C. 310[11], where Lord Oliver provided that in cases of psychiatric injury, Claimants "*Broadly… divide into two*

11 **Alcock v Chief Constable of South Yorkshire Police** [1992] 1 A.C. 310

categories, that is to say, those cases in which the injured plaintiff was involved, either mediately or immediately, as a participant, and those in which the plaintiff was no more than the passive and unwilling witness of injury caused to others."

Once this is done, the practitioner can begin to analysis the facts of the claim, consider what evidence needs to be gathered, and ensure that they are applying the relevant legal control mechanisms and tests to the issue of liability.

Primary and secondary victims are covered in greater depth later in this text but in essence, the distinction flows from a Claimant either being at direct risk of harm (so as to be classed as a primary victim), or not at direct risk of harm (a secondary victim) due to the act of alleged negligence.

What kind harm needs to be foreseen?

When we consider the issue of the forseebalility of harm, the outcome is dependent on what kind of claim we are dealing with, and how any psychiatric injury is said to be caused by it.

In a case where a Claimant is the primary victim of an act of negligence that causes nervous shock, the decision of **Page v Smith** [1996] A.C. 155[12] (whilst considered in greater depth later in this text) establishes that the foreseeability of psychiatric injury is not treated any differently from the foreseeability of physical harm. A Defendant's duty to a primary victim is, as was case in **Page**[13], is the duty to take care not to cause personal injury to the Claimant, not to take care not to cause physical injury to the Claimant. Addressing the issue of foreseeability of harm, it was only necessary for a Court to ask if the Defendant should have

12 **Page v Smith** [1996] A.C. 155

13 **Page v Smith** [1996] A.C. 155

foreseen that the Claimant might suffer personal injury (be it physical or psychiatric) due to their negligence.

In cases of nervous shock the question of if a Defendant should have foreseen the risk of psychiatric injury to the Claimant only needs to be considered in cases involving secondary victim cases, where different control mechanisms apply and the Court will need to ask itself if it was reasonably foreseeable that a person of reasonable fortitude would suffer some psychiatric injury due to the Defendant's breach of duty (the same being considered in depth later in this text).

In cases where the development of psychiatric injury is not based on nervous shock but exposure to stressful events which lead to the development of a recognisable psychiatric injury the guidelines laid down in **Hatton v Sutherland** [2002] EWCA Civ 76 (and considered in greater depth later in this text) apply. The Court will need to be satisfied the injury was foreseeable due to the stress that the Defendant created, as opposed to stress from other events outside of its control, and duty.

An actionable claim?

There are a number of areas explored in this text where a claim for psychiatric injury, due to its underlying factual basis will not be actionable due to reasons of public policy, and the need to control the number of potential Claimants. As set out by Lord Wilberforce in **McLoughlin v O'Brian** [1983] 1 AC 410, Nd reiterated more recently by Spencer J in **Young v Downey** [2020] EWHC 3457 (QB), a Defendant "*cannot be expected to compensate the world at large*".

It's not possible to provide an exhaustive list of such claims, but practitioners need to be aware that in claims based on psychiatric injury, certain types of claim cannot succeed for reasons of public policy. These include;

a. A claim for personal injury which develops out of the fear of an event that is yet to come to pass, where the Claimant is never at any actual risk of harm;

b. A secondary victim who witnesses the death of a family member following them reiving treatment by medical professionals;

c. A Claimant who after bringing a claim in the Employment Tribunal, seeks to bring a claim based on the same facts in the County Court.

Causation and material contribution

The development of a psychiatric injury is multifactorial, textured and subjective. Unexpected life events can cause psychiatric injury, but can also assist in an injured Claimant's recovery. The mind is complex, and doesn't heal in the same manner as flesh and bone. The effects of trauma can rest in a Claimant's subconscious for years, only to be reawakened by a stressful and threatening situation, at which point they manifest into a psychiatric disorder which but for the Claimant's benign traumatic memories, would not have been the case.

In nearly any claim for psychiatric injury there will be numerous stressors relevant to the development of a recognisable psychiatric disorder that are outside of the scope of a Defendant's negligence. These can include

a. A history of violent or sexual abuse;

b. Troubled and emotionally toxic relationships;

c. Bereavement;

d. Substance abuse; and

e. Underlying or pre-existing psychiatric conditions and vulnerability.

These factors are not exhaustive and itis not uncommon that upon careful examination of a Claimant's medical records, that an alternative or competing cause of the complained of psychiatric injury is identified.

When dealing with claim for psychiatric injury, the Court will need in the main to apply the "*but for*" test. A Claimant needs to satisfy a Court that there is a causative link between a Defendant's negligent conduct complained of, and the development of the psychiatric injuries they have suffered. When dealing with claims for psychiatric injury it is advisable to seek to be pragmatic and to ask, 2 questions;

a. Firstly "*what would have happened (in so far as the Claimant's injuries are concerned), had the Defendant not breach their duty of care?*"; and

b. Secondly, *"what is the evidential basis for this?"*

It may seem reductive to break the process down to such base elements, but this can help bring clarity to factually complex matters, and focus as to where further enquires need to be made.

The answer to this question is almost always going to require the practitioner to consider if the injury can be said to be divisible and capable of apportionment (for example, are or competing causes of injury?) or if it is indivisible. Whilst both types of divisibility are covered later in this text, it is not uncommon in cases of psychiatric injury for a Claimant to be able to establish that the alleged breach of duty "*materially contributed to their injury*" (**Fairchild v Glenhaven Funeral Services** [2002] UKHL 22[14]). Where a Claimant can do this, then compensation for the entirety of their psychiatric injury is possible, despite any other competing causes or events.

A Court will need to ask if it is even possible to separate the injury suffered from all of its competing causes, or was it the totality of a

14 **Fairchild v Glenhaven Funeral Services** [2002] UKHL 22

Claimant's experience which caused injury to their psyche? This can be especially true in claims for stress at work involving allegations of bullying or overworking. Factually these claims often involve a Claimant being exposed over to unreasonable and hazardous levels of stress for lengthy period of time. They will almost all feature a moment that can be described as "*the straw that broke the camel's back*", when their stress becomes unbearable, and psychiatric injury is suffered. Without understanding the prior events however, the reaction and its severity cannot be understood.

It is advisable that when seeking to "*unpick the patchwork quilt*"[15] that is the causation of psychic injury to remember that;

a. A Claimant in the current legal landscape only needs to establish that the complained of act materially contributed to the injury which they suffered from;

c. Material in this context means more than negligible;

d. Practically, it's not the highest of hurdles to clear, but any attempt to jump it must need to be supported with robust psychiatric evidence.

Apportionment

Once a Claimant has succeeded in establishing causation of their injury is due to a breach of duty committed by a Defendant the Court should always ask if it needs to consider the issue of apportionment. In cases of more commonly encounter orthopaedic injuries this will rarely be the case. For example, it's unlikely that there will be several causes for a

15 **White v Chief Constable of South Yorkshire** [1999] 2 AC 455 *where* Lord Steyn said that the law on the recovery of compensation for pure psychiatric harm *"is a patchwork quilt of distinctions which are difficult to justify."*

broken leg in a car crash, but in psychiatric injury claims the waters run deeper and can be turbulent.

Practically when approaching the issue, a Court is firstly going to seek to identify if the injury can be seen as either divisible, or indivisible. In the case of an indivisible injury (as set out above), with two separate wrongdoers but no external or alternative contributing factors then the Claimant is entitled to recovery in full from either of the wrongdoers.

If we work on an assumption that a Claimant can establish at least a material contribution towards the symptoms which they suffer, the next logical step is to consider if it is possible to divide the injury itself and apportion it against the prevailing causes.

Where an injury is divisible, this will often result in extensive and opposing medical opinion. Seriously psychiatrically injured Claimants (especially in stress at work claims) will have often been exposed to a number of events over a lengthy period of time, all of which will have served increase lowered their susceptibility to psychiatric injury. In such cases, a lengthy and detailed interrogation of the Claimant's medical history is going to be required in order to understand and evidence what apportionment of injury should be reached.

Assistance can be taken from **Bailey v Ministry of Defence** [2008] EWCA civ 883[16], and the Judgment of Waller LJ siting in the Court of Appeal. **Bailey** is a tragic case where the Claimant had been a patient in a hospital managed by the MOD. She had undergone an unsuccessful procedure to remove a gallstone, the view of which had been obscured by bleeding during the procedure. Following the procedure, there was a period of lack of care and in particular a failure to resuscitate. The Claimant was diagnosed as having possibly developed pancreatitis. Her condition continued to deteriorate and she was moved to an intensive care unit where she underwent additional procedures, including surgery

16 **Bailey v Ministry of Defence** [2008] EWCA civ 883

to the liver, and it was confirmed that she had pancreatitis. She was then moved to another hospital, where she swallowed her own vomit and went into cardiac arrest and suffered hypoxic brain damage.

The Claimant's case was that physical cause of her final brain damage was her weakness and inability to react to her vomit, and that the contributory cause of her weakness was the negligent treatment she had received, which in turn made a material contribution to her overall weakness. "*But for*" these negligent acts, she could have reacted to the vomit and her injury, on the balance of probabilities, been avoided.

The Claimant succeeded in her claim in the High Court and the Defendant appealed. The Court of Appeal upheld the decision of the lower Court, with Waller LJ taking time to set out the common laws approach to the but for test with "*In my view one cannot draw a distinction between medical negligence cases and others. I would summarise the position in relation to cumulative cause cases as follows. If the evidence demonstrates on a balance of probabilities that the injury would have occurred as a result of the non-tortious cause or causes in any event, the Claimant will have failed to establish that the tortious cause contributed... If the evidence demonstrates that "but for" the contribution of the tortious cause the injury would probably not have occurred, the Claimant will (obviously) have discharged the burden. In a case where medical science cannot establish the probability that "but for" an act of negligence the injury would not have happened but can establish that the contribution of the negligent cause was more than negligible, the "but for" test is modified, and the Claimant will succeed*".

Practitioners are also assisted by the case of **Dickins v O2** [2008] EWCA Civ 1144[17] and **BAE Systems (operations) ltd v Konczak** [2017] EWCA Civ 1188[18] which in cases of psychiatric injury reinforced that the concept of a material contribution applies (discussed at some length later). The Court of Appeal in **Konczak** through the Judgment of

17 **Dickins v O2** [2008] EWCA Civ 1144

18 **BAE Systems (operations) ltd v Konczak** [2017] EWCA Civ 1188

Underhill LJ made it clear at paragraph 71 that "*What is therefore required in any case of this character is that the tribunal should try to identify a rational basis on which the harm suffered can be apportioned between a part caused by the employer's wrong and a part which is not so caused. I would emphasise, because the distinction is easily overlooked, that the exercise is concerned not with the divisibility of the causative contribution but with the divisibility of the harm. In other words, the question is whether the tribunal can identify, however broadly, a particular part of the suffering which is due to the wrong; not whether it can assess the degree to which the wrong caused the harm*".

Acceleration and exacerbation of symptoms

When dealing with a Claimant who was already psychiatrically symptomatic and unwell prior to any alleged negligence, medical opinion can conclude a breach of duty has caused their pre-existing symptoms to be in some way been accelerated, exacerbated or worsened for a definable and finite period of time. As already avered to, it is not uncommon for psychiatrically injured Claimants to have a history of poor mental health and this will give rise to alternative avenues of argument for Defendants when causation of injury and apportionment is considered.

Acceleration or exacerbation arguments can prove to be a useful tool for a Defendant Practitioner by creating a metaphorical line in the sand for the recoverability of damages to advance to, but no further as the Claimant on passing this point in time, would be in the same position as they are now due their constitutional psychiatric issues.

It can be a tactically astute and attractive argument to advance before a Court demonstrating not only a reasonableness on the part of the Defendant, but also providing a sound and stable route to Judgment in cases of conflicting expert evidence. Considering the thought process that this catalyses, a Court may ask itself if both experts agree that a psychiatric injury has been caused to the Claimant and the only question is the period of injury, not its intensity, since both experts agree that this finite period has been caused by, how on the balance of probabilities can any opinion to go beyond this period be safely preferred?

It is an issue to remain conscious of, and practitioners where they can foresee the possibility it may arise are advised to not only research the psychiatric science behind an injury to make sure it is capable of acceleration or exacerbation, but also what the actual factual causes of any such material change are. This list of matters to consider is wide ranging and needs to be expert led, but can include;

a. Where a Claimant's medical records show and evidence a history of deterioration in their psychiatric state, is further future deterioration probable, and if so over what time scale;

b. Whether the Claimant has a genetic predisposition to the developing a psychiatric disorders, or any form of underlying relevant condition present in their family history that needs to be considered;

c. If there is any evidence in the Claimant's medical history which demonstrates a worsening tendency to react violently, harmfully and aggressively to stressors in their life;

d. Are there other sources of records relating to the Claimant which can be used to identify a pattern of deteriorating behaviour, such a probation or social service files.

e. Evidence that the Claimant has been actively misusing drugs, alcohol or engaging in harmful activity, and if so, how would this interact or aggravate any underlying condition they may have.

CHAPTER THREE

DIAGNOSIS

The bedrock of any claim for a psychiatric injury, is identifying its presence and cause. For any alleged psychiatric injury to be actionable, it must be capable of classification as a recognisable psychiatric disorder, and will fall into the diagnostic criteria of either ICD 11 or DSM 5. A Claimant's grief, anger or upset is not going to be enough to give rise to a claim for personal injury.

Whilst reliable, robust and persuasive part 35 CPR compliant expert evidence is central to the success of any claim for psychiatric injury, the practitioner should never unquestioningly adopt their conclusions reached by any expert psychiatrist. Such expert evidence must be capable of withstanding scrutiny and challenge.

This chapter is intended to give a practical outline of how this can be achieved. It is not designed to replace the need for psychiatric evidence, but to sign post issues that may arise in claims involving psychiatric injury.

Clinically significant symptoms

When seeking to either understand or undermine an expert's diagnosis of psychiatric injury, the practitioner must never lose sight of the fact that both DSM-5 and ICD-11 require that the reported symptoms are "*clinically significant*".

ICD-11 makes it clear that "*Mental, behavioural and neurodevelopmental disorders are syndromes characterised by clinically significant disturbance in an individual's cognition, emotional regulation, or behaviour that reflects a dysfunction in the psychological, biological, or developmental processes that underlie mental and behavioural functioning. These disturbances are usually associated with distress or impairment in personal, family, social, educational, occupational, or other important areas of functioning*".

DSM-5 largely aligns with ICD-11, and defines a mental disorder as "*a syndrome that is characterized by clinically significant disturbances in an individual's cognition, emotion regulation, or behaviour. These disturbances must reflect a dysfunction in the psychological, biological, or developmental processes that underlie mental functioning*".

In the main, it will be obvious and apparent when these criteria are satisfied. It is also advisable when considering the issues of both causation and quantum, that the requirement of reported symptoms to remain of clinical significance is not lost. Where and when an expert fails to a provide a proper and objective assessment of the clinical significance of the Claimant's symptoms in reaching their diagnosis, it is often the first sign of a weak point in a case, or an expert who may not be stand up to scrutiny.

Commonly encountered psychiatric injuries

Whilst this text cannot replace the worth and knowledge that is to be gained from reading the diagnostic criteria of ICD-11 and DSM-5, the classification of psychiatric injuries that are most commonly encountered in claims of psychiatric injury are reactionary, or consequential to a Defendant's alleged breach of duty.

As a result of the likely factual aetiology of injury, practitioners far more likely to encounter psychiatric injuries capable of classification as either a mood disorder (ICD-11 6A) or a anxiety of fear based disorder (ICD-11 6B)

Depression

Depression is a word that is used with increasing frequency in the modern world. It's not uncommon to hear someone say "*I'm depressed*" in relation to disappointment or some minor adverse event, but depression as an illness is far worse and quite different.

A single episode depressive disorder is characterised by the presence or history of one depressive episode when there is no history of prior depressive episodes. This episode is characterised in ICD-11 6A70 as "*a period of depressed mood or diminished interest in activities occurring most of the day, nearly every day during a period lasting at least two weeks accompanied by other symptoms such as difficulty concentrating, feelings of worthlessness or excessive or inappropriate guilt, hopelessness, recurrent thoughts of death or suicide, changes in appetite or sleep, psychomotor agitation or retardation, and reduced energy or fatigue. There have never been any prior manic, hypomanic, or mixed episodes, which would indicate the presence of a bipolar disorder*".

Where there is a history of depression or multiple instances of it, the Claimant may suffer from a recurrent reperceive disorder. ICD-11 6A71 classes recurrent depressive disorder as being "*characterised by a history of at least two depressive episodes separated by at least several months without significant mood disturbance. A depressive episode is characterised by a period of depressed mood or diminished interest in activities occurring most of the day, nearly every day during a period lasting at least two weeks accompanied by other symptoms such as difficulty concentrating, feelings of worthlessness or excessive or inappropriate guilt, hopelessness, recurrent thoughts of death or suicide, changes in appetite or sleep, psychomotor agitation or retardation, and reduced energy or fatigue. There have never been any prior manic, hypomanic, or mixed episodes, which would indicate the presence of a Bipolar disorder*".

Depressive Disorders are characterised by a depressive mood (e.g., sad, irritable, empty) or loss of pleasure accompanied by other cognitive, behavioural, or neurovegetative symptoms that significantly affect the individual's ability to function. Symptoms commonly encountered in case of depression can include;

a. A persistent and continuous low mood

b. Feeling hopeless and helpless

c. Low self-esteem

d. Feelings of guilt

e. Feeling tearful

f. A lack of motivation

g. Constant procrastination

h. Suicidal thoughts

i. Inability to sleep

Depression can also manifest with physical symptoms and these can include a number of points, but most notably:

a. Weight gain or loss

b. Constipation

c. Unexplained aches and pains

d. Feeling of no energy or vitality

e. Low sex drive (loss of libido)

f. Disturbed sleep

Depression is sadly a common but serious psychiatric illness. In personal injury claims it is not uncommon to see an injured Claimant react to a physical injury or disability with some form of a depressive reaction. It is also possible that Claimants who suffer from depression will be vulnerable to future relapses of their condition or a reduced life expectancy. Practically, the danger of this future deterioration should always be considered, and contingencies made in any schedules of loss to reflect the same.

Anxiety or fear-related disorders

Almost everyone at some point in their life is going to feel anxious, be it before receiving exam results, speaking to new people or even going to somewhere new and different. However, what happens when that sense of anxiety, becomes so heighted, and the person who experiences it, so vulnerable to an overly intense anxious reaction that it starts to impact on their life negatively? This may be one form of an anxiety disorder. Anxiety is (perhaps obviously) the main symptom of several other conditions which a practitioner can only be alive to, these include:

a. Panic disorders;

b. Phobias – such as agoraphobia;

c. Post-traumatic stress disorder (PTSD);

d. Social anxiety disorder (of particular use in cases where Claimants have to deal with customers in their workplace).

ICD-11 6B helpful defines anxiety and fear-related disorders as being "*characterised by excessive fear and anxiety and related behavioural disturbances, with symptoms that are severe enough to result in significant distress or significant impairment in personal, family, social, educational, occupational, or other important areas of functioning. Fear and anxiety are closely related phenomena; fear represents a reaction to perceived imminent threat in the present, whereas anxiety is more future-oriented, referring to perceived anticipated threat. A key differentiating feature among the Anxiety and fear-related disorders are disorder-specific foci of apprehension, that is, the stimulus or situation that triggers the fear or anxiety. The clinical presentation of Anxiety and fear-related disorders typically includes specific associated cognitions that can assist in differentiating among the disorders by clarifying the focus of apprehension*".

Generalized Anxiety

ICD-11 at 6B00 defines a generalised anxiety disorder as being *"characterised by marked symptoms of anxiety that persist for at least several months, for more days than not, manifested by either general apprehension (i.e. 'free-floating anxiety') or excessive worry focused on multiple everyday events, most often concerning family, health, finances, and school or work, together with additional symptoms such as muscular tension or motor restlessness, sympathetic autonomic over-activity, subjective experience of nervousness, difficulty maintaining concentration, irritability, or sleep disturbance. The symptoms result in significant distress or significant impairment in personal, family, social, educational, occupational, or other important areas of functioning. The symptoms are not a manifestation of another health condition and are not due to the effects of a substance or medication on the central nervous system"*.

It is essential that any Claimant who complains of such a disorder can evidence the following features;

a. *"Marked symptoms of anxiety manifested by either;*

b. *General apprehensiveness that is not restricted to any particular environmental circumstance (i.e., 'free-floating anxiety'); or*

c. *Excessive worry (apprehensive expectation) about negative events occurring in several different aspects of everyday life (e.g., work, finances, health, family);*

d. *Anxiety and general apprehensiveness or worry are accompanied by additional characteristic symptoms, such as muscle tension or motor restlessness.*

e. *Sympathetic autonomic overactivity as evidenced by frequent gastrointestinal symptoms such as nausea and/or abdominal distress, heart palpitations, sweating, trembling, shaking, and/or dry mouth;*

f. *Subjective experience of nervousness, restlessness, or being 'on edge'.*

g. *Difficulty concentrating;*

h. *Irritability;*

i. *Sleep disturbances (difficulty falling or staying asleep, or restless, unsatisfying sleep);*

j. *The symptoms are not transient and persist for at least several months, for more days than not;*

k. *The symptoms are not better accounted for by another mental disorder (e.g., a Depressive Disorder);*

l. *The symptoms are not a manifestation of another medical condition (e.g., hyperthyroidism) and are not due to the effects of a substance or medication on the central nervous system (e.g., caffeine, cocaine), including withdrawal effects (e.g., alcohol, benzodiazepines);*

m. *The symptoms result in significant distress about experiencing persistent anxiety symptoms or significant impairment in personal, family, social, educational, occupational, or other important areas of functioning. If functioning is maintained, it is only through significant additional effort.*"

DSM-5 requires that a Claimant demonstrate "*excessive anxiety and worry (apprehensive expectation), occurring more days than not for at least 6 months, about a number of events or activities (such as work or school performance), and that the person finds it difficult to control the worry*", and that this has caused "*clinically significant distress or impairment in social, occupational, or other important areas of functioning*". The Claimant must also show that their "*anxiety and worry are associated with three or more of the following six symptoms (with at least some symptoms present for more days than not for the past 6 months)*".

a. Restlessness or feeling keyed up or on edge;

b. Being easily fatigued;

c. Difficulty concentrating or mind going blank;

d. Irritability;

e. Muscle tension;

f. Sleep disturbance (difficulty falling or staying asleep, or restless unsatisfying sleep).

Adjustment disorders

In practice, an adjustment disorder is one of the most common injuries encountered in psychiatric injury claims. They are often temporary, meaning that they will persist and improve over time, but in essence cover situations where, due to a stressful or traumatic experience, the affected persons varies their behaviour to deal with it. Most people will experience such a disorder in their life and it is often brought on by the death a loved one, the loss of a job or the ending of a relationship. The symptoms of adjustment disorders can include:

a. A constant sense of anxiety;

b. Avoidance behaviours;

c. A constant feeling of upset;

d. Social withdrawal;

e. A lack of concentration;

f. Fatigue.

ICD-11 6B43 defines it an adjustment disorder as a "*maladaptive reaction to an identifiable psychosocial stressor or multiple stressors (e.g. divorce, illness or disability, socio-economic problems, conflicts at home or work) that usually emerges within a month of the stressor. The disorder is characterised by preoccupation with the stressor or its consequences, including excessive worry, recurrent and distressing thoughts about the stressor, or constant rumination about its implications, as well as by failure to adapt to the stressor that causes significant impairment in personal, family, social, educational, occupational or other important areas of functioning. The symptoms are not better explained by another mental disorder (e.g., Mood Disorder, another Disorder Specifically Associated with Stress) and typically resolve within 6 months, unless the stressor persists for a longer duration*".

ICD-11 makes it mandatory that the following symptoms are present in a Claimant for the diagnose to be made;

a. "*Maladaptive reaction to an identifiable psychosocial stressor or multiple stressors (e.g., single stressful event, ongoing psychosocial difficulty or a combination of stressful life situations) that usually emerges within a month of the stressor. Examples include divorce or loss of a relationship, loss of a job, diagnosis of an illness, recent onset of a disability, and conflicts at home or work;*

b. *The reaction to the stressor is characterized by preoccupation with the stressor or its consequences, including excessive worry, recurrent and distressing thoughts about the stressor, or constant rumination about its implications;*

c. *The symptoms are not better accounted for by another mental disorder (e.g., a Mood Disorder, another Disorder Specifically Associated with Stress);*

d. *Once the stressor and its consequences have ended, the symptoms resolve within 6 months.*

e. *Failure to adapt to the stressor results in significant impairment in personal, family, social, educational, occupational or other important areas of functioning. If functioning is maintained, it is only through significant additional effort*".

DSM-5 defines them broadly as "*excessive anxiety and worry (apprehensive expectation), occurring more days than not for at least 6 months, about a number of events or activities (such as work or school performance)*". Further, DSM-5 requires that "*the development of emotional or behavioural symptoms in response to an identifiable stressor(s) occurring within 3 months of the onset of the stressor(s)*". There is also additional requirement that the "*symptoms or behaviours are clinically significant, as evidenced by one or both of the following:*

a. *Marked distress that is out of proportion to the severity or intensity of the stressor, taking into account the external context and the cultural factors that might influence symptom severity and presentation;*

b. *Significant impairment in social, occupational, or other important areas of functioning*".

Post-traumatic stress disorder

Post-traumatic stress disorder can be a crippling illness. Claimants afflicted with post-traumatic stress disorder will often relive the traumatic event endured through nightmares and flashbacks. They may also experience feelings of isolation, irritability, and guilt.

Our understanding and opinions of PTSD (Post-Traumatic Stress Disorder) have evolved significantly over the years, shaped by advances in medical science, changes in cultural attitudes, and experiences drawn from military conflicts, among other factors. Here's how our views on PTSD have shifted.

It seems clear that throughout history, humans who have experienced trauma have suffered from PTSD. Plutarch's Life of Marius written around 100AD speaks of Marius suffering from night terrors, harassing dreams, excessive drinking and flashbacks to previous battles when he found himself under severe stress towards the end of his life.

PTSD has been historically poorly understood and was labelled with terms like "*shell shock*" or "*combat fatigue*" during World War I and World War II. These terms were mainly used to describe psychological symptoms seen in soldiers exposed to combat, but the underlying causes were not fully understood, with the afflicted soldiers being stigmatized as weak or cowardly.

Following the Vietnam War PTSD was formally recognized in the psychiatric community, being added to DSM-3 in 1980, and later being added to ICD-10 in 1992. This marked a turning point, acknowledging that trauma can have long-lasting psychological impacts.

To assist early identification, persons affected by PTSD will often display a combination of the following symptoms.

a. Trouble sleeping,

b. Suffer a lack of concentrations;

c. Are irritable;

d. Can be socially withdrawn;

e. Have difficulty controlling their temper;

f. Have an exaggerated startle response.

A core issue in a claim for PTSD is that the injured person will have been exposed generally to events which have caused them to fear for their own, or another's life, and physical integrity. The injury is often categorised by the presence of flashback. Practically, it can be helpful when dealing with a Claimant's evidence to understand what these flashback are. They will often assist a medical expert in identifying what breach has been causative of this injury.

For example, in a case relating to a road traffic accident, the flash back will likely be to the accident itself. In a case of stress at work, it may well relate to specific parts of the Claimant's experiences. The need to balance the issues of causation with breach are considered later in this work. There is growing recognition that PTSD can result from many types of emotionally shocking experience including an accumulation of small, individually non-life-threatening events in which case the resultant PTSD is referred to as Complex PTSD (C-PTSD).

ICD11 6B40 defines PTSD as being a disorder which "*may develop following exposure to an extremely threatening or horrific event or series of events. It is characterised by all of the following;*

a. *re-experiencing the traumatic event or events in the present in the form of vivid intrusive memories, flashbacks, or nightmares;*

b. *Re-experiencing may occur via one or multiple sensory modalities and is typically accompanied by strong or overwhelming emotions, particularly fear or horror, and strong physical sensations;*

c. *Avoidance of thoughts and memories of the event or events, or avoidance of activities, situations, or people reminiscent of the event(s); and*

d. *Persistent perceptions of heightened current threat, for example as indicated by hypervigilance or an enhanced startle reaction to stimuli such as unexpected noises. The symptoms persist for at least several weeks and cause significant impairment in personal, family, social, educational, occupational or other important areas of functioning*".

It is essential in ICD-11 that a Claimant evidences;

a. "*Exposure to an event or situation (either short- or long-lasting) of an extremely threatening or horrific nature. Such events include, but are not limited to, directly experiencing natural or human-made disasters, combat, serious accidents, torture, sexual violence, terrorism, assault or acute life-threatening illness (e.g., a heart attack); witnessing the threatened or actual injury or death of others in a sudden, unexpected, or violent manner; and learning about the sudden, unexpected or violent death of a loved one;*

b. *Following the traumatic event or situation, the development of a characteristic syndrome lasting for at least several weeks, consisting of all three core elements;*

   i. *Re-experiencing the traumatic event in the present, in which the event(s) is not just remembered but is experienced as occurring again in the here and now. This typically occurs in the form of vivid intrusive memories or images; flashbacks, which can vary from mild (there is a transient sense of the event occurring again in the present) to severe (there is a complete loss of awareness of present surroundings), or repetitive dreams or nightmares that are thematically related to the traumatic event(s). Re-experiencing is typically accompanied by strong or overwhelming emotions, such as fear or horror, and strong physical sensations. Re-experiencing in the present can also involve feelings of being overwhelmed or immersed in the same intense emotions that were experienced during the traumatic event, without a prominent cognitive aspect, and may occur in response to reminders of the event. Reflecting on or ruminating about the event(s) and remembering the feelings that one experienced at that time are not sufficient to meet the re-experiencing requirement;*

   ii. *Deliberate avoidance of reminders likely to produce re-experiencing of the traumatic event(s). This may take the form either of active internal avoidance of thoughts and memories related to the event(s), or external avoidance of people, conversations, activities, or situations reminiscent of the event(s). In extreme cases the person may change their environment (e.g., move to a different city or change jobs) to avoid reminders;*

iii. Persistent perceptions of heightened current threat, for example as indicated by hypervigilance or an enhanced startle reaction to stimuli such as unexpected noises. Hypervigilant persons constantly guard themselves against danger and feel themselves or others close to them to be under immediate threat either in specific situations or more generally. They may adopt new behaviours designed to ensure safety (e.g., not sitting with ones' back to the door, repeated checking in vehicles' rear-view mirrors)".

ICD 11 finally requires that the "*disturbance results in significant impairment in personal, family, social, educational, occupational or other important areas of functioning. If functioning is maintained, it is only through significant additional effort*". DSM-5 has a similar rigid framework.

In summary a partitioner is likely to encounter the following reported symptoms from a Claimant, which can be of a case of PTSD;

a. <u>Continuous symptoms</u>

i. A Claimant who reports recurrent and intrusive distressing recollections of the event, including images, thoughts or perceptions (flashbacks);

ii. A Claimant who reports recurrent distressing dreams of the event;

iii. A Claimant who reports acting or feeling as if the traumatic event were recurring, this can sometimes occur when they are being spoken to about the events underlying their injury;

iv. A Claimant who demonstrates intense psychological distress when they encounter things which refer to of symbolise an aspect of the traumatic event.

b. Persistent avoidance

i. A Claimant demonstrates that they take effort to avoid thoughts, feelings or conversations associated with the trauma;

ii. A Claimant demonstrates that they take effort to avoid activities, places or people that arouse recollections of the trauma;

iii. A Claimant demonstrates an inability to recall an important aspect of the trauma;

iv. A Claimant demonstrates that they take now have a diminished interest or participation in activities and life;

v. A Claimant reports that feel of detached or estrangement from others;

vi. A Claimant reports that they have a restricted range of emotions, (such as not being able to have affectionate feelings);

vii. A Claimant who reports a sense of a foreshortened future (such as not expecting to have a career, marriage, children or a normal life span).

c. Persistent symptoms

i. A Claimant reports that they have difficulty falling or staying asleep.

ii. A Claimant reports that they suffer from irritability or outbursts of anger;

iii. A Claimant reports that they have difficulty concentrating.

iv. A Claimant reports and demonstrates that they suffer from hyper vigilance.

v. A Claimant reports and demonstrates that they suffer from an exaggerated startle response.

These points represent a check list which a Claimant can look to address and answer by way of their witness evidence. Further, in dealing with medical experts, the criteria above represent "*watchwords*" which to a trained professional will indicate a case of PTSD.

Complex PTSD (C-PTSD)

The concept of Complex PTSD (C-PTSD) has been an evolving one for a number of years. It can be summarised as a disorder where a Claimant suffers from all of the above symptoms associated with PTSD, but was never placed in a position where their life, of the life of another was threatened.

It is recognised in ICD-11 at 6B41 as being a "*disorder that may develop following exposure to an event or series of events of an extremely threatening or horrific nature, most commonly prolonged or repetitive events from which escape is difficult or impossible (e.g. torture, slavery, genocide campaigns, prolonged domestic violence, repeated childhood sexual or physical abuse). All diagnostic requirements for PTSD are met. In addition, Complex PTSD is characterised by severe and persistent 1) problems in affect regulation; 2) beliefs about oneself as diminished, defeated or worthless, accompanied by feelings of shame, guilt or failure related to the traumatic event; and 3) difficulties in sustaining relationships and in feeling close to others. These symptoms cause significant impairment in personal, family, social, educational, occupational or other important areas of functioning*".

It is essential that before such a diagnosis to be made that a Claimant can demonstrate and evidence the following;

a. *"Exposure to an event or series of events of an extremely threatening or horrific nature, most commonly prolonged or repetitive events from which escape is difficult or impossible. Such events include, but are not limited to, torture, concentration camps, slavery, genocide campaigns and other forms of organized violence, prolonged domestic violence, and repeated childhood sexual or physical abuse;*

b. *Following the traumatic event, the development of all three core elements of Post-Traumatic Stress Disorder, lasting for at least several weeks:*

   i. *Re-experiencing the traumatic event after the traumatic event has occurred, in which the event(s) is not just remembered but is experienced as occurring again in the here and now, as set out above in cases of PTSD;*

   ii. *Deliberate avoidance of reminders likely to produce re-experiencing of the traumatic event(s). This may take the form either of active internal avoidance of thoughts and memories related to the event(s), or external avoidance of people, conversations, activities, or situations reminiscent of the event(s). In extreme cases the person may change their environment (e.g., move house or change jobs) to avoid reminders;*

   iii. *Persistent perceptions of heightened current threat, for example as indicated by hypervigilance or an enhanced startle reaction to stimuli such as unexpected noises".*

Such Claimants are identified as being likely to display the following severe and pervasive problems in their self-regulation which can include;

a. *"Heightened emotional reactivity to minor stressors;*

b. *Violent outbursts;*

c. *Reckless or self-destructive behaviour;*

d. *Dissociative symptoms when under stress, and;*

e. *Emotional numbing, particularly the inability to experience pleasure or positive emotions;*

f. *Persistent beliefs about oneself as diminished, defeated or worthless, accompanied by deep and pervasive feelings of shame, guilt or failure related to the stressor;*

g. *Persistent difficulties in sustaining relationships and in feeling close to others. The person may consistently avoid, deride or have little interest in relationships and social engagement more generally*".

The disturbance must also result "*in significant impairment in personal, family, social, educational, occupational or other important areas of functioning. If functioning is maintained, it is only through significant additional effort*" as in cases of PTSD.

Somatisation

Somatisation is a rare, but serious psychiatric disorder and takes the form of a Claimant's psychological or emotional factors demonstrating them self as physically. Practically, this can take the form of stress causing headaches and nausea to the lower end its severity, and disabling chronic pain and fatigue in its most severe forms.

A somatisation disorder is defined by ICD-11 6C20 as "*bodily distress disorder is characterised by the presence of bodily symptoms that are distressing to the individual and excessive attention directed toward the symptoms, which may be manifest by repeated contact with health care providers. If another health condition is causing or contributing to the symptoms, the degree of attention is clearly excessive in relation to its nature and progression. Excessive attention is not alleviated by appropriate clinical examination and investigations and appropriate reassurance. Bodily symptoms are persistent, being present on most days for at least several months. Typically, bodily distress disorder involves multiple bodily symptoms that may vary over time. Occasionally there is a single symptom—usually pain or fatigue—that is associated with the other features of the disorder. The symptoms and associated distress and preoccupation have at least some impact on the individual's functioning (e.g. strain in relationships, less effective academic or occupational functioning, abandonment of specific leisure activities)".*

A Claimant must evidence;

a. *"The presence of bodily symptoms that are distressing to the individual. Typically, this involves multiple bodily symptoms that may vary over time. Occasionally the focus is limited to a single symptom, usually pain or fatigue;*

b. *Excessive attention is directed toward the symptoms, which may manifest in;*

c. *Persistent preoccupation with the severity of the symptoms or their negative consequences. In individuals who have an established medical condition that may be causing or contributing to the symptoms, the degree of attention related to the symptoms is clearly excessive in relation to the nature and severity of the medical condition;*

d. *Repeated contacts with health care providers related to the bodily symptoms that are substantially in excess of what would be considered medically necessary;*

e. *Excessive attention to the bodily symptoms persists despite appropriate clinical examination and investigations or appropriate reassurance by health care providers;*

f. *Bodily symptoms are persistent; that is, some symptoms are present (though not necessarily the same symptoms) on most days during a period of at least several months (e.g., 3 months or more);*

g. *The bodily symptoms and related distress and preoccupation result in significant impairment in personal, family, social, educational, occupational or other important areas of functioning;*

h. *The symptoms or the associated distress and preoccupation are not better accounted for by another mental disorder (e.g., Schizophrenia or Other Primary Psychotic Disorder, a Mood Disorder, or an Anxiety or Fear-Related Disorder*)".

In essence it is where psychiatric issues cause a physical manifestation of the same. such cases often lead to unhelpful allegations of malingering and fundamental dishonesty. Practically speaking, it is not unheard of for a Claimant who suffers from for example, Fibromyalgia, to see an accident of set of events re aggravating or worsening this pre-existing injury. Expert evidence is likely the be needed from the relevant expert on this point but it is not an area of the claim that should be jettisoned simply as it does not appear to flow form the alleged breaches.

Conclusion

The early receipt of well-reasoned and thoroughly researched psychiatric expert evidence is essential in claims of psychiatric injury. Practitioners are well advised to ensure that the instructed expert has access to both the Claimant's medical and treatment records (if applicable) as well as proof of evidence to assist in focusing their minds. They also must not be afraid or cautious in seek to test the evidence. If there is a problem, or a weakness in a case, the sooner it is identified, the sooner steps can be taken to correct it, or mitigate its impact.

CHAPTER FOUR

NERVOUS SHOCK

What is nervous shock

Nervous shock is not a sperate cause of action, but rather it is a description of the factual mechanism through which a Claimant's psychiatric injury is said to be caused. This will almost always arise from a Defendant's breach of a duty of care owed to a Claimant. Despite being classed as an "*outdated*" definition, it remains a well understood and applied concept in claims involving psychiatric injuries.

Lord Ackner in **Alcock v Chief Constable of South Yorkshire** [1992] 1 AC 310[19] encapsulated the modern approach by setting out that there was "*nothing unusual or peculiar in the recognition by the law that compensable injury may be caused just as much by a direct assault upon the mind or the nervous system... This is no more than the natural and inevitable result of the growing appreciation by modern medical science*".

Practically the concept is most commonly encountered arising from circumstances where a Claimant is placed into a situation where they genuinely fear they are at risk of suffering immediate harm, or consequence of witnessing a traumatic event, such as an accident involving or impearling a Claimant's family member. The former, in the main gives rise to the Claimant being classed as a primary victim, the later a secondary victim.

Due to the nature of events which can give rise to psychiatric injury often being what a lay person would describe as "*shocking*" it is advisable that any practitioner in this field of litigation has a grounding in not only how the law presently works, but how it has developed. Not being so armed

19 **Alcock v Chief Constable of South Yorkshire** [1992] 1 AC 310

can and does lead to confusion when it comes to how the law is to be applies to the facts of case. It can also create the situation where what may appear initially to be attractive arguments as to how liability should be dealt by a Court, becoming hollow and of little to no weight legally.

Nervous shock vs stress

Nervous shock is quite different from a claim arising from stress. The latter is considered in more depth later in this text and is most commonly encounter in the aptly named "*stress at work*" claims.

It is practically helpful within the context of dealing with such cases to apply the common meaning of the words shock and stress to the facts when seeking to decide into which class of claims a matter falls.

A claim based on stress operates on the basis that a Defendant in breach of a duty owed to a Claimant causes them to be exposed to a foreseeable risk of injury created by such stress. The operation of the law in such cases is governed by the **Hatton v Sutherland** [2002] EWCA Civ 76 guidelines, and is addressed in more depth later in this text. Practically, it is advisable to always think of such cases as being;

a. A case based on exposure to stress;

b. To treat such a cases as you would nearly any case based on exposure;

c. To focus on how the stress that is caused can be said to pose the foreseeable risk of imminent injury, as opposed to just establishing it existed.

The current test for Nervous Shock

In order to succeed in a claim based on a Claimant suffering from nervous shock, the Court will then need to consider if the Claimant is to be classed as a primary victim, or secondary victim. A Claimant will in any event need to establish;

a. That the Defendant who is responsible for the events complained of, owed the Claimant a duty of care to avoid causing harm to the Claimant;

b. That these events caused the Claimant to experience "*sudden appreciation by sight or sound of a horrifying event, which violently agitates the mind*"[20];

c. That these events are experienced through the Claimant's own unaided senses.

Primary victim test

If the Claimant can be classed a primary victim, meaning that they can be said to have been placed at the risk of physical injury by the negligence of the Defendant, the **Page v Smith** [1996] A.C. 155[21] principal as to the foreseeability of injury applies, and the Claimant only needs to establish that they were placed at the risk of foreseeable harm. This is to be assessed by applying an objective standard of proof by the Court and is addressed below, and later in this text in more detail. As should be clear from the previous chapter addressing diagnosis, these are the type of events that due to their nature may give rise to the development of PTSD like symptoms.

A Primary victim will need to satisfy a Court of the following;

a. That the Defendant who is responsible for the events complained of, owed the Claimant a duty of care to avoid causing harm to the Claimant;

b. That the Claimant due to this breach of duty, was placed at risk of injury;

---

20 **Alcock v Chief Constable of South Yorkshire** [1992] 1 AC 310

21 **Page v Smith** [1996] A.C. 155

c. That the shock of the events complained of caused them to develop a recognisable psychiatric injury.

Secondary victim test

If a Claimant doesn't fall to be classed at having been at risk of actual injury due to the Defendants, then the Claimant will be almost certainly classed as a secondary victim.

They are unlikely to be capable of being classed as a primary victim due to them having no proximity to the accident in question (although the facts of a case and what risks were presented need to be considered carefully), and the control mechanisms regulating this class of Claimants as established in **Alcock v Chief Constable of South Yorkshire** [1992] 1 AC 310 will. apply[22].

A Secondary victim in order to succeed needs to satisfy the Court that;

a. They held close ties of love and affection with the primary victim of a Defendant's act of negligence;

b. They were present at the accident or its immediate aftermath;

c. It was reasonably foreseeable that the Defendant's negligence might cause them to suffer psychiatric injury;

d. The shock of the events complained of caused them to develop a recognisable psychiatric injury.

Whilst a secondary victim doesn't need to be present at the scene of a negligent act, they must be able to show that they were present at the immediate aftermath in order to be sufficiently proximate[23], with the

22 **Alcock v Chief Constable of South Yorkshire** [1992] 1 AC 310

23 **Paul v Royal Wolverhampton NHS Trust** [2024] UKSC 1.

common law maintaining a necessary degree of flexibility in how it should assess the events which make up the accident, and its aftermath.

The development of the law

In order to understand where the common law currently rests, it is important we understand how it has developed over the years, which in turn allows us to better understand how a Court will decide a matter, and what issues and facts are likely to give rise to difficulty or controversy. Whilst the law deal in with cases of nervous shock has developed dealing with the claims of both primary and secondary victims (and both are separately considered in detail later in this text), both are considered below, due to the common component of nervous shock being present in both types of claim.

The phrase "*nervous shock*" was first used in the context we are considering in **Victorian Railway Commissioners v James & Mary Coultas** (1888) 13 App. Cas. 222[24]. The case was Australian in origin and is one of the more factually interesting that this work considers. At around 9pm, the Claimant, her husband and brother were travelling home by horse drawn car. Their route home passed over a railway crossing. When they arrived at the crossing, the crossing keeper opened the first gate for them. As they were crossing, they saw a train travelling at speed towards them. In fear of injury and to avoid a collision they rushed across the tracks, only avoiding the collision by a narrow of margin. These events were so terrifying that the Claimant fainted and the evidence before the Court indicated that she had been injured due by the nervous shock.

The Privy Council dismissed the claim, reasoning that; "*According to the evidence of the female plaintiff her fright was caused by seeing the train approaching, and thinking they were going to be killed. Damages arising from mere sudden terror unaccompanied by any actual physical injury, but*

[24] **Victorian Railway Commissioners v James & Mary Coultas** (1888) 13 App. Cas. 222

occasioning a nervous or mental shock, cannot under such circumstances, their Lordships think, be considered a consequence which, in the ordinary course of things, would flow from the negligence of the gatekeeper." The judgment, despite being nearly 150 years old makes to reference to flood gate litigation with; "... *it would be extending the liability for negligence much beyond what that liability has hitherto been held to be. Not only in such a case as the present, but in every case where an accident caused by negligence had given a person a serious nervous shock, there might be a claim for damages on account of mental injury. The difficulty which now often exists in cases of alleged physical injuries of determining whether they were caused by the negligent act would be greatly increased, and a wide filed opened for imaginary claims.*"

Following this, opinions changed with the passage of time, and the law began to develop. In the case of **Wilkinson v Downton** [1897] 2 Q.B. 57[25] Wright J decided that in a case where a Defendant's actions had been intended to cause harm, then the risk of psychiatric injury was foreseeable and the claim actionable. This was a modest and incremental development of law, and served to deter the intentional infliction of psychiatric harm by potential Defendants through permitting an injured Claimant to seek a legal remedy.

Four years later, in **Dulieu v White & Sons** [1901] 2 K.B. 669 KBD the Court decided that mental shock caused to a Claimant who was put in fear for their own physical safety was actionable, with Kennedy J concluding that "*If impact be not necessary, and if, as must be assumed here, the fear is proved to have naturally and directly produced physical effects, so that the ill results of the negligence which caused the fear are as measurable in damages as the same results would be if they arose from an actual impact, why should not an action for those damages lie just as well as it lies where there has been an actual impact? It is not, however, to be taken that in my view every nervous shock occasioned by negligence and producing physical injury to the sufferer gives a cause of action. There is, I am inclined to think,*

25 **Wilkinson v Downton** [1897] 2 Q.B. 57

at least one limitation. The shock, where it operates through the mind, must be a shock which arises from a reasonable fear of immediate personal injury to oneself."

Twenty-four years later and building on the above, the law took a further modest step forward in **Hambrook v Stokes Bros** [1925] 1 K.B. 141[26]. In this case Claimant who was 4 months pregnant, suffered nervous shock due to her fear for the lives and safety of her children following learning of a serious lorry accident. Unbeknownst to her at the time, the lorry had narrowly missed two of her children but sadly injured the third. She suffered nervous shock which eventually caused her death. Factually, she was never in fear for herself but in fear for his children. This was an important fact that distinguished the case from that preceding it.

The claim was brought by her husband, and while Branson J had initially directed the jury that fear for the life of someone else was insufficient to ground liability, the decision was overturned by a Court of the Appeal majority. Bankes LJ held that a Claimant" *would establish a cause of action if he proved to the satisfaction of the jury all the material facts on which he relies – namely, that the death of his wife resulted from the shock occasioned by the-running away of the lorry, that the shock resulted from what the plaintiff's wife either saw or realized by her own unaided senses, and not from something which someone told her, and that the shock was due to a reasonable fear of immediate personal injury either to herself or to her children*"

Fourteen years later, the law took another tentative step forward in the case **Owens v Liverpool Corp** [1939] 1 KB 394[27]. In this case, a tram collided with a hearse, overturning the coffin being carried by it causing the attendant Family and mourner's nervous shock. The deceased's mother, uncle, cousin and the cousin's husband succeeded in bringing claims against the Defendant, even though they apprehended no risk to the lives or health of themselves or anyone else (the primary victim was

---

26 **Hambrook v Stokes Bros** [1925] 1 K.B. 141

27 **Owens v Liverpool Corp** [1939] 1 KB 394

already dead, and beyond risk of suffering physical harm). The Court of Appeal's Judgment, delivered through Mackinnon LJ first breathed life into the "*egg-shell skull*" principal with "*one who is guilty of negligence to another must put up with idiosyncrasies of his victim that increase the likelihood or extent of damage to him: it is no answer to a claim for a fractured skull that its owner had an unusually fragile one*".

The House of Lords in **Bourhill v Young** [1943] A.C. 92[28] some 5 years later, decided that the law had expanded too far and too fast in **Owens** and modified the test to be applied. **Bourhill** arose from a difficult and unique set of facts in which a pregnant Edinburgh fishwife who had just gotten off a tram, heard the impact a car colliding with a motorcycle. She had not seen or heard anything prior to the collision which occurred some 45–50 feet away from her, with the tram obscuring her view of the accident site. The motorcyclist was killed in the collision and after his body was removed, she saw his blood on the road surface which she claimed, caused her to suffer nervous shock and led to her suffering a premature stillbirth. Her claim failed on the basis that the negligent motorcyclist could not have foreseen that his excessive speed might cause injury to the Claimant. Furthermore, the Claimant was not in the area of potential danger arising as the result of his negligence, and accordingly he owed her no duty to her due to her lack of proximity.

The Judgment makes reference to the Court needing to be mindful of questions raised by such claims and the wider concept of public policy in stating that a "*driver of a car or vehicle, even though careless, is entitled to assume that the ordinary frequenter of the streets has sufficient fortitude to endure such incidents as may from time to time be expected to occur in them, including the noise of a collision and the sight of injury to others, and is not to be considered negligent towards one who does not possess the customary phlegm*". It also criticises the decision of **Owens** as extending the principles of liability too far.

28 **Bourhill v Young** [1943] A.C. 92

Ten years later, in **King v Phillips** [1953] 1 Q.B. 429, the Court of Appeal affirmed the **Bourhill** scope of duty as being the governing test when assessing if a claim was actionable, with Lord Denning setting out that the "*that the test of liability for shock [remained] foreseeability of injury by shock. But this test is by no means easy to apply. The test is not what the negligent party himself could reasonably have foreseen, for he rarely has time to foresee anything. The test is what a hypothetical reasonable observer could reasonably have foreseen. It is difficult to decide where the line is to be drawn*".

The next major development of the common law occurred in **McLoughlin v O'Brian** [1983] 1 A.C. 410[29]. This was a tragic and difficult claim, again arising from a specific and rarely encountered set of facts, which where that;

a. One of the Claimant's children was killed and her husband and two other children severely injured in a road accident;

b. The facts of the accident were reported to her while she was at her home, some two miles from the scene. On learning of what had transpired, she attended the hospital where her family members were being cared for;

c. At the hospital she saw the extent of the injuries to her family and heard of the death of her daughter;

d. As a result of this, she suffered severe and persisting nervous shock for which she claimed damages.

The House of Lords in finding for the Claimant, extended liability for nervous shock to all cases where it was reasonably foreseeable that a Claimant would suffer such injury irrespective of any limitations of time and space. The test for a Defendant's liability from this point onwards in regards to a Claimant suffering nervous shock, was the ordinary test of

---

[29] **McLoughlin v O'Brian** [1983] 1 A.C. 410

reasonable foreseeability. If it was reasonably foreseeable that a Claimant would suffer nervous shock, even though they were nowhere near the scene of the accident, they would be entitled to recover damages. The Judgment is seminal not only for how it approaches and reformulates of the legal tests applied to cases dealing with nervous shock, but it also addresses and explores the issues of public policy such claims create. Lord Wilberforce sets out that "*It is necessary to consider three elements inherent in any claim: the class of persons whose claims should be recognised; the proximity of such persons to the accident; and the means by which the shock is caused. As regards the class of persons, the possible range is between the closest of family ties – of parent and child, or husband and wife – and the ordinary bystander. Existing law recognises the claims of the first: it denies that of the second, either on the basis that such persons must be assumed to be possessed of fortitude sufficient to enable them to endure the calamities of modern life, or that Defendants cannot be expected to compensate the world at large. In my opinion, these positions are justifiable, and since the present case falls within the first class, it is strictly unnecessary to say more. I think, however, that it should follow that other cases involving less close relationships must be very carefully scrutinised. I cannot say that they should never be admitted. The closer the tie (not merely in relationship, but in care) the greater the claim for consideration. The claim, in any case, has to be judged in the light of the other factors, such as proximity to the scene in time and place, and the nature of the accident*".

Turning to the question of proximity, Lord Wilberforce concluded "*As regards proximity to the accident, it is obvious that this must be close in both time and space. It is, after all, the fact and consequence of the Defendant's negligence that must be proved to have caused the "nervous shock." Experience has shown that to insist on direct and immediate sight or hearing would be impractical and unjust and that under what may be called the "aftermath" doctrine one who, from close proximity, comes very soon upon the scene should not be excluded.*"

Grappling with the issue of public policy the following 4 issues were identified,

a. Extension of the law may lead to a proliferation of claims, and possibly fraudulent claims;

b. An extension of liability would be unfair to Defendants, as imposing damages out of proportion to the negligent conduct complained of;

c. To extend liability beyond the most direct and plain cases would greatly increase evidentiary difficulties and tend to lengthen litigation;

d. An extension of the scope of liability ought only to be made by Parliament, after careful research.

Nine years later, one of the most important Judgments in cases of psychiatric injury was delivered in **Alcock v Chief Constable of South Yorkshire** [1992] 1 AC 310[30] where the House of Lords took the opportunity to codify and regulate claims brought by secondary victims. The claim arise from the Hillsborough disaster and covered in detail later on in this text, it was emphasised that the nervous shock complained of must arise from a "*sudden and unexpected shock to the plaintiff's nervous system*". The House of Lords determined that for the purposes of establishing liability in negligence, Claimants who suffered pure psychiatric injury from witnessing an event at which they are not physically present were not to be classed as sufficiently proximate for a duty to be owed by a Defendant.

In this case the Claimants in question were secondary victims who had watched the disaster unfolding and being reported via television. The House of Lords determined that in order for a such Claimants to be able to establish a claim for psychiatric injury resulting from such shock it was necessary for them to demonstrate that;

30 **Alcock v Chief Constable of South Yorkshire** [1992] 1 AC 310

a. The psychiatric injury suffered by the Claimant was reasonably foreseeable;

b. Applying Lord Wilberforce's judgment in **McLoughlin v O'Brian**[31], that there was a close tie or relationship between the Claimant and the injured person;

c. That the Claimant was proximate to the accident in both time and space, and;

d. That the injury was caused by direct perception of the accident or its immediate aftermath.

As previously identified in **McLoughlin**[32], **Alcock**[33] made it clear that a Claimant must be able to demonstrate their proximity (or closeness) in time and space to the complained of accident or its immediate aftermath. If they could not, then they would not be able to bring an actionable claim. In practical terms, has served to significantly restrict the that the class of potential secondary victims. Lord Ackner in dealing with this issue stated that "*The necessary element of proximity between plaintiff and Defendant is furnished, at least in part, by both physical and temporal propinquity and also by the sudden and direct visual impression on the plaintiff's mind of actually witnessing the event or its immediate aftermath. To use Lord Wilberforce's words in* ***McLoughlin****... "As regards proximity to the accident, it is obvious that this must be close in both time and space. . . . The shock must come through sight or hearing of the event or of its immediate aftermath*".

When assessing what could be said to be the immediate aftermath and an act of negligence, he continued; "*Grief, sorrow, deprivation and the necessity for caring for loved ones who have suffered injury or misfortune*

31 **McLoughlin v O'Brian** [1983] 1 A.C. 410

32 **McLoughlin v O'Brian** [1983] 1 A.C. 410

33 **Alcock v Chief Constable of South Yorkshire** [1992] 1 AC 310

must, I think, be considered as ordinary and inevitable incidents of life which, regardless of individual susceptibilities, must be sustained without compensation. It would be inaccurate and hurtful to suggest that grief is made any the less real or deprivation more tolerable by a more gradual realisation, but to extend liability to cover injury in such cases would be to extend the law in a direction for which there is no pressing policy need and in which there is no logical stopping point. In my opinion, the necessary proximity cannot be said to exist where the elements of immediacy, closeness of time and space, and direct visual or aural perception are absent. I would agree with the view expressed by Nolan L.J. that there may well be circumstances where the element of visual perception may be provided by witnessing the actual injury to the primary victim on simultaneous television... the televised images seen by the various plaintiffs cannot be equiparated with sight or hearing of the event".

... What constitutes the immediate aftermath of an accident must necessarily depend upon the surrounding circumstances. To essay any comprehensive definition would be a fruitless exercise. In ***McLoughlin v O'Brian*** *the immediate aftermath extended to a time somewhat over an hour after the accident and to the hospital in which the victims were waiting to be attended to. It appears that they were in very much the same condition as they would have been had the mother found them at the scene of the accident. In these appeals the visits to the mortuary were made no earlier than nine hours after the disaster and were made not for the purpose of rescuing or giving comfort to the victim but purely for the purpose of identification. This seems to me to be a very different situation from that in which a relative goes within a short time after an accident to rescue or comfort a victim. I consider that not only the purpose of the visits to the mortuary but also the times at which they were made take them outside the immediate aftermath of this disaster".*

The Judgment concluded that the Claimants in **Alcock**[34] did not demonstrate "*the degree of immediacy required to sustain a claim for damages for nervous shock. That they were sufficient to give rise to worry and*

[34] **Alcock v Chief Constable of South Yorkshire** [1992] 1 AC 310

concern cannot be in doubt, but in each case... the plaintiff learned of the death of the victim at second hand and many hours later... To extend the notion of proximity in cases of immediately created nervous shock to this more elongated and, to some extent, retrospective process may seem a logical analogical development... I cannot for my part see any pressing reason of policy for taking this further step along a road which must ultimately lead to virtually limitless liability".

Finally, the ever looming shadow of flood gate litigation was addressed with; "*pragmatic extensions of the accepted concepts of what constitutes proximity must be approached with the greatest caution.* ***McLoughlin v O'Brian*** *[1983] 1 A.C. 410 was a case which itself represented an extension not, as I think, wholly free from difficulty and any further widening of the area of potential liability to cater for the expanded and expanding range of the media of communication ought, in my view, to be undertaken rather by Parliament, with full opportunity for public debate and representation, than by the process of judicial extrapolation.*"

Page v Smith [1996] A.C. 155

With that above set out and a better understanding of the law's development provided, we turn to what is probably, one of if not the most influential cases in establishing how the Courts should approach cases in which a primary victim suffers psychiatric injury.

The House of Lords in **Page v Smith** [1996] A.C. 155[35] concluded that in cases of a primary victims of negligence, the foreseeability of them suffering from psychiatric injury as a result, should be treated in the same way as physical injury, and there was and to be no special or unique control mechanism applied. What was important and effectively determinative, was to ask if the Claimant a primary victim?

The claim itself arose from a minor road traffic accident in which the Claimant, who was not injured, went on to suffer from a severe

35 **Page v Smith** [1996] A.C. 155

reoccurrence of chronic fatigue syndrome brought on by the shock of the accident, a condition he had suffered from some 20 years prior to the accident but that had been in remission. These facts were understandably unknown to the Defendant. The Judgment identifies that the vehicles in question were found by the Court to have collided at 30mph. The Claimant's vehicle had been "*written off*", due to the force of the collision. My suspicion on reading the Judgement Ios that there may well have been a psychical injury suffered by Mr Page, but it that it was not advanced for reasons unknown.

Previously, the Court of Appeal had held that in similar claims where no physical injury had been caused to a Claimant, it was not reasonably foreseeable that a person of reasonable fortitude would suffer psychiatric illness as a result of an act of admitted or alleged negligence. Therefore, on the facts of **Page**, there could not be a duty of care owed to the Claimant in respect of his psychiatric injury. The House of Lords disagreed. Lord Lloyd in delivering the leading Judgment set out that; "*In an age when medical knowledge is expanding fast, and psychiatric knowledge with it, it would not be sensible to commit the law to a distinction between physical and psychiatric injury, which may already seem somewhat artificial, and may soon be altogether outmoded. Nothing will be gained by treating them as different 'kinds' of personal injury, so as to require the application of different tests in law….*

Liability for physical injury depends on what was reasonably foreseeable by the Defendant before the event. It could not be right that a negligent Defendant should escape liability for psychiatric injury just because, though serious physical injury was foreseeable, it did not in fact transpire. Such a result in the case of a primary victim is neither necessary, logical nor just. To introduce hindsight into the trial of an ordinary running-down action would do the law no service".

He continued setting out the test for foreseeability of injury. It is helpful to consider the wider aspects of his reasoning in these circumstances which were that; "*Before a Defendant can be held liable for psychiatric injury suffered by a primary victim, he must at least have foreseen the risk of physical injury. So that if, to take the example given by my noble and learned friend, Lord Jauncey of Tullichettle, the Defendant bumped his neighbour's car while parking in the street, in circumstances in which he could not reasonably foresee that the occupant would suffer any physical injury at all, or suffer injury so trivial as not to found an action in tort, there could be no question of his being held liable for the onset of hysteria. Since he could not reasonably foresee any injury, physical or psychiatric, he would owe the plaintiff no duty of care. That example is, however, very far removed from the present.*

The test in every case ought to be whether the Defendant can reasonably foresee that his conduct will expose the plaintiff to risk of personal injury. If so, then he comes under a duty of care to that plaintiff...In the case of a primary victim the question will almost always turn on whether the foreseeable injury is physical. But it is the same test in both cases, with different applications. There is no justification for regarding physical and psychiatric injury as different 'kinds' of injury. Once it is established that the Defendant is under a duty of care to avoid causing personal injury to the plaintiff, it matters not whether the injury in fact sustained is physical, psychiatric or both.

... Applying that test in the present case, it was enough to ask whether the Defendant should have reasonably foreseen that the plaintiff might suffer physical injury as a result of the Defendant's negligence, so as to bring him within the range of the Defendant's duty of care. It was unnecessary to ask, as a separate question, whether the Defendant should reasonably have foreseen injury by shock; and it is irrelevant that the plaintiff did not, in fact, suffer any external physical injury".

In the case of **Page**, addressing the facts of the case, and having established that physical injury and psychiatric injury should not be seen as different types of injury in cases of primary victims, he concluded that; "*When cars collide at 30 miles per hour, the possibility that those involved will suffer nervous shock, resulting in some form of psychiatric illness, is not something to be brushed aside. In my opinion, the Court of Appeal were wrong to find that psychiatric illness, in some form, was not a foreseeable* *consequence of the accident in a person of normal fortitude. But for reasons already mentioned, I do not regard that as the relevant test.*

In conclusion, the following propositions can be supported. 1. In cases involving nervous shock, it is essential to distinguish between the primary victim and secondary victims. 2. In claims by secondary victims the law insists on certain control mechanisms, in order as a matter of policy to limit the number of potential Claimants. Thus, the Defendant will not be liable unless psychiatric injury is foreseeable in a person of normal fortitude. These control mechanisms have no place where the plaintiff is the primary victim. 3. In claims by secondary victims, it may be legitimate to use hindsight in order to be able to apply the test of reasonable foreseeability at all. Hindsight, however, has no part to play where the plaintiff is the primary victim. 4. Subject to the above qualifications, the approach in all cases should be the same, namely, whether the Defendant can reasonably foresee that his conduct will expose the plaintiff to the risk of personal injury, whether physical or psychiatric. If the answer is yes, then the duty of care is established, even though physical injury does not, in fact, occur. There is no justification for regarding physical and psychiatric injury as different 'kinds of damage.' 5. A Defendant who is under a duty of care to the plaintiff, whether as primary or secondary victim, is not liable for damages for nervous shock unless the shock results in some recognised psychiatric illness. It is no answer that the plaintiff was predisposed to psychiatric illness. Nor is it relevant that the illness takes a rare form or is of unusual severity. The Defendant must take his victim as he finds him".

CHAPTER FIVE

PRIMARY VICTIMS INVOLVING PHYSICAL INJURY

Primary victims

Applying **Page v Smith** [1996] A.C. 155[36] our hypothetical Claimant must demonstrate in a case where they allege that nervous shock has caused them to suffer a recognisable psychiatric injury;

a. That they are owed a duty by the Defendant that has been breached;

b. That are placed in the sphere of danger by the above act of negligence so as to be classed as a primary victim;

c. That the Defendant could reasonably foresee that their conduct would expose the Claimant to the risk of personal injury, whether physical or psychiatric. If the answer is yes, then the duty of care is established, even though physical injury does not, in fact, occur;

d. That the psychiatric consequences complained of must be capable of being classed a recognisable psychiatric disorder;

e. It is no answer for the Defendant to say that the Claimant was predisposed to psychiatric illness, nor is it relevant that the illness takes a rare form or is of unusual severity. The Defendant must take his victim as he finds him.

---

36 **Page v Smith** [1996] A.C. 155

Lord Wilberforce's Judgment in the House of Lords decision of **McLoughlin v O'Brian** [1983] 1 A.C. 410[37] remains helpful authority when dealing with claims of what appear to be a disproportionate psychiatric reaction to a breach. It provides a firm basis to show that the Courts have long accepted that such injuries can be caused through; "... *English law, and common understanding, have moved some distance since recognition was given to this symptom as a basis for liability. Whatever is unknown about the mind-body relationship (and the area of ignorance seems to expand with that of knowledge), it is now accepted by medical science that recognisable and severe physical damage to the human body and system may be caused by the impact, through the senses, of external events on the mind. There may thus be produced what is as identifiable an illness as any that may be caused by direct physical impact.*"[38]

A Claimant may well develop an actionable psychiatric injury as a consequence of suffering a physical injury. Such injuries are not caused in the main by the nervous shock created by the Defendant's negligence, but are often secondary to the physical injuries a Claimant suffers. For example, it's not uncommon in a case where a Claimant suffers from a significant physical injury which limits them, for them to develop a recognisable psychiatric reaction secondarily in relation to this (such as a depressive reaction). It is important that any part 35 CPR compliant medical evidence sets out factual basis of what an expert says has caused the Claimant top suffer injury, and not just report its presence.

Cases involving physical injury and psychiatric injury

On the basis that psychiatric injury is caused either by, or as a result of a physical injury suffered by a Claimant, there is little controversy as to the principal of the Claimant being able to recover damages of this psychiatric injury as a primary victim. Where there is no physical injury,

37 **McLoughlin v O'Brian** [1983] 1 A.C. 410

38 **McLoughlin v O'Brian** [1983] 1 A.C. 410

this has proven a little more complicated, and is considered later in this text.

Historically, the issue had not been as straightforward as it currently is, as exemplified by the House of Lords decision in **Bourhill v Young** [1943] A.C. 92[39] and the requirements that any psychiatric injury suffered by the Claimant needed to be foreseeable in a person of "*customary phlegm*", with a "*normal standard of susceptibility*" to developing psychiatric injury as a consequence of any breach. We have moved beyond the **Bourhill** framework following **Page v Smith** [1996] A.C. 155[40] with only the risk of harm, not the exact nature of the harm being required to be foreseeable. After all, in a claim based in negligence, the Defendant's duty owed to a Claimant is the duty to take care not to cause personal injury. As our hypothetical Claimant has already suffered a physical injury, there is not going to be any issue as to foreseeability of psychiatric injury.

To ground this in a practical context it is not uncommon for a practitioner to encounter;

a. Claimants who are involved in road traffic collisions where personal injury is suffered who develop an anxiety or adjustment disorders consequential to the collision;

b. Claimants who in cases of serious and life endangering personal injury suffer from symptoms of PTSD arising from the cause of their injury;

c. In cases involving Claimants who have suffered a disabling physical injury, for the Claimant to develop a depressive reaction as a result of the disability and its restrictions on them.

---

39 **Bourhill v Young** [1943] A.C. 92

40 **Page v Smith** [1996] A.C. 155

Minor injuries, serious psychiatric reactions and the "eggshell personality"

Whilst uncommon in the public at large, it is not so uncommon to encounter Claimants who have a "*eggshell personality*"[41] when it comes to their predisposition and vulnerability of developing psychiatric injuries. This trait is often the very underlying reason for their claim, as it may have caused them to develop an acute psychiatric reaction to what can only be objectively classed as minor breaches.

The factual mechanism and causes of psychiatric injury has proven to be a fertile area of litigation between Claimants and Defendant insurers with polarising positions often adopted by the parties as to the causation of injury, and truthfulness of the Claimant (the later point is addressed in more detail at the end of this chapter). Applying the balance of probabilities test to the evidence available, it is necessary to;

a. Identify how a Claimant is said to have become injured and what stressors this event objectively created;

b. To understand the Claimant's past psychiatric history and in particular, what their vulnerabilities to developing a recognisable psychiatric disorder are;

c. To apply the identified stressors forensically to the Claimant's psychiatric history and reported symptoms to identify which parts can be said to form a recognisable psychiatric injury, and which parts are a non-compensable reaction;

d. To consider what objective and verifiable evidence can be gathered to support such claims of injury and symptomology;

---

41 **Owens v Liverpool Corp** [1939] 1 KB 394

e. In cases of longer lasting psychiatric injury, consider the wider question of causation of injury and if the Claimant would have suffered such effects in any event;

f. To ensure that such claims for injury are supported by a part 35 CPR compliant medical report that not only is supportive, but can evidence and demonstrate that an objective and evidence based conclusion has been reached.

It is possible to encounter a class of claims which on their bare facts, appear to be of a modest value, but upon further investigation and the gathering of expert evidence grow exponentially in quantum, with claims for consequential losses for loss of earnings, future care and adaptations, quickly transforming what began as a low value claim for personal injury into a complex multi- discipline, high value litigation. Practically if a practitioner finds themselves in this situation;

a. The need for robust and cogent medical evidence cannot be overstated. The evidence needs to consider comprehensively the Claimant's past medical history;

b. This evidence must comply with the part 35 CPR declaration, and be provided to assist the Court and objective. This may be done by way of reference to the diagnostic criteria, but also relevant psychiatric literature and studies that support any conclusions reached;

c. Such evidence should not simply repeat whatever a Claimant says and then seek to automatically allocate these symptoms to a negligent act, but rather, explain why they should be allocated and apportioned to it.

Claimants who find themselves in a such position will find support in the House of Lords decision in the **British Steel Plc v Simmons** [2004] UKHL 20. In this case the Claimant was employed as a burner by the Defendant in Cambuslang. Whilst in the course of his employment he tripped and fell from a burning table and struck his head on a metal stanchion. He sustained a severe blow to the head and after the accident experienced an exacerbation of a pre-existing skin condition. He further developed a change in his personality which resulted in a severe depressive illness. These later developments were said by the Defendant to be entirely unforeseeable. The Defendant had been previously found to be responsible for the Claimant's physical injuries, and on appeal the finding on liability was not challenged.

A complicating feature of this case was that the Claimant had, prior to his injury, warned the Defendant of the potential danger that his work exposed him to the risk of personal injury. The Claimant was angry after the accident, and in part, the fact he had warned the Defendant of the risk to him beforehand played some part in increasing the levels of anger he experienced. Whilst the claim for consequential psychiatric injury failed at first instance with the Claimant was not able to establish that it was caused by the Defendant's negligence, but rather his anger and absence from work, the Judgment itself appears to indicate it was seen as being too remote.

In essence, there was in any event the absence of a clear linking thread between the negligent act, and the onset of the symptoms complained of on the analysis applied. The matter moved through the appellate Courts, and on reaching the House of Lords it was held that in any event, the physical injury had made a material contribution to the Claimant's psychiatric injuries and therefore, the Claimant could recover damages. The fact that the Claimant has sustained physical injuries for which his employer had been found liable made it unnecessary to ask whether the psychiatric injury he had also suffered was reasonably foreseeable.

In dealing with Remoteness, Lord Hope provided that "*The fact that the pursuer sustained physical injuries in the accident for which the defenders have been found liable makes it unnecessary, applying* ***Page v Smith****, to ask whether the psychiatric injury from which he has also been suffering was reasonably foreseeable. The pursuer is in the position of a primary victim of the accident on Lord Lloyd's analysis, which has been followed and applied*

....So no distinction needs to be made between his initial physical injuries and his subsequent mental state. The duty of care which the defenders owed to the pursuer extended to the psychiatric symptoms as well as to the physical consequences. They must take their victim as they find him, so the aggravation of his psoriasis and the anger which led to his depressive mental illness can both be assumed to fall within the scope of their liability, so long as there was a causal connection between these symptoms and the accident".

He continued, "*An analogy can be drawn between this case and* ***Wardlaw v Bonnington Castings Ltd****, where there were two sources of dust, one of which came from defective swing grinders and was due to the fault of the defenders. The pursuer's pneumoconiosis could not be wholly attributed to the material from one source or the other. Lord Reid said (p 32):*

'It appears to me that the source of his disease was the dust from both sources, and the real question is whether the dust from the swing grinders materially contributed to the disease. What is a material contribution must be a question of degree. A contribution which comes within the exception de minimis non curat lex is not material, but I think that any contribution which does not fall within that exception must be material. I do not see how there can be something too large to come within the de minimis principle but yet too small to be material.'

In this case there were several causes of the pursuer's anger. It was enough that one of them arose from the fault of the defenders. The pursuer did not need to prove that that cause would of itself have been enough to cause the anger which produced the exacerbation. He was entitled to succeed if it made a material contribution to it (see also ***McGhee v National Coal Board****, per Lord Reid at p 53)*".

Lord Roger summed it up more simply at paragraphs 55 with "*Since the pursuer in the present case actually suffered physical injuries as a result of the defenders' fault and negligence, the starting point is that he is a primary victim in terms of Lord Lloyd's classification. Senior counsel for the defenders argued, however, that the pursuer's psoriasis and his depressive illness sprang not from the accident itself, but from his anger at the happening of the accident. Hence, he could not recover damages. I see no reason to give effect to such a distinction, even supposing that it can be realistically drawn in a given case. Regret, fear for the future, frustration at the slow pace of recovery and anger are all emotions that are likely to arise, unbidden, in the minds of those who suffer injuries in an accident such as befell the pursuer. If alone or in combination with other factors, any of these emotions results in stress so intense that the victim develops a recognised mental illness, there is no reason in principle why he should not recover damages for that illness*".

He concluded at paragraph 67 that "*Once liability is established, any question of the remoteness of damage is to be approached along the following lines which may, of course, be open to refinement and development. (1) The starting point is that a defender is not liable for a consequence of a kind which is not reasonably foreseeable… (2) While a defender is not liable for damage that was not reasonably foreseeable, it does not follow that he is liable for all damage that was reasonably foreseeable: depending on the circumstances, the defender may not be liable for damage caused by a novus actus interveniens or unreasonable conduct on the part of the pursuer, even if it was reasonably foreseeable … (3) Subject to the qualification in (2), if the pursuer's injury is of a kind that was foreseeable, the defender is liable, even if the damage is greater in extent than was foreseeable or it was caused in a way that could not have been foreseen …. (4) The defender must take his victim as he finds him … (5) Subject again to the qualification in (2), where personal injury to the pursuer was reasonably foreseeable, the defender is liable for any personal injury, whether physical or psychiatric, which the pursuer suffers as a result of his wrongdoing*"

The delayed onset of psychiatric injury following injury

A challenging occurrence in psychiatric injury litigation (and one that is often met with some scepticism by Defendants), is the situation where a Claimant following suffering a physical injury, at a later date develops a psychiatric injury. Practically if and when such a situation arises, it is going to pose real and significant hurdles as to causation and whilst it can be argued successfully (with supportive and robust evidence), it is better to view success on such as a point as being possible, rather than assured.

This issue was visited in tragic circumstances in the case of **Corr v IBC Vehicles Ltd** [2008] UKHL 13[42]. In this matter, the Claimant was the widow of Mr Thomas Corr who died on 23rd May 2002 when he committed suicide. Mr Corr had been a maintenance engineer, working for Vauxhall motorcars. In 1996 on his production line was an automated arm with a sucker for lifting the vehicles which were being assembled whilst panels were connected to them. During the course of the working day, one of the arms malfunctioned and due to this, the Claimant and a colleague were instructed to repair the fault. During their repair procedure, suddenly and without warning the machine picked up a panel and lifted it out of the press causing it to strike him on the right side of his head, severing most of his ear.

The Claimant underwent reconstructive surgery for this ear which was a long and painful process. Due to his physical injury, the Claimant suffered from disfigurement, unsteadiness, mild tinnitus, severe headaches and difficulty in sleeping. Whilst these physical injuries were in and of themselves bearable, he went on to develop Post Traumatic Stress Disorder which caused him to begin to suffer from nightmares, and to struggle in his daily life and work. The Claimant's symptoms worsened and he plummeted into an intensifying spiral of psychiatric depression. On the 23rd May 2002 killed himself by jumping from the top of a multistorey car park. Mrs Corr, his widow, brought a claim against the Defendant on behalf of her deceased husband's estate and under the Fatal Accidents Act 1976. She was awarded £85,000.00 in respect of the claim on behalf of the estate but, the claim under the Fatal Accidents Act 1976 was dismissed by the Judge. In dismissing the claim he found that the deceased's suicide was not reasonably foreseeable by the Defendant and the damages sought to be recovered in relation to the suicide fell outside the scope of the Defendant's duty of care.

The evidence which was produced in the claim showed that it had been an agreed fact between the parties' respective experts at trial, that the

42 **Corr v IBC Vehicles Ltd** [2008] UKHL 13

depression which the Claimant suffered from to the accident had driven the Claimant to suicide. This evidence showed that about 10% of severely injured persons, took their own lives. Mrs Corr appealed to the Court of Appeal who found in her favour, and the Defendant in turn appealed to the House of Lords where she succeeded on the following basis;

a. Depression, possibly very severe, was a foreseeable consequence of the Defendant's breach of duty. It was not incumbent on the Claimant to show that suicide itself was foreseeable since a tortfeasor who reasonably foresaw the occurrence of some damage need not foresee the precise form which the damage might take (**Hughes v Lord Advocate** [1963] A.C. 837[43]),

b. Some manifestations of severe depression could be held to be so unusual and unpredictable as to be outside the bounds of what was reasonably foreseeable, but suicide could not be so regarded. It was not a usual manifestation, but it was not uncommon;

c. Whilst a suicide could be a novus actus if the deceased took their own life as a conscious decision in the absence of any disabling mental illness, the Claimant's suicide was not a voluntary, informed decision taken by him as an adult of sound mind making and giving effect to a personal decision about his future;

d. It was the response of a person suffering from a severely depressive illness which impaired his capacity to make reasoned and informed judgments about his future, and such illness was a consequence of the Defendants negligence.

e. Since the suicide was not a novus actus it was impossible to hold that the damages attributable to the death as being too remote because the Claimant's conduct was unreasonable.

---

43 **Hughes v Lord Advocate** [1963] A.C. 837

Lord Justice Neuberger delivering the lead Judgment at paragraph 68 – 69 set out; "*In my judgment, in a case such as this, it would represent a failure to take into account the importance of personal autonomy, and would be inconsistent with the reasoning in Reeves's case, if we were to hold that, save where the deceased was of entirely sound mind at the relevant time, it would be inappropriate in principle to reduce the damages awarded under the 1976 Act on the grounds of contributory negligence, where the deceased had taken his own life. The mere facts that his mental state was impaired to some extent by a condition for which the Defendant was responsible, and that he would not have killed himself but for that impairment, cannot, in my opinion, without more justify rejecting the contention that there could have been a degree of "fault" on his part.*

In the end, I consider that the question to be addressed is the extent to which the deceased's personal autonomy has been overborne by the impairment to his mind attributable to the Defendant. Where it has not been so overborne at all, the contribution, and hence the reduction in damages, may well be 50% (as in Reeves's case); where it has been effectively wholly overborne, there will be no reduction. In other cases, the answer will lie somewhere between those two extremes. In such cases, the question, while a relatively easy question to formulate, will, I strongly suspect, be a relatively difficult question to answer, at least in many circumstances".

He concludes at paragraph 70 that "*Almost any exercise which involves assessing the degree of contributory negligence must inevitably be somewhat rough and ready, and that is particularly so where one has to decide on the extent to which a person, whose mental capacity is impaired to a degree, is responsible for his own suicide. However, even bearing that in mind, and acknowledging the force of Lord Scott's view to the contrary, I am in agreement with Lord Mance in that I do not consider it appropriate for your Lordships to determine the appropriate degree of responsibility (if any) to apportion to Mr Corr for his suicide in the present case. The question does not seem to have been the subject of significant evidence or argument at first instance, and it was hardly touched on in argument in the Court of Appeal. Not only do I doubt whether it is possible to answer that question on the basis of the evidence and limited argument before us, and in the absence of any finding in the Courts below; it would also be unfair on the Claimant to consider a reduction in her damages on this ground as, for essentially the same reasons, she has not had a proper opportunity to deal with the question. It is not as if it is inevitable that there would have been some discount on this ground: it would be for the Defendant to establish any deduction on the basis of evidence and argument*".

The case itself whilst tragic, highlights how it is possible that with the appropriate and robust expert evidence secured, a Claimant can progress a claim for damages flowing from similar facts. A key point to remember is that in **Corr** there was an agreement to a certain degree between the parties' experts on breach of duty and injury. In the absence of this is it is likely that the case would have ended differently.

Fundamental Dishonesty and psychiatric injury claims

Since the diagnosis of a recognisable psychiatric injury is heavily based on the account a Claimant provides, it is not difficult to understand how and why a Defendant may allege that a Claimant has either fabricated or significantly exaggerated their symptoms. This has become a more notable trend in claims for psychiatric injury post the 1st October 20213 and the enactment of the Enterprise and Regulatory Reform Act 2013, and with it the incorporation of Quantitative One-way Costs Shifting (QOCS) into the CPR.

Rule 44.14 (1) CPR provides that "*subject to rules 44.15 and 44.16, orders for costs made against a Claimant may be enforced without the permission of the Court but only to the extent that the aggregate amount in money terms of such orders does not exceed the aggregate amount in money terms of any orders for, or agreements to pay or settle a claim for, damages, costs and interest made in favour of the Claimant*".

In practical terms, if a Claimant fails to establish liability or causation of injury and recovers nil, the level of costs that can be enforced against them personally (without any order from the Court) will be nil. Some commentators have opined that this unintentionally created a situation in which Claimants feel emboldened to present claims that have a low prospect of success, which in the previously in a costs bearing regime would not have been presented. The fact that a Claimant may feel that they face little to no personal commercial risk in presenting such a claim, is often identified as the root of this issue. A finding of fundamental dishonesty can displace this. Such a finding does not have to be related to the claim entire, it can relate to only a single component in that;

a. The Claimant could succeed in proving and recovering damages for physical injuries section 57 (1) (a) of the Criminal Justice and Courts Act 2015); but

b. Be found to be fundamentally dishonest as to their claim for psychiatric injury (section 57 (1) (b) of the Criminal Justice and Courts Act 2015)

If such a finding is made by the Court (the finding being on the balance of probabilities) then the Court upon an application by the Defendant;

a. Must dismiss the claim (section 57 (2) of the Criminal Justice and Courts Act 2015); unless it is satisfied that the Claimant would suffer substantial injustice if the claim were dismissed;

b. Any order for costs against the Claimant may be enforced to the full extent of the order with the permission of the Court, where the claim is found on the balance of probabilities to be fundamentally dishonest (rule 44.16 (1) CPR);

c. Further the Claimant may face proceedings for contempt of Court.

The Courts interpretation of the facts of the claim and the evidence presented at trial will be what determines if a Court makes such a finding. There is no half way house, a Claimant either is, or isn't fundamentally dishonest. Being "*unconvincing*" or "a *unreliable historian*" is not going to be enough. The Defendant bears the burden of proof. When we turn to consider how the Court approaches this issue, **Howlett v Davies** [2017] EWCA Civ 1696[44] provides important practical guidance on two points. First, and whilst obiter Newey LJ explained at paragraph 39 that "*where a witness' honesty is to be challenged, it will always be best if that is explicitly put to the witness. There can then be no doubt that honesty is in issue. But what ultimately matters is that the witness has had fair notice of a challenge to his or her honesty and an opportunity to deal with it. It may be that in a particular context a cross-examination which does not use the words "dishonest" or "lying" will give a witness fair warning*".

Secondly, as set out at paragraph 16 of the judgment (as per **Gosling v Hailo** (unreported) 29 April 2014[45]) that "*The corollary term to 'fundamental' would be a word with some such meaning as 'incidental' or 'collateral. A Claimant should not be exposed to costs liability merely because he is shown to have been dishonest as to some collateral matter or perhaps as to some minor, self-contained head of damage. If, on the other hand, the dishonesty went to the root of either the whole of his claim or a substantial part of his claim, then it appears to me that it would be a fundamentally dishonest claim: a claim which depended as to a substantial or important part of itself upon dishonesty*".

These principals were reemphasised in **London Organising Committee of the Olympic and Paralympic Games v Sinfield** [2018] EWHC 51 (QB)[46] where Knowles J held at paragraph 62, that "*a Claimant should be found to be fundamentally dishonest if he has acted dishonestly and has thus substantially affected the presentation of his case in a way which potentially adversely affects the Defendant in a significant way*", and at paragraph 63 that "*substantially affects*" is intended to "*convey the same idea as the expressions "going to the root" or "going to the heart" of the claim*".

44 **Howlett v Davies** [2017] EWCA Civ 1696

45 **Gosling v Hailo** (unreported) 29 April 2014

46 **London Organising Committee of the Olympic and Paralympic Games v Sinfield** [2018] EWHC 51 (QB)

Spencer J in **Pegg v Webb** [2020] EWHC 2095 (QB)[47] made it clear at paragraphs 19 and 21 of the Judgment that if the dishonesty in questions went to the "*root of either the whole of the claim or a substantial part of his claim*" then it would be a fundamentally dishonest claim. Further, in **Alpha Insurance v Roche** [2018] EWHC 1342 (QB)[48] Yip J made it clear that at paragraph 12 that the Courts considered it to be a matter of public interest in maintaining the integrity of the legal system by identifying false claims, and that Claimants who pursue such claims should be required to meet the costs of the litigation.

The practical impact of the above should not be underestimated in cases involving psychiatric injury. It has a natural synergy with such claims due to diagnosis being dependent on the Claimant's account given to their appointed medical expert. If they are found to have been untruthful in this aspect, or exaggerate their claim then a finding of fundamental dishonest could be made.

Further, it enables a Defendant to not only sidestep the protective costs aspect of QOCS, but also to legitimately place pressure on a Claimant to settle or withdraw from a litigation in fear of personal, monetary and legal consequences. Afterall, if a Court finds a Claimant has exaggerated or made up their symptoms how can he be anything but dishonest? There are further issues with a Defendant in alleging fundamental dishonesty being seen as seeking to pressurise an genuinely injured Claimant into compromising claims or discontinuing but in the main, where such allegations are raised they are rarely done without any evidential basis.

It's all about the evidence

Medical evidence as stressed, is of significant importance in claims involving psychiatric injury, but the practitioner should not underestimate the power and importance of witness evidence which

47 **Pegg v Webb** [2020] EWHC 2095 (QB)

48 **Alpha Insurance v Roche** [2018] EWHC 1342 (QB)

clearly sets out the progression and development of a Claimant's symptoms. In most cases where there is a physical injury (due to the concept of "*material contribution*") there is not in the majority of cases likely to be a stern battle as to the causation of some injury, but rather the extent, apportionment, and prognosis of any psychiatric injury.

CHAPTER SIX

PRIMARY VICTIMS WHERE THERE IS NO PHYSICAL INJURY: PURE NERVOUS SHOCK CLAIMS

Having dealt with cases where physical injury is caused to a Claimant and the Claimant goes onto develop a recognisable psychiatric injury, the principals of material contribution, causation and remoteness and how they apply to claims for personal injury should be clear. However what about claims where there is an act of negligence, but no physical injury is caused to a Claimant, but they develop a recognisable psychiatric injury as a result?

It is possible for a Claimant in these situations to successfully bring a claim, but these hypothetical Claimants will need to identify that they have suffered from such an event and to be classed as causing "*nervous shock*", which has been dealt with in the previous chapters. The points raised as to causation, and fundamental dishonesty continue to apply with equal force to this class of claims.

The test

In order for a Claimant to be able to succeed in such a clam, they must be able to evidence that that were;

a. Placed in the "*zone of danger*" created by the Defendant's breach of duty;

b. By either good fortune, circumstance or fate escape without physical injury; but

c. Suffer a "*sudden and unexpected shock to the plaintiff's nervous system*"; and

d. Develop a recognisable psychiatric injury due to the breach

As established previously, when addressing the issue of the foreseeability of injury and following **Page v Smith** [1996] A.C. 155[49], once it has been established that the Claimant is to be treated as a primary victim and has suffered a recognisable psychiatric injury due to the Defendants breach, the Court should approach the claim in the following manner;

a. The Court should ask, could the Defendant reasonably foresee that its conduct would expose the Claimant to the risk of personal injury, whether physical or psychiatric?

b. If the answer is yes, then the duty of care is established, even though physical injury does not, in fact, occur;

c. There is no justification for regarding physical and psychiatric injury as different kinds of damage. A Defendant who is under a duty of care to the Claimant as primary victim, is not liable for damages for nervous shock unless the shock results in some recognised psychiatric illness;

d. In the event that the Claimant does suffer a recognisable psychiatric injury, the Defendant must take his victim as he finds him.

Page was applied by the Court of Appeal in **Young v Charles Church (Southern) Ltd** (The Times 1 May 1997)[50], where the Claimant, a construction worker, suffered a psychiatric illness after witnessing the death of his colleague from a distance of some six to ten feet. His colleague was killed instantly when a scaffold pole (which the Claimant)

---

49 **Page v Smith** [1996] A.C. 155

50 **Young v Charles Church (Southern) Ltd** (The Times 1 May 1997)

had just handed him came into contact with a live overhead electric power line, electrocuting him. Another of the Claimant's colleagues who was standing nearby suffered burns.

On the factual matrix of the claim and unlike the car driver in **Page**[51], the Claimant's psychiatric illness was caused by the impact upon him of the harrowing injuries and death of his colleague. With this distinction of factual causation in mind, the Court of Appeal nonetheless held that that distinction was not significant within the context of the claim, since the Claimant was at risk of physical injury from an accident which could be foreseen, and his illness was caused by the accident which did occur as a result of the Defendant's negligence. He was therefore a primary victim under the **Page**[52] test and able to recover damages for his psychiatric illness.

No objective danger posed to a Claimant but a subjective belief that there was

This is a more complex issue and one in which the law may well be subject to movement and further development in the future. At present, such cases are not actionable. It is entirely possible for a Claimant to suffer from what they believe to be a "*sudden and unexpected shock*", but it arises in circumstances where they are not at any objective risk of danger. Whilst there is a natural friction between what a Claimant may well state they experienced and believed, and what the actual evidence in a case show when it is viewed objectively, it can often be the case that it is agreed that the events complained of have caused the Claimant to suffer from a recognisable psychiatric injury.

The Courts have been required to deal with how, and when a Claimant can reasonably be said to at the risk of foreseeable physical harm for reasons of public policy as opposed to dealing with purely causation of

---

51 **Page v Smith** [1996] A.C. 155

52 **Page v Smith** [1996] A.C. 155

injury. Afterall, if the law only required a Claimant to state they believed they were at risk of physical injury to be classed as a primary victim, without any interrogation of the reasonableness of that belief, then any person who witnessed the consequences of an accident that created a risk of physical injury could potentially recover damages.

Whilst it is foreseeable that a Claimant who narrowly avoids death or serious injury (such as being narrowly missed by a falling building) may be at risk of suffering a to psychiatric injury due to nervous shock, it is challenging to see in what circumstances the law should permit a Claimant who objectively was not within the danger zone of injury created by a Defendant's negligence (such as being outside of a safety cordon erected around falling building) to have a recognisable claim for psychiatric injury caused by their fear of a non-existent risk of physical injury. This is not to say that such a Claimant cannot be injured psychiatrically by these events, but that public policy cannot as a general principal, allow such claims to succeed.

It cannot be correct that the scope of liability in such claims should be permitted to expand without close and careful control, but it is important that the question of how wide and broad any sphere of proximity to danger is to be drawn remains fluid and flexible.

A helpful illustration of this is found in the case of **McFarlane v EE Caledonia** [1993] EWCA Civ 13[53] which has already been discussed. The need for a Claimant to identify that they were objectively at risk of danger remains absolute. The reasoning and logic of the ratio was underlined further in the case of **Hegarty v EE Caledonia Ltd** [1997] 2 Lloyd's Rep 259[54], a later claim brought by another workman who had been on the same support vessel. In this case the Claimant claimed that he fell within this second category identified by Stuart-Smith LJ in

53 **McFarlane v EE Caledonia** [1993] EWCA Civ 13

54 **Hegarty v EE Caledonia Ltd** [1997] 2 Lloyd's Rep 259

McFarlane[55], namely that the "*sudden and unexpected*" nature of the explosion led to his psychiatric injury. Whilst the Court of Appeal accepted that the plaintiff was a person of reasonable fortitude and that he had genuinely feared that he was in danger, it did not agree that this this fear was a reasonable one. The decision is understandable, but one can see how the control measures governing how wide such claims should be cast, was applied.

This approach has been confirmed by the House of Lords in **Rothwell v Chemical & Insulating Co Ltd** [2007] UKHL 39[56]). In this matter the appellants appealed against a decision that pleural plaques caused by negligent exposure to asbestos, which were not in themselves damage that could give rise to a cause of action, did not become actionable damage when aggregated with the risk of future disease and consequent anxiety. The presence of such plaques did not usually occasion any symptoms. The plaques did not cause asbestos-related diseases, but they signalled the presence in the lungs and pleura of asbestos fibres that might independently cause life-threatening or fatal diseases. The appeals were dismissed on the following grounds;

a. The symptomless plaques were not damage that could found a cause of action;

b. It was not merely that the plaques caused no immediate symptoms, the important point was that, save in the most exceptional case, the plaques would never cause any symptoms, did not increase the susceptibility of the Claimants to other diseases or shorten their expectation of life;

c. They had no effect upon their health at all;

---

55 **McFarlane v EE Caledonia** [1993] EWCA Civ 13

56 **Rothwell v Chemical & Insulating Co Ltd** [2007] UKHL 39

d. Neither the risk of future disease nor anxiety about the possibility of that risk materialising amounted to damage for the purpose of creating a cause of action,

It was acknowledged that although the law allowed the risk of future disease and consequent anxiety to be considered in computing the loss suffered by someone who had actually suffered some compensable physical injury, in the absence of such compensable injury, there was no cause of action under which damages could be claimed and, therefore, there could be no computation of loss in which the risk and anxiety could be considered.

Pertinently, paragraphs and 33 and 34 of the Judgment provide that "*in the present case, the foreseeable event was that the Claimant would contract an asbestos-related disease. If that event occurred, it could no doubt cause psychiatric as well as physical injury. But the event has not occurred. The psychiatric illness has been caused by apprehension that the event may occur. The creation of such a risk is, as I have said, not in itself actionable. I think it would be an unwarranted extension of the principle in Page v Smith to apply it to psychiatric illness caused by apprehension of the possibility of an unfavourable event which had not actually happened.*

In ***Creuzfeldt-Jakob Disease Litigation Group B Plaintiffs v Medical Research Council*** *[2000] Lloyd's Rep Med 161*[57] *Morland J observed that if* ***Page*** *were given the wide interpretation for which counsel for Mr Grieves argues, psychiatric injury caused by the apprehension of illness related to exposure to asbestos, radiation, or contaminated food would become actionable, even though the Claimants had actually suffered no physical injury. Whether such liability would have the disastrous consequences for society which the judge predicted may be debatable, but it would involve an extension of the principle to cases which I do not think were contemplated. I do not think it would be right to do so*".

57 **Creuzfeldt-Jakob Disease Litigation Group B Plaintiffs v Medical Research Council** [2000] Lloyd's Rep Med 161

Further, paragraphs 54 – 55 and 59 of the Judgment set out the following framework and checklists that need to be applied;

a. In **Frost v Chief Constable of South Yorkshire** [1999] 2 AC 455[58], 500, Lord Steyn said that, in view of the difficulties that they gave rise to, the only prudent course was to treat the categories as reflected in authoritative decisions such as **Alcock v Chief Constable of South Yorkshire Police** [1992] 1 AC 310[59] and **Page v Smith** [1996] AC 155[60] as settled for the time being;

b. The category of primary victim should be confined to persons who suffer psychiatric injury caused by fear or distress resulting from involvement in an accident caused by the Defendant's negligence or its immediate aftermath;

c. A Claimant who suffers psychiatric injury because of something that he may experience in the future as a result of the Defendant's past negligence is in an entirely different category as the immediacy that is characteristic of the situation that applies to primary victims as contemplated in **Page**[61] is lacking;

d. **Page**[62] concerned with an immediate response to a sudden and alarming accident, for the consequences of which the plaintiff had no opportunity to prepare himself;

e. Claimants, who are at risk of developing a harmful disease and have entirely genuine feelings of anxiety as to what they may face in the future, should be denied a remedy;

---

58 **Frost v Chief Constable of South Yorkshire** [1999] 2 AC 455.

59 **Alcock v Chief Constable of South Yorkshire Police** [1992] 1 AC 310.

60 **Page v Smith** [1996] AC 155.

61 **Page v Smith** [1996] AC 155.

62 **Page v Smith** [1996] AC 155.

f. But they have not yet sustained an injury for which the law can give them a remedy in damages.

A real prospect of harm

The decision in the case of **Page**[63] as alluded to has proved to be far-reaching when dealing with the issue of the recoverability of damages for psychiatric injuries when it comes to considering the issues and concepts of the fortitude and resilience of the Claimant involved. The irony is that the decision judgment rather gives the impression of Mr Page being too stoic to present a claim for physical injury, and being seen as meritorious Claimant.

The principal significance of the foreseeability aspect of the Judgment is that where a primary victim is physically put in danger due a Defendant's negligence, then that Claimant no longer will be required to identify and evidence that an individual of ordinary fortitude in their position would have been injured. The Court is only interested in if injury was foreseen, not a express psychiatric reaction.

The bypassing of the requirement for the satisfaction of the ordinary fortitude test which had been in place since **Bourhill v Young** [1943] A.C. 92[64] does mean that individuals of low mental fortitude may well be placed into a position where a completely unforeseeable psychiatric reaction becomes is recoverable. What the law requires is that there is a risk of harm present.

To illustrate the application of this principle, a dramatic example of this can be found in the case of **Donachie v Chief Constable of Greater Manchester Police** [2004] EWCA Civ 405[65]. In this matter the

---

63 **Page v Smith** [1996] AC 155.

64 **Bourhill v Young** [1943] A.C. 92

65 **Donachie v Chief Constable of Greater Manchester Police** [2004] EWCA Civ 405

Claimant was a police detective who was required to place a tracking device on the underside of a car, being used by a suspected group of criminals. This car was parked in a street, and near a pub, in which the suspects were drinking. Understandably, during the act of moving to the vehicle, placing the tracking device and then leaving, the Claimant was placed in fear. This was amplified since due to the Defendant's negligence the batteries on the tracking device failed a number of times, and the Claimant was required to go back to the device some 9 times.

Unbeknownst to the Defendant, the Claimant suffered from hypertension which rendered him particularly vulnerable to stress. After the incident, this caused him to suffer an abnormal psychiatric reaction, which in turn caused him to suffer a serious stroke. At first instance, his claim for damages for personal injury was not successful, with a finding that neither the Claimant's psychiatric reaction nor his stroke had been reasonably foreseeable as consequences of the events.

However, the Court of Appeal overturned the decision through the proper application of the principals of **Page**[66]. The rationale was that as the Defendant's negligence had exposed the Claimant to a foreseeable risk of physical injury. Therefore the finding that psychiatric injury had not been foreseeable was not sustainable. All that was of importance following this analysis, was the result of the negligent act. Practically, this will mean that when dealing with similar claims, a detailed and balanced analysis of the factual context of the claim needs to be made at an early stage.

In the case of **Schofield v Chief Constable of West Yorkshire** [1999] I.C.R. 193[67] provides us with a further example of the application of these principles. In this mater, the Claimant, a police constable attended a premises with a colleague, following the report of firearms being present on the property. On arrival, without any warning, her colleague found a

66 **Page v Smith** [1996] A.C. 155

67 **Schofield v Chief Constable of West Yorkshire** [1999] I.C.R. 193

firearm, picked it up and fired it into nearby bedding material. The lady who had reported the weapons was present and the Claimant moved to protect her. Interestingly, she stated in her evidence that she didn't believe herself to be in any danger, but went onto develop post-traumatic stress disorder, and had to leave the Defendants employ.

The Court at first instance held that the actions of the Claimant's colleague gave rise to the risk of foreseeable injury, and on the basis of **Page**[68] the Claimant was entitled to bring a claim for damages, despite her not suffering any physical injury. The Defendant appealed, but the Court of Appeal dismissed the appeal. It was found that the relationship between the Claimant and the Defendant was of sufficient proximity for the Claimant not to be classed as a bystander. Furthermore, involvement did not require the Claimant to be involved in the negligent act, but rather in the event during which the negligent act took place.

How wide can the duty be?

In the case of **A v Essex County Council** [2003] EWCA Civ 1848[69] adoptive parents suffered psychiatric injury as a result of the violent and destructive behaviour of a young boy placed with them by the Defendant local authority. They brought an action against the Defendant authority and were successful on the basis that the authority had failed provide them with information about the child when the placement was made. Whilst the Court of Appeal accepted that the authority had failed to provide the relevant information to the Claimants, it was difficult to accept that psychiatric illness had been a foreseeable result of the breach.

The local authority had information about the child's serious behavioural difficulties, including violent behaviour, his need for constant adult supervision, and for child guidance and specialised respite care. During this child's 14-month placement, and subsequent adoption, the child

---

68 **Page v Smith** [1996] A.C. 155

69 **A v Essex County Council** [2003] EWCA Civ 1848

attacked both parents and their natural child and was diagnosed with attention deficit hyperactivity disorder and prescribed Ritalin. After a period in local authority accommodation, he returned to live with the adoptive parents. The parents claimed damages in respect of the local authority's negligence in not fully informing them of what was known about the boy before placing him with them. The claim included damages for psychiatric injury. The Judge held that the local authority was liable to the parents in negligence for failing to provide them with "*all relevant information*" about the two children they were preparing to adopt.

However, this was in main, somewhat irrelevant since the application of **Page** allowed the Claimants to sidestep these issues. Lady justice Hale provided in the main Judgment "... *it is difficult to accept that psychiatric illness was a foreseeable result of placing this child with those adopters. But it was foreseeable that William might assault them and damage their property. In those circumstances, the principle in* ***Page v Smith*** *[1996] AC 155 indicates that there is liability for whatever harm ensues*".

CHAPTER SEVEN

RESCUERS AND INVOLUNTARY PARTICIPANTS

Rescuers

The law, and wider society have an obvious incentive to encourage members of the public to help out in situations of danger for the greater good. There is a clear moral argument that an individual who altruistically goes to the aid of others and whilst not suffering physical injury, suffers psychiatric injury as a result of what they experience, should be entitled to recover damages.

This rationale however that an altruistic rescuer should be protected by the law in the event that their heroism causes them to suffer injury, creates legal fiction since unless a rescuer actively perceives danger to themselves (for example rushing into a flaming building to save an infant), then in cases where there is no objective risk to a Claimant (for example the same rescuer collecting an infant from a house he merely believes could be on fire) there is unlikely to be an objective and reasonable perception of imminent danger. Therefore the claim would be likely to fail.

It's a difficult point to reconcile, but the law must draw a line as to which classes of potential Claimants are able to present claims. Afterall, it is foreseeable that if the law expands the pool of potential Claimants to include anyone who believes they are placing themselves in peril to rescue an injured person, is going to lead to unexpected consequences and a potential explosion of flood gate litigation.

The current test

The duty owed to a rescuer is independent of any duty owed to the person who has been endangered. It is free standing. At present;

a. Where a Defendant through negligence creates a situation which places people in peril and danger;

b. That Defendant owes a duty of care to those whom they ought reasonably to foresee may come to the rescue of people imperilled by their negligence, and do so at risk to their own safety;

c. The Claimant however must;

   i. Show that they provided more than "*trivial or peripheral assistance*" and

   ii. That they exposed themselves to danger, or reasonably believed that they were doing so in going to the rescue of injured persons;

   iii. And that this caused the Claimant to suffer personal injury.

Rescuers and the laws development

In order to understand the current legal test, we need to understand the decisions which underpin the above. This class of Claimants was addressed in **Chadwick v British Railways Board** [1967] 1 WLR 912[70]. In this matter, the Claimant lived some 200 yards from the train crash site in Lewisham, in which 90 people died and many more were injured. Courageously, he spent many hours of the night crawling under the wreckage to help and comfort the victims of the crash. The Claimant became psychoneurotic as a result of what he had witnessed, and received

70 in **Chadwick v British Railways Board** [1967] 1 WLR 912

hospital treatment for it. He died 6 months later due to unrelated reasons. His claim was effectively that his experiences in acting as a rescuer had caused him to suffer nervous shock. Waller J in dealing with the case held that the Claimant's estate were able to recover damages. The Judgment sets out the following;

a. That damages were recoverable for nervous shock even where the shock was not caused by fear for oneself or the safety of one's children;

b. That in the circumstances the Claimant's injury due to shock was foreseeable;

c. That the Defendant ought to have foreseen the existence of a rescuer and accordingly owed him a duty.

There have been a number of claims dealing with rescuers in the upper Courts and whilst they have not always succeeded, the Courts have given the area detailed and careful consideration in deciding how to approach such claims. This may be reflective of the moral dilemma created by the friction between the actions of a courageous passerby, and the needs of public policy.

Following **Chadwick**[71], it was not till the Hillsborough tragedy that the question of whether a rescuer could be classed as a primary victim was revisited by the Courts in the case of **White v Chief Constable of South Yorkshire** [1999] 2 A.C. 455[72]. The claim arose from the Hillsborough disaster. The Defendant was responsible for the policing of a football match at which, due to overcrowding in part of the stadium, 97 people died and many more sustained injuries in what was the horrific, and well reported collapse of the lower tier stand. Police officers attended the scenes of the disaster and experienced the full horror of what had

71 in **Chadwick v British Railways Board** [1967] 1 WLR 912

72 **White v Chief Constable of South Yorkshire** [1999] 2 A.C. 455

transpired. Following this a large number of police officers brought claims for psychiatric injury suffered as a result of tending victims of the tragedy.

In **White**[73] liability was admitted and damages assessed in relation to those officers who were active in the immediate area where the deaths and injuries occurred. Five Claimants were selected as representative of the various roles carried out by the remaining Claimants' matter. It was not in issue that these Claimants had suffered post-traumatic stress disorder caused by their experiences arising from the tragedy. Four of them had been on duty at the stadium and the fifth had been responsible for stripping bodies and completing casualty forms at a hospital. Waller J dismissed the Claimants' claims since;

a. Although a relationship analogous to master and servant existed between the first Defendant and the Claimants giving rise to a duty of care and embracing psychiatric injury, that duty did not arise where the Claimant was a secondary victim, unless he could be classed as a rescuer;

b. Such a duty could not place a police officer in a better position than a bystander, and it would be unattractive and not just and reasonable that Police Officers could recover whereas bystanders could not.

The Court of Appeal, by a majority, allowed the appeals by the four plaintiffs who had been on duty at the time of the disaster on the ground that a Chief Constable's duty of care to a police officer in relation to psychiatric injury caused in the course of employment arose irrespective of whether the employee would otherwise have been classified as a primary or a secondary victim and, that a tortfeasor likewise owed a rescuer a duty of care in respect of psychiatric injury sustained during the rescue, even if the rescuer would otherwise be classified as a secondary

---

73 **White v Chief Constable of South Yorkshire** [1999] 2 A.C. 455

victim, so that each of the plaintiffs who was present at the ground was owed a duty of care as a servant or as a rescuer or both.

The matter progressed to the House of Lords where the appeals were dismissed (with Lord Goff and lord Griffiths dissenting). It was held;

a. That whilst an employer owes a duty of care to employees not to cause them physical harm;

b. There was no authority to support a finding of liability for psychiatric injury caused by witnessing horrific injuries to others;

c. With regards to rescuers, their status as rescuers did not automatically place them as primary victims;

d. To be classed as a primary victim, even a rescuer must demonstrate that they are in the zone of physical danger;

e. Since the Claimants were not themselves at risk of physical injury, their claims could not succeed.

There I expect, more than a little policy-based decision making at play in House of Lords judgment, with Lord Steyn concluding after a detailed assessment of the development of the law in the area that; "*One is considering the claims of police officers who sustained serious psychiatric harm in the course of performing and assisting their duties in harrowing circumstances. That is a weighty moral argument: the police perform their duties for the benefit of us all. The difficulty is, however, twofold. First, the pragmatic rules governing the recovery of damages for pure psychiatric harm do not at present include police officers who sustain such injuries while on duty. If such a category were to be created by judicial decision, the new principle would be available in many different situations, e.g. doctors and hospital*

workers who are exposed to the sight of grievous injuries and suffering. Secondly, it is common ground that police officers who are traumatised by something they encounter in their work have the benefit of statutory schemes which permit them to retire on pension. In this sense they are already better off than bereaved relatives who were not allowed to recover in the ***Alcock*** *case. The claim of the police officers on our sympathy, and the justice of the case, is great but not as great as that of others to whom the law denies redress.*

... The law has long recognised the moral imperative of encouraging citizens to rescue persons in peril. Those who altruistically expose themselves to danger in an emergency to save others are favoured by the law.

... In order to recover compensation for pure psychiatric harm as rescuer it is not necessary to establish that his psychiatric condition was caused by the perception of personal danger.... But in order to contain the concept of rescuer in reasonable bounds for the purposes of the recovery of compensation for pure psychiatric harm the plaintiff must at least satisfy the threshold requirement that he objectively exposed himself to danger or reasonably believed that he was doing so. Without such limitation, one would have the unedifying spectacle that, while bereaved relatives are not allowed to recover as in the ***Alcock*** *case, ghoulishly curious spectators, who assisted in some peripheral way in the aftermath of a disaster, might recover. For my part the limitation of actual or apprehended dangers is what proximity in this special situation means. In my judgment it would be an unwarranted extension of the law to uphold the claims of the police officers. I would dismiss the argument under this heading*".

He summarised the position with "*The law on the recovery of compensation for pure psychiatric harm is a patchwork quilt of distinctions which are difficult to justify. There are two theoretical solutions. The first is to wipe out recovery in tort for pure psychiatric injury.... The second solution is to abolish all the special limiting rules applicable to psychiatric harm. ... In my view the only sensible general strategy for the Courts is to say thus far and no further. The only prudent course is to treat the pragmatic categories as reflected in authoritative decisions such as the* ***Alcock*** *case [1992] 1 A.C. 310 and* ***Page v. Smith*** *[1996] A.C. 155 as settled for the time being but by and large to leave any expansion or development in this corner of the law to Parliament. In reality there are no refined analytical tools which will enable* *the Courts to draw lines by way of compromise solution in a way which is coherent and morally defensible. It must be left to Parliament to undertake the task of radical law reform*".

What we can take from the decision, and it remains a telling point to this day is that the House of Lord asked for Parliament to consider law reform on the issue. It is very rare that the Highest Court in the land asks for such, and exemplifies the gravity of the friction such cases generate.

This common law was more recently revisited, and summarised more briskly by Mr Leggatt QC at paragraph 23 of **Monk v PC Harrington Ltd** [2008] EWHC 1879 (QB)[74] where it was identified that a rescuer must establish;

a. That they provided more than "*trivial or peripheral assistance*";

b. That they exposed themselves to danger, or reasonably believed that they were doing so in going to the rescue of injured persons.

If these criteria are met, then the rescuer establishes the requisite components of foreseeability, proximity and duty of care. However, the rescuer still needs to satisfy the Court of an act of negligence and causation of a recognisable psychiatric injury flowing from this, but in principal if this can be done the case can succeed.

Rescuing the rescued?

It is possible for claims to be presented against the actual subject of the rescue by the rescuer. In **Harrison v British Railways Board** [1981] 3 All E.R. 679[75] the Claimant was a guard on a passenger train, which the second Defendant, a late-arriving passenger, attempted to board as it was pulling out of the station.

74 **Monk v PC Harrington Ltd** [2008] EWHC 1879 (QB)

75 **Harrison v British Railways Board** [1981] 3 All E.R. 679

The Claimant was not able to signal the driver to stop the train which continue to move out of the station. He tried to grab hold of the passenger (the second Defendant) to pull him aboard but the second Defendant lost his grip and fell dragging the Claimant from the moving train and caused them both to suffer serious physical injuries. It was held that a person who, through lack of care for his own safety, put himself into a dangerous situation and who, as a reasonable man, ought to have foreseen that some other person might endanger himself by attempting to help, was liable for injuries sustained by the rescuer during the rescue attempt. Applying the ratio of **Page**[76], there is no immediate reasons why a claim for psychiatric injury in such circumstances could not be presented.

In the more recent case of **Dunnage v Randall & UK Insurance Ltd** [2015] EWCA Civ 673[77], where the Claimant was seriously injured while attempting to prevent his schizophrenic uncle from setting fire to himself, the Court held that the uncle was under a duty to take care. Arden LJ at paragraph 153 of the Judgment held that "*The objective standard of care reflects the policy of the law. It is not a question of the law discriminating unfairly against people with physical or mental illness. The law takes the view as a matter of policy that everyone should owe the same duty of care for the protection of innocent victims. It would after all, in many cases, be open to a person who knows he has reduced abilities to take account of those abilities in what he does: that is why Mansfield was decided the other way from Morriss. There will be hard cases, as this case may be one, where a person does not know what action to take to avoid injury to others. However, his liability is no doubt treated in law as the price for being able to move freely within society despite his schizophrenia*".

---

76 **Page v Smith** [1996] A.C. 155

77 **Dunnage v Randall & UK Insurance Ltd** [2015] EWCA Civ 673

Unjust outcomes?

Practically in this framework, the importance of evidence, and the acknowledgment by the Courts that claims should be tried and not simply dismissed, was emphasised by the Court of Appeal in **Cullin v London Fire and Civil Defence Authority** [1999] P.I.Q.R. P314[78]. In this matter the Claimants, who were firefighters employed by the Defendant all suffered psychiatric injury due to being involved in in rescues, were not able to recover damages. Two of the Claimants, a Mr White and Mr Sheehan attended a fire at which part of a building collapsed in particular a wall, whilst the fire was being fought by firefighters employed by the Defendant, and four of the men were caught inside as a result of the collapse. One of the men was buried and died. These two Claimants assisted in the removal of the debris and the rescue of the body of the deceased.

In another fire four firefighters were lost inside a building, and two of the men asphyxiated in the building and died. Mr Cullin was part of a different team and went to search for the men who were lost, but was unable to find them. The two firefighters who died were found by other firefighters and brought out of the building. Mr Cullen saw the bodies and witnessed the unsuccessful attempts to resuscitate them.

All three of the above firefighters sought damages for psychiatric injuries suffered by the above events, and their involvement. It was conceded, and legally correct that the Claimants could not in these circumstances overcome the **Alcock**[79] control measures so as to be classed as secondary victims, so the only hope they had of recovering damages was if they could be classed as primary victims in the ordinary way or as rescuers.

78 **Cullin v London Fire and Civil Defence Authority** [1999] P.I.Q.R. P314.

79 **Alcock v Chief Constable of South Yorkshire** [1992] 1 A.C. 310.

The Defendant sought to persuade the Court that their claims should be struck out on a single basis, namely that for the Claimants to be classed as primary victims in respect of psychiatric injury caused through shock sustained by what had happened to others, it was necessary for them to be involved in the same accident/incident as gave rise to the death or injury of those others. Furthermore, as rescuers, none of the Claimants could identify that they believed they were placed in danger when their injuries arose.

Fortunately for the Claimants the Court or Appeal dismissed the application to strike out the claim highlighting that the Claimants could potentially establish they were primary victims, namely that they were "*directly involved in the accident and well within the range of foreseeable physical injury*". Secondly it was possible they could establish legal requirements to be classed relating to rescuers seeking compensation for psychiatric harm i.e., a Claimant can show that he had objectively exposed himself to danger, or had reasonably believed that he was doing so. In either of these scenarios, it was possible that they might be entitled to damages. For the purpose of determining whether a Claimant was the primary victim of an accident or incident, that accident or incident had to be regarded broadly, and as in all cases, the facts carefully considered and scrutinised.

It can be argued that it is inequitable that rescuers who come to a scene of a disaster where the immediate risk of danger has passed, or they are situated outside of a danger zone, cannot successfully pursue claims as rescuers for nervous shock and consequential psychiatric injuries caused through the trauma of being involved in the aftermath of a disaster. It may well be that the law develops to encompass these claims in certain situations but on a personal note, the inequity of the situation is stark.

At present, unless a rescuer actively perceives they are being exposed to danger caused through an act of negligence (for example rushing into a collapsing building to save people trapped therein) then the claim on balance will fail. Compare this to cases where there is no subjective risk to a Claimant, for example the same rescuer providing first aid to a seriously injured person who has been pulled from the same building such as seeking to staunch the bleeding from a severed limb, but does so at a safe distance. They are not able to say they believed they were in danger, and therefore cannot recover damages as a rescuer despite their actions being just as meritorious in the sense of the preservation of life. Whilst there is a factual distinction with a rescuer removing someone from a dangerous situation, the provision of effective and immediate first aid is surely not less meritorious? At present this second class of person would appear to actually be a secondary victim, and due to the **Alcock**[80] control mechanisms would be very unlikely, if not unable to bring successful claims.

Involuntary participants

In cases where a party believes they have caused harm or death to a Claimant then in certain and very specific circumstances, a narrow and small class of potential Claimants exists, that of the involuntary participant. On the basis that a duty of care can be established, such a case can succeed, but it will be exceptionally fact dependent. As Lord Olivier in **Alcock**[81] set out if: "*the negligent act of the Defendant has put the plaintiff in the position of being, or of thinking that he is about to be or has been, the involuntary cause of another's death or injury and the illness complained of stems from the shock to the plaintiff of the consciousness of this supposed fact. The fact that the Defendant's negligent conduct has foreseeably put the plaintiff in the position of being an unwilling participant in the event establishes of itself a sufficiently proximate relationship between them and the principal question is whether, in the circumstances, injury of that type to that plaintiff was or was not reasonably foreseeable*".

The law relating to such claims is highly fact specific and will be dependent on the evidence called, and circumstances of the claim, but practically, the most common versions of facts which tend to give rise to

80 **Alcock v Chief Constable of South Yorkshire** [1992] 1 A.C. 310

81 **Alcock v Chief Constable of South Yorkshire** [1992] 1 A.C. 310

this are either workplace situations where there is belief that a co-worker has been injured or killed, or in child sex abuse cases arising from fostering.

Accident cases

In the case of **Dooley v Cammell Laird Ltd** [1951] 1 Lloyd's Rep. 271[82] the Claimant was employed as a crane operator, had been leant by the first Defendant along with his crane to the second Defendant, who was working on a ship being outfitted in the first Defendant' yard. A crane sling provided by the second Defendants broke, causing material to fall into the ship's hold, where workers were present. The Claimant believed that he had been the cause of their death or injury, and suffered injury due to nervous shock. Donovan J held that;

a. The first Defendants had breached regulations 33 and 36 of the Shipbuilding Regulations, 1931, making them liable to the Claimant as these breaches contributed to his injury;

b. The second Defendants owed a duty of care to the Claimant, which they breached by supplying a defective sling, and the resulting damage he suffered was not too remote; and

c. That the first Defendant was entitled to indemnified by the second Defendants as to three-quarters of the damages and costs awarded to the Claimant.

In **Galt v British Railways Board** [1983] 133 NLJ 870[83] a train driver succeeded in recovering damages for nervous shock following him driving the train around a bend and seeing two men on the track only 30 yards away. As the train moved forward, he believed he had killed them

82 **Dooley v Cammell Laird Ltd** [1951] 1 Lloyd's Rep. 271

83 **Galt v British Railways Board** [1983] 133 NLJ 870

(see also the case of **Monks v Cann Hall Primary School** [2013] EWCA Civ 826[84] as set out above).

In **Hunter v British Coal Corp** [1999] Q.B. 140[85] the Court of Appeal reached a different conclusion due to the factual basis of the Claimant's actual proximity to seeing the harm caused. In this case, the Claimant was driving on a roadway in a mine owned by the Defendant when he collided with a hydrant, causing it to leak. The Claimant with a colleague, tried to stop the leak, and left to find a hose to divert the water. While the Claimant was away, the hydrant exploded, killing his colleague. Although the Claimant did not witness the accident and was kept from returning to the scene, he experienced shock upon hearing of his colleagues' death. The Claimant went on to develop a depressive illness, blaming himself for hitting the hydrant and causing the fatality. Brooke LJ identified that the case raised a two novel issues of law that needed to be considered, namely;

a. In what circumstances does the law provide compensation for survivor's guilt?

b. Should a workman who was not present at the scene of a fatal accident to a work colleague for which he believed himself to be responsible be compensated for the reactive depression he suffered as a consequence?

He summarised the legal propositions to be applied with "*In my judgment, the effect of these statements of the law is to identify as the relevant factor the physical participation of the plaintiff in the event which resulted from the employer's breach of duty, which participation caused the plaintiff to believe that he was responsible for his fellow employee's death or injury. If so, the employer is liable for the nervous shock and psychiatric injury caused to the plaintiff as a result of his having participated in the event. It puts the*

84 **Monks v Cann Hall Primary School** [2013] EWCA Civ 826

85 **Hunter v British Coal Corp** [1999] Q.B. 140

plaintiff into the same class as a "primary" victim; it puts him and his injury within the scope of the duty of care which the employer owes to him. The test then becomes one of causation; the ***Alcock*** *criteria, or "control mechanisms" (see per Lord Lloyd of Berwick in* ***Page v. Smith*** *[1996] A.C. 155, 197), cease to be determinative".*

Provided that the plaintiff can in the present case prove (as, on the judge's findings, he has proved) the causal relationship between the Defendants' breach of duty and his participation in the incident and between that participation and his suffering nervous shock, and provided that he has proved the foreseeability of nervous shock to him as a possible consequence of the breach of duty, the plaintiff has discharged the burden of proof that rests upon him. He is entitled to recover damages for his injury from the Defendants".

However, since the Claimant was not at the scene of the accident, not at any real physical risk of injury or a witness to the accident, he could not be said to be personally involved as an unwilling participant, and there weas an insufficient degree of proximity in time and space by which the Claimant could be classed as primary victim, who believed himself to have been the involuntary cause of another's death.

The Court concluded that "*it would be quite wrong for this Court to push forward the frontiers of liability... particularly as the case was not very fully argued, at a time when the Law Commission, whose report on this topic has not yet been published, has just completed a major review of this area of the law. I am wholly unpersuaded that Mr. Hunter is to be treated as a participant in the accident, as the law now stands, and the concept that he believed himself to be still psychologically involved as a participant in an accident which had occurred at least a quarter of an hour before he was told that his workmate had died is not one which is currently recognised by English law. It must of course be remembered that a direct victim can recover even if he/she is not a person of ordinary fortitude, so that this control mechanism would be wholly absent in "survivor's guilt"" cases ... Employers will then be liable for damages suffered by the most nervous of their employees in such circumstances, since they must take their direct, or primary, victims as they find them. The present law, of course, makes recovery less easy for a nervous wife or mother who suffers post-traumatic stress disorder but does not qualify as a direct victim*".

Service cases

It is hard to find a better example of the operation of the law on this point, and in particular the heavy emphasis placed on the need for the facts of a case to considered and analysed by a Court, than **W v Essex CC** [2001] 2 A.C. 592[86].

In this tragic case, the Claimants who were foster carers, sued the local authority, who, despite the Claimants' stipulation that they would not house a child known or suspected of being a child abuser, placed G with them. G was known by the local authority to have previously committed sexual offences and G went on to subsequently seriously abuse the Claimants' children. The Claimants brought claims against the local Authority for damages for psychiatric injury suffered upon learning of the abuse to their children and originating from a sense of responsibility for G's actions. The case was initially struck out as having no prospect of success but the house of Lords reinstated it on the basis that the Claimants may well be able to prove their case, it was impossible to say without hearing evidence. Lord Lynn provided that; "*Whilst I accept that there has to be some temporal and spatial limitation on the persons who can claim to be secondary victims, very much for the reasons given by Lord Steyn in the Frost case, it seems to me that the concept of "the immediate aftermath" of the incident has to be assessed in the particular factual situation. I am not persuaded that in a situation like the present the parents must come across the abuser or the abused "immediately" after the sexual incident has terminated. All the incidents here happened in the period of four weeks before the parents learned of them. It might well be that if the matter were investigated in depth a judge would think that the temporal and spatial limitations were not*

86 **W v Essex CC** [2001] 2 A.C. 592

satisfied. On the other hand he might find that the flexibility to which Lord Scarman referred indicated that they were.

If this were, on the authorities, a clear cut case, I would not hesitate to strike it out. However I wholly agree with the decision of Hooper J and the majority of the Court of Appeal as to the children's claim and I have come to the conclusion that the parents' claim cannot be said to be so certainly or clearly bad that they should be barred from pursuing it to trial".

CHAPTER EIGHT

SECONDARY VICTIMS

Secondary victim claims invariably involve shocking events, harrowing circumstances and devastating losses to the Claimants involved. They are emotionally charged, legal complicated and an area where what a Claimant may perceive as natural justice, can be denied to them for reason of public policy, adding insult and cost to their injury.

They are claims which require that the Claimant to satisfy a number of prescriptive legal control mechanism, and are more often than not contested. Due to this, objectivity in the assessment of if a claim is actionable at the earliest of stages is vital. Court

Definition

Secondary victims are classed as individuals who suffer injury as a result of an event but inhabit the somewhat unique position that during the occurrence of, or becoming aware of the event on which their cause of action is based, were not in any physical danger. The psychiatric injury upon which any claim is predicated will have been caused through either their perception of, or the hearing of the death or injury to others.

The test for determining whether a Claimant is a primary victim or a secondary victim is excellently encapsulated in Hale LJ's judgment in **Hatton v Sutherland** [2002] EWCA Civ 76[87], at paragraph 19: "*Where psychiatric harm is suffered, the law distinguishes between 'primary' and 'secondary' victims. A primary victim is usually someone within the zone of foreseeable physical harm should the Defendant fail to take reasonable care... A secondary victim is usually someone outside that zone: typically, such a*

[87] **Hatton v Sutherland** [2002] EWCA Civ 76

victim foreseeably suffers psychiatric harm through seeing, hearing or learning of physical harm tortiously inflicted upon others".

The current test

In **Paul v Royal Wolverhampton NHS Trust** [2024] UKSC 1[88] the Supreme Court updated and modified the legal tests to be applied for modern use. The well understood control mechanisms a Claimant must overcome, created in **Alcock v Chief Constable of South Yorkshire Police** [1992] 1 A.C. 31[89] remain in place, and whilst the decision has attracted criticism, it has brought a clarity and increased the focus on a secondary victim's proximity to an accident, and the duties owed to a Claimant.

In order to succeed, a secondary victim must.

a. Establish that they held close ties of love and affection with the primary victim;

b. That they were present at the accident or its immediate aftermath;

c. That it was reasonably foreseeable that the Defendant's negligence might cause them to suffer psychiatric injury;

d. That they suffered psychiatric injury due to their direct perception of the accident or its immediate aftermath.

These criteria have long been understood to be relevant by the Courts as show in **McLoughlin v O'Brian** [1983] 1 A.C. 410[90] where House of Lords extended liability for nervous shock to all cases where it was reasonably foreseeable that a Claimant would suffer injury, irrespective

---

88 **Paul v Royal Wolverhampton NHS Trust** [2024] UKSC 1

89 **Alcock v Chief Constable of South Yorkshire Police** [1992] 1 A.C. 31

90 **McLoughlin v O'Brian** [1983] 1 A.C. 410

of any limitations of time and space, and Lord Wilberforce held that; "*It is necessary to consider three elements inherent in any claim: the class of persons whose claims should be recognised; the proximity of such persons to the accident; and the means by which the shock is caused. As regards the class of persons, the possible range is between the closest of family ties – of parent and child, or husband and wife – and the ordinary bystander. Existing law recognises the claims of the first: it denies that of the second, either on the basis that such persons must be assumed to be possessed of fortitude sufficient to enable them to endure the calamities of modern life, or that Defendants cannot be expected to compensate the world at large. In my opinion, these positions are justifiable, and since the present case falls within the first class, it is strictly unnecessary to say more. I think, however, that it should follow that other cases involving fewer close relationships must be very carefully scrutinised.... The claim, in any case, has to be judged in the light of the other factors, such as proximity to the scene in time and place, and the nature of the accident.*

As regards proximity to the accident, it is obvious that this must be close in both time and space. It is, after all, the fact and consequence of the Defendant's negligence that must be proved to have caused the "nervous shock." Experience has shown that to insist on direct and immediate sight or hearing would be impractical and unjust and that under what may be called the "aftermath" doctrine one who, from close proximity, comes very soon upon the scene should not be excluded".

The Alcock control mechanisms

The most important development in the law of secondary victims came less than 10 years later in the case of **Alcock v Chief Constable of South Yorkshire Police** [1992] 1 A.C. 310[91], the claim which dealt with horrors of the Hillsborough Disaster. The decision continues to frame how the Courts approach cases of secondary victims. **Alcock**[92] was the lead case in

91 **Alcock v Chief Constable of South Yorkshire Police** [1992] 1 A.C. 310.

92 **Alcock v Chief Constable of South Yorkshire Police** [1992] 1 A.C. 310.

a number of related appeals arising out of the disaster. Whilst well documented, in summary an officer of the South Yorkshire Police negligently allowed Sheffield Wednesdays football stadium to become overcrowded, as a result of which 95 spectators were crushed to death and more than 400 were injured. These events due to the nature of the event were televised showing individuals being crushed, injured, and killed. the fatal events were happening.

The Claimants were relatives or friends of spectators caught up in the disaster. Some witnessed the unfolding tragedy from other parts of the stadium, some watched it live on television and some heard of it from friends or the radio and later saw recorded television pictures. They all claimed damages from the Defendant police authority on the ground that the impact of what they had seen and heard caused them severe nervous shock. The House of Lords held that in order to establish a claim for psychiatric injury arising from the incident, it was necessary to show, not only that psychiatric illness suffered by the particular Claimant was reasonably foreseeable, but also, drawing upon Lord Wilberforce's judgment in **McLoughlin v O'Brian** [1983] 1 A.C. 410[93], that there was a close tie or relationship between the Claimant and the injured person, that the Claimant was proximate to the accident in both time and space, and that the injury was caused by means of a sudden and unexpected shock.

Alcock[94] established that the persons to whom a duty of care may be owed was not be the restricted to those with a particular, familial, relationship with the primary victim, as in the case of husband and wife or parent and child but that the relationship needed to be based on close ties of love and affection. There would need to be a claim-by-claim consideration and reflection on this relationship in order to determine whether the degree of love and affection felt by the Claimant for the victim so as to make it just that the Defendant ought to have foreseen

93 **McLoughlin v O'Brian** [1983] 1 A.C. 410

94 **Alcock v Chief Constable of South Yorkshire Police** [1992] 1 A.C. 310

that the Claimant may suffer psychiatric harm. Applying these principles, it was held that the claims by those at the ground failed. The relationships of the Claimants to the deceased victims included those of brother, brother-in-law, uncle and a particular friend, and none of them had proved a sufficiently close relationship of love and affection as to make his claim reasonably foreseeable by the Defendant. That control measures created in **Alcock**[95] are;

a. <u>The Dearness Test</u> – The Claimant must have had close ties of love and affection with the victim.

b. <u>The Nearness Test</u> – The Claimant must have been present at the accident itself or its immediate aftermath;

c. <u>The Hearness Test</u> – The psychiatric injury has to be caused by the direct perception of the accident or its immediate aftermath. The Claimant must establish that his psychiatric illness was caused by directly hearing or seeing the traumatic event, or its immediate aftermath. The event must be perceived through the Claimant's own unaided senses. Therefore, a Claimant cannot recover if he receives the news of the traumatic event or its immediate aftermath through a third party;

The Dearness test

Secondary victims need to be able to demonstrate a "*close tie*" of love and affection, with the primary victim. Whilst there are no fixed categories of relationships that fall into this definition, the Courts have been shown to generally acknowledge such ties between;

a. Spouses;

b. Fiancés;

95 **Alcock v Chief Constable of South Yorkshire Police** <u>[1992] 1 A.C. 310.</u>

c. Parents and their children;

d. Cohabitees who although not married have lived as married couple for at least 2 years.

It's a high bar, and necessarily so for reasons of public policy. The Courts have to be prescriptive and rigid on who can be said to satisfy it. Underlining this, siblings, best friends and also grand-parents and grandchildren will need to prove and evidence such a close tie. This does create an arbitrary bar for Claimants since whilst the other aspects of the control measures can be more easily debated, the nature of a relationship is something which is far more difficult to define as it is subjected to the Claimant.

The requirement that a Claimant must demonstrate a close relationship with the primary victim is likely to prevent rescuers from successfully claiming damages as secondary victims for those they attempt to rescue.

This has generated evidential burdens in workplace accident cases as shown in as **Robertson v Forth Road Bridge Joint Board** (No.2) 1996 S.L.T. 263[96]. In this claim two employee of the Defendant had suffered the nervous shock after witnessing a colleague's death when he was blown off the Forth Road Bridge. They had worked alongside the deceased for most of their careers, both as coopers at a local distillery and as bridge workers, and they often commuted together and socialized once a week. Both Claimants argued that because they were engaged in the same task as the deceased, they were sufficiently involved in the accident to fall within the scope of the employer's duty of care. They also claimed that they were in a similar position to rescuers and should not be required to prove close ties of love and affection with the deceased. The Court of Session (Inner House, First Division) dismissed the appeal on the basis that;

[96] **Robertson v Forth Road Bridge Joint Board** (No.2) 1996 S.L.T. 263

a. The Defendant employer did not owe the Claimants a duty of care solely based on their status as employees;

b. A requisite relationship of proximity was still required and lacking on the facts of the case; and

c. As both Claimants could not demonstrate the necessary close ties of love and affection with the deceased, they did not meet the criteria to be considered rescuers, nor could they be regarded as involuntary causes of another's injury, as outlined in **Alcock**[97].

The Court as to issues of public policy identified that secondary victims claims by ordinary bystanders' cases for nervous shock are generally rejected, either on the grounds that individuals are expected to have sufficient resilience to cope with life's tragedies, or because it was unreasonable to hold Defendants liable to an indeterminate number of potential Claimants. Lord Hope concluded that in cases where "*the employees are merely bystanders or witnesses, as the pursuers were in this case, the ordinary rule must apply. They must be assumed to be possessed of sufficient fortitude to enable them to endure the shock caused by witnessing accidents to their fellow employees. Unless they can bring themselves within one of the other recognised categories, their claim for damages for this kind of illness must be refused*".

Whilst being an example of a primary victim case, the operation of this control measure was well identified in the case of **Farrell v Avon HA** [2001] Lloyd's Rep. Med. 458[98]. In this case, the Claimant had sexual intercourse with a woman on a single occasion and as a result of this, she became pregnant. There was no romance, and the two went their separate ways with the Claimant later forming a relationship with another woman, who he later married. When the lady whom he had engaged in a single sexual encounter with (not his partner) gave birth she telephoned

97 **Alcock v Chief Constable of South Yorkshire** [1992] 1 A.C. 310

98 **Farrell v Avon HA** [2001] Lloyd's Rep. Med. 458

the Claimant to tell him that their baby was not well. The Claimant went to the hospital immediately and when he arrived, he was told that his baby had died. Quite shockingly, he was allowed to hold the dead baby but, there had been a mix up. Be it a fortunate cruelty, he was told later that in fact, his baby had survived, and he was told this after some 20 minutes. He was then taken to see his new-born son, and as he was very upset only stayed about five minutes. The Claimant then left the hospital and following this had no contact with his biological son.

Whilst it was decided by the Court that there was in fact, no primary victim on who the Claimant could predicate his case, even if he was a secondary victim, then on the facts before the Court, he had not established any close ties of love or affection. Therefore, considering the actual relationship between the two and the actions of the Claimant had he been a secondary victim, say if his child had actually died, there was no way he could have succeeded in proving a close tie of love and affection. However, the trial judge concluded that he must be a primary victim because there was no other primary victim. He found that the Claimant was involved directly and immediately in the incident.

The nearness test

The secondary victim also needs to satisfy the Court that they either witnessed the accident or its immediate aftermath which injured, or put in peril the primary victim. Practically, the law now focuses on what this accident is said to be, and how its consequences manifested.

<u>The need for an accident</u>

Paul[99] defines an accident at paragraphs 52 of the Judgment as being "*an unexpected and unintended event which caused injury (or a risk of injury) by violent external means to one or more primary victims*". At paragraphs 95 – 96 the Supreme Court as to the timing of when an accident occurs held that "*Typically in accident cases, the accident and the Defendant's*

---

[99] **Paul v Royal Wolverhampton NHS Trust** <u>[2024] UKSC 1</u>[99]

negligent act or omission which caused the accident to occur at much the same time.... However... there is nothing in any of the House of Lords authorities to suggest that the right to recover damages for personal injury caused by witnessing a person's death or injury in an accident is affected by the length of time between the negligent act or omission and the accident.... They do not include any requirement of closeness in space and time to the Defendant's breach of duty".

As to the need importance of a secondary victim's proximity to the accident is covered at paragraph 107 – 110 of the Judgment, and can be summarised as follows;

a. Since accident is, by definition, a discrete event, whether someone was present at the scene and whether they directly perceived an accident is (in most cases) straightforward (paragraphs 108).

b. Witnessing an accident involving a close family member is itself likely to be a disturbing and upsetting event even if that person escapes unharmed. Distinguishing between Claimants who actually witness the accident in which a close relative was killed and those who did not was an intelligible place to draw a line (paragraph 109);

c. It is often difficult or arbitrary to distinguish between primary and secondary victims. As the Courts accept that compensation can be recovered for psychiatric injury sustained without any physical injury, no distinction could reasonably be drawn between injury caused by fear for the Claimant's own safety and by fear for the safety of a close family member (paragraph 110).

Paul[100] focused on if in clinical negligence claims, a failure to diagnose and treat an underlying health condition resulting in the sudden and shocking death of the primary victim, amounted to an accident giving rise to a secondary victim claim. The Supreme Court held that it did not

---

100 **Paul v Royal Wolverhampton NHS Trust** [2024] UKSC 1

since as set out at paraphs 107 – 117, these Claimant could not place themselves at the scene of any alleged act of negligence. At paragraph 116, the clear conclusion is reached that "*situations where the Claimant witnesses the death or illness of a relative from disease would give rise to unacceptable and unfair differences in treatment between different categories of Claimant. It would be impossible to explain to an ordinary reasonable person why, for example, damages can be recovered by a daughter who sees her parent die from a heart attack or pulmonary embolism which should have been avoided, but compensation is denied to, say, a mother who did not witness a road accident in which her child was fatally injured or its "immediate aftermath" but identifies the mutilated body afterwards in the mortuary or is present at the hospital when her child dies many days later from injuries sustained in the accident. Such unjust differences in outcome could, of course, be avoided by removing the second and third requirements for claims by secondary victims established by the House of Lords in* ***Alcock*** *and confirmed in* ***Frost****. But it would not, in our view, be right to contemplate such a radical departure from settled law*".

There was no proper analogy in the context of an accident, to be drawn between this definition, and an event where a Claimant suffers personal injury by witnessing a loved one's suffering or death brought about by a negligently untreated injury, illness or disease. Whilst the distinction may seem arbitrary and policy based, it does help in preserving such claims to the remit of what they initially appear to have been intended to cover. As for the requirement of a secondary victim to be physical present at the accident or its aftermath, the Courts have interpreted this fairly strictly, and the two hours or so that elapsed in **McLoughlin** between the accident and the Claimant's arrival at the hospital was felt to be the "*upon the margin of what the process of logical progression would allow*". The law has however remained flexible, with the focus being on the factual basis of a claim, as opposed to hard and fast rules.

Within the context of clinical negligence claims, **Paul**[101] reflects a natural extension of the direction of travel the Courts were taking in **North Glamorgan NHS Trust v Walters** [2002] EWCA Civ 1792[102], **Taylor v Novo (UK) Limited** [2013] EWCA Civ 194[103], **Liverpool Women's Hospital NHS Foundation Trust v Ronayne** [2015] EWCA Civ 588[104] and **Shorter v Surrey and Sussex Healthcare NHS Trust** [2015] EWHC 614 (QB)[105]).

As made clear in paragraph 141 of the Judgment in **Paul**[106] "*the persons whom doctors ought reasonably to have in contemplation when directing their minds to the care of a patient do not include members of the patient's close family who might be psychologically affected by witnessing the effects of a disease which the doctor ought to have diagnosed and treated. Hence there does not exist the proximity in the relationship between the parties necessary to give rise to a duty of care.* However **Paul**[107] deals with claims in a very specific environment. Cases relating to genuine accidents, remain largely unchanged.

The aftermath of an accident

Galli-Atkinson v Seghal [2003] EWCA Civ 697[108] provides a helpful authority that the aftermath of an accident can be made up of a number of components. Provided that they make up the aftermath of an accident,

---

101 **Paul v Royal Wolverhampton NHS Trust** [2024] UKSC 1

102 **North Glamorgan NHS Trust v Walters** [2002] EWCA Civ 1792

103 **Taylor v Novo (UK) Limited** [2013] EWCA Civ 194

104 **Liverpool Women's Hospital NHS Foundation Trust v Ronayne** [2015] EWCA Civ 588

105 **Shorter v Surrey and Sussex Healthcare NHS Trust** [2015] EWHC 614 (QB)

106 **Paul v Royal Wolverhampton NHS Trust** [2024] UKSC 1

107 **Paul v Royal Wolverhampton NHS Trust** [2024] UKSC 1

108 **Galli-Atkinson v Seghal** [2003] EWCA Civ 697

they can retain sufficient proximity to the accident. In this matter, the Claimant appealed against a decision that she could not recover damages for nervous shock following the death of her 16 year-old daughter in a road traffic accident. She had suffered an extreme reaction to L's death and, as a result, a psychiatric condition which eventually led to her having to give up work. She had arrived at the scene of the accident approximately one hour after the accident had occurred and whilst she didn't see her daughter's body, she was aware that there had been a serious accident, and she was told by a policeman that her daughter had been killed, and about 2 hours later, she had to identify her disfigured body at a mortuary.

At first instance, the judge applying the ratio of **McLoughlin v O'Brian** [1983] 1 A.C. 410[109], and **Alcock v Chief Constable of South Yorkshire** [1992] 1 A.C. 310[110], concluded that the events that took place at the mortuary could not be said to have been part of the aftermath of the accident, and that there was no remedy in law for shock caused by being told of death. The Court of Appeal disagreed, with Latham LJ when approaching the factual basis of the claim, at paragraph 25 – 27 of the Judgment that; "*an event itself may be made up of a number of components.... Likewise, in my judgment, [so] can the aftermath, provided that the events alleged to constitute the aftermath retain sufficient proximity to the event...*

*In the present case, the immediate aftermath, in my view, extended from the moment of the accident until the moment that the appellant left the mortuary. The judge artificially separated out the mortuary visit from what was an uninterrupted sequence of events, quite unlike the visit to the mortuary under consideration in **Alcock**. The visit with which we are concerned was not merely to identify the body. It was to complete the story so far as the appellant*

109 **McLoughlin v O'Brian** [1983] 1 A.C. 410

110 **Alcock v Chief Constable of South Yorkshire** [1992] 1 A.C. 310

was concerned, who clearly at that stage did not want — and one can understand this — to believe that her child was dead.

... the judge was wrong to have excluded what happened at the mortuary from consideration. If, therefore, it could properly be said, on the basis of the psychiatric evidence, that the whole of that sequence of events which was witnessed by the appellant played a part in producing the illness from which she undoubtedly suffered, then the appellant is entitled to succeed in her claim".

While unreported **Jones v Ramshaw** [2011] Unreported 5th September 2011[111] supports the approach taken in **Galli-Atkinson v Seghal** [2003] EWCA Civ 697[112]. In **Jones** the Claimant's daughter was one of four teenage girls being driven in the back of a car by the Defendant on a mountain road between Garnlydan and Llangydnidr in Wales. The Defendant lost control of his vehicle which left the road and crashed tragically killing all four girls. The fathers of the other three girls attended the Claimant's home at around 10pm concerned about their absence and returned shortly afterwards with news of the accident and on hearing this, the fathers headed to the scene of the accident. When the four fathers approached the accident site they were met by a police cordon approximately a mile from the scene.

Whilst it was obvious there had been a serious incident, no details were provided at this point in time. Within a short period of time of arriving the fathers as well as many other people were milling around trying to find out what had happened. Whilst the Claimant could not see the scene of the accident itself, he had a vivid sight of the helicopter hovering overhead with the search light beaming down into the area of the accident. He could hear the sirens and calls of the emergency services as well as witness their presence on the ground at the scene of the accident. Sadly, and soon after this, the parents present, including the Claimant

111 **Jones v Ramshaw** [2011] Unreported 5th September 2011

112 **Galli-Atkinson v Seghal** [2003] EWCA Civ 697

were then bluntly informed that all four of the young girls were dead. The Claimant took his wife home before they attended the police station. Following an assertion to the contrary that some of the girls may have been alive it was confirmed that all four were tragically dead. The Claimant attended the hospital, and the Claimant's wife identified his deceased daughter. The Claimant did not see her body, the distressing details of her condition were relayed to him. Following this it appears that the Claimant developed a psychiatric injury.

It was found that the Defendant was liable to the Claimant as a secondary victim for the following reasons. Firstly, the extreme nature of the facts and the distressing and traumatic scene which they experienced at the accident site. Secondly, the scene at the police cordon was exceptionally harrowing and became worse when the news of the girl's deaths was bluntly given. Thirdly, although the attendance at the hospital was some nine hours later, the Claimant's involvement in the trauma had been unrelenting and could not be dissected into individual parts and fourthly, that the qualitative distinction between direct and reported perception of the body was insufficient to break the sequence of events.

The case **of Monk v PC Harrington Ltd** [2008] EWHC 1879 (QB)[113] provides a different factual scenario, and accordingly a different outcome. In this case, during the course of construction work at the new Wembley Stadium, a temporary working platform was dislodged from the top of a concrete core by a tower crane. It hit two men who were working below. One of the men died at the scene shortly afterwards and the other sustained a badly broken leg. At the time of the accident Mr Monk was working as a self-employed foreman for PC Harrington Ltd. About two weeks before the accident he had supervised the erection and placing on top the core of the platform that fell. When he heard there had been an accident, he made his way to the scene and crawled under the platform

[113] **Monk v PC Harrington Ltd** [2008] EWHC 1879 (QB)

to see if he could help specifically, to comfort the man with the broken leg.

Subsequently, as a result of the accident, Mr Monk began to suffer from symptoms of post-traumatic stress disorder (PTSD) and associated depression amounting to a psychiatric illness for which he received various treatments and medications. Later, Mr Monk ceased to go to work. The psychiatric experts agreed that as a result of his involvement Mr Monk suffered from PTSD and associated depression. The Defendant admitted liability and the issue for determination was whether Mr Monk fell within the class of persons to whom the law would afford a remedy for psychiatric injury caused by the admitted negligence of an employer.

The Claimant's case was that his involvement in the accident was such that he satisfied the necessary conditions to recover compensation as a rescuer and even if he was unable to bring himself within the rescuer category of primary victim, he could nevertheless establish the necessary proximity to the accident, which he believed he had caused, in order that he could be regarded as an unwilling participant. The Judge accepted that the Claimant provided a significant help in comforting the injured men until the emergency services arrived. He accepted that the assistance was neither trivial nor peripheral and entitled him to be regarded as a rescuer.

However, the evidence showed that it was improbable that in rushing to the aid of the injured men, the Claimant believed he was putting his own physical safety at risk and if he did hold such a belief, it was unreasonable. This meant that the Claimant could not establish that he was a primary victim on the basis of his involvement as a rescuer. The Judge then turned to the question the Claimant case relied on him still being a primary victim as an unwilling participant. Who can be classed as an "*involuntary participant*" was set out by Lord Oliver in **Alcock**[114] where he divided plaintiffs into two broad categories: "*That is to say, those cases in which the*

[114] **Alcock v Chief Constable of South Yorkshire** [1992] 1 A.C. 310

injured plaintiff was involved, either immediately or immediately, as a participant, and those in which the plaintiff was no more than the passive and unwilling witness of injury caused to others."

Having referred to a series of cases Lord Oliver continued: "*These are all cases where the plaintiff has, to a greater or lesser degree, been personally involved in the incident out of which the action arises, either through the direct threat of bodily injury to himself or in coming to the aid of others injured or threatened... where the negligent act of the Defendant has put the plaintiff in the position of being, or thinking that he is about to be or has been, the involuntary cause of another's death or injury and the illness complained of stems from the shock to the plaintiff of the conscious- ness of this supposed fact.*

The fact that the Defendant's negligent conduct has foreseeably put the plaintiff in the position of being an unwilling participant in the event establishes of itself a sufficiently proximate relationship between them and the principal question is whether, in the circumstances, injury of that type to that plaintiff was or was not reasonably foreseeable."

The Judge held that to succeed Mr Monk had to show that his injuries were induced by a genuine belief that he had caused another person's injury or death. Although the traumatic effects of the accident upon Mr Monks' health were increased by a belief that he might have caused the accident, there was no reasonable basis for such a belief. Accordingly, it was not reasonably foreseeable that someone in his position would suffer psychiatric injury as a result of such a belief. This left Mr Monk as a secondary victim and as he had no ties of love and affection to the victims therefore his claim failed.

The Hearness test

In **Alcock** it was held that a secondary victim's perception of events scenes on television did not create the necessary degree of proximity to the accident. Lord Ackner set out at paragraph that; "*Although the television pictures certainly gave rise to feelings of the deepest anxiety and distress, in the* *circumstances of this case the simultaneous television broadcasts of what occurred cannot be equated with the "sight or hearing of the event or its immediate aftermath." Accordingly shocks sustained by reason of these broadcasts cannot found a claim*".

Practically, where a Claimant can establish the requisite degree of proximity, this component is unlikely to pose any real issues.

That it was reasonably foreseeable that a person of reasonable fortitude would suffer some psychiatric injury?

This particular component continues to cause a number of issues practically when dealing with claims for secondary victims. On the one hand a practitioner confronted with a genuinely injured Claimant, who has suffered an extreme reaction to a shocking and sudden event, may still be restricted from being able to successfully purse a claim on the basis that the injury suffered cannot be said to have been objectively foreseeable. The issue flows from the decision in **Bourhill**[115] (already considered in this text) where their Lordships held that in deciding the question the Defendant can assume that the Claimant was a person of "*customary phlegm*", with the "*normal standard of susceptibility*". In cases where a Claimant suffers from an "*eggshell personality*" then their mental injury is unlikely to be reasonably foreseeable unless heightened vulnerability is known, or should be known to a Defendant. This creates a useful and sensible restriction in the bringing of such a claim.

Paul[116] has helpfully modified this test and brought some clarity to the issue. Paragraphs 75 – 76 of the judgement in set out that; "*It is of course necessary for a Claimant to show that it was reasonably foreseeable that the Defendant's negligence might cause her injury. If, for example, a Claimant with a history of psychiatric illness develops such an illness after witnessing a minor accident in which his wife sustains some cuts and bruises, his claim*

[115] **Bourhill v Young** [1943] A.C. 92

[116] **Paul v Royal Wolverhampton NHS Trust** [2024] UKSC 1

might fail that test. But we can see no justification for super-imposing an additional, separate requirement that the event witnessed by the Claimant was "horrifying".

Although said to involve an "objective standard", such a test is in truth unavoidably subjective. There is no available Richter scale of horror. The test pushes judges to compare the facts of the case before them with the facts of other cases and engage in an exercise of deciding whether or not the facts are similarly "horrifying". As Tomlinson LJ put it in ***Ronayne****, at para 15, the judge's task is to "allocate to [the] case its appropriate place on the spectrum between circumstances which attract compensation and those which do not".*

The increased flexibility now provided for coupled with the movement away from seeking to compare one secondary victim to a theoretical reasonable person is helpful, since causation of psychiatric injury is very much dependent on what the secondary victim experienced and their own vulnerabilities Practically, the point to raise with oneself must be whether psychiatric injury would have been reasonably foreseeable in a person of "*ordinary fortitude*" in the circumstances that the practitioner finds themselves dealing with. What an unusually sensitive secondary victim may not be able to successfully pursue a claim for damages as a secondary victim in circumstances which do not satisfy this, the increased focus and clarity brought to what the Court should class as an accident, has the effect of re directing focus in a practical manner the facts which underpin the claim, and what can be shown as having occurred.

Whilst the decision in **Paul**[117] seems to have shut down any secondary victim claim based on witnessing the results of clinical negligence, there may yet be circumstances in which such claims could be made.

However the law has moved forward significant in how it approaches this issue outside of the context of clinical negligence as demonstrated by the

[117] **Paul v Royal Wolverhampton NHS Trust** [2024] UKSC 1

case of **Tranmore v T E Scudder Ltd** [1998] EWCA Civ 733[118] presents an interesting example of how the Judgement in **Paul**[119] may assist secondary victims.

In this matter, the Defendants were demolition contractors. They employed the Claimant's son who was killed on the 16th May 1995 when a building collapsed onto him. The Claimant was told of the collapse at about 7.30 p.m. on his return home from work and arrived at the site at about 8.00 p.m. having been driven there by his other son.

He arrived to a scene of police and emergency services and was denied entry to the site. It was not until about 10 p.m. that the plaintiff was told that the rescue services had been able to get into the building and to ascertain that they could not help his son and that his son was dead. He did not see his son's body fortunately until he attended the mortuary some 24 hours later. Lord Justice Roch although with noted sympathy to the Claimant dismissed his claim stating that; "*We, however, have to apply English law as we find it. In our hierarchy of Courts, it is not, in my judgment, for this Court to break new ground, and I do not find it possible to hold that this plaintiff could successfully bring himself within the "immediate aftermath" line of cases. He did not go to the accident site for two hours after the accident happened. By that time all the immediate work of the police and the emergency services had finished. Even during the brief period when he was inside the shattered building, his son was buried in rubble two floors above him. He never saw any part of his son's body until he visited the mortuary about 24 hours later. I do not consider that any of these matters, taken in isolation, would necessarily be decisive, but their combined effect is in my judgment overwhelming*".

118 **Tranmore v T E Scudder Ltd** [1998] EWCA Civ 733

119 **Paul v Royal Wolverhampton NHS Trust** [2024] UKSC 1

Secondary victims in a clinical negligence

Following the decision in **Paul**[120], it appears that secondary victim claims are closed in all but most the most extreme of circumstances since;

a. A victim must have witnessed an accident or its aftermath caused by the Defendant's negligence, and as *"an accident is, by definition, a discrete event in the ordinary sense of that word, meaning something which happens at a particular time, at a particular place, in a particular way. Whether someone was present at the scene and whether they directly perceived an accident are in most cases questions which admit of a clear and straightforward answer;*

b. That's this would mean that secondary victim would need to be present during a Claimant's treatment;

c. That further, "*as the class of victims doctors ought reasonably to have in contemplation when directing their minds to the care of a patient do not include members of the patient's close family who might be psychologically affected by witnessing the effects of a disease which the doctor ought to have diagnosed and treated. there does not exist the proximity in the relationship between the parties necessary to give rise to a duty of care*"[121] there is no duty on which a claim can be based.

It is sensible at this point to identify an example of a claim which may despite the above judgment still succeed. The case of **RE (A Minor) v Calderdale and Huddersfield NHS Foundation Trust** [2017] EWHC 824 (QB)[122] itself is tragic, and involved three members of the same

---

120 **Paul v Royal Wolverhampton NHS Trust** [2024] UKSC 1

121 **Paul v Royal Wolverhampton NHS Trust** [2024] UKSC 1, paragraphs 141.

122 **RE (A Minor) v Calderdale and Huddersfield NHS Foundation Trust** [2017] EWHC 824 (QB)

family, RE a child being born, LE, the child's mother and DE the mother's grandmother who was present during the birth. The issue before the Court with regards to LE and DE's claims was solely whether they were entitled to recover damages either as primary or secondary victims with causation of injury and quantum being agreed. The claim arose from complications during the birth of RE who suffered a hypoxic brain injury because of a negligent delay in her delivery. Goss J at paragraph 31 – 33 of the Judgment found that RE started to sustain negligently caused damage when her head was crowned but her body remained in the birth canal. At this stage, the law would consider her to be "*in utero*" and therefore RE and LE were both considered to be the same legal being (as per **Wild v Southend University Hospital NHS Foundation Trust** [2014] EWHC 4053 (QB)[123]).

Since RE and LE were the same legal entity when injury was inflicted to RE, LE was classed as a primary victim of the Defendant's negligence. This resulted in LE being able to sidestep the draconian control measures imposed by **Mcloughlin v O'Brian** [1983] AC 410[124] and **Alcock**[125]. Goss J was of the opinion that DE (who was present at the time of injury) had to be classed as a secondary victim. It was clear in evidence that she had witnessed a particularly traumatic birth, and believed her newly born granddaughter to be dead. As per **Mcloughlin**[126] and **Alcock**[127]. Mr Justice Goss summarised the test for secondary victims articulately at paragraph 35 of the judgment as being effectively a two-stage process, namely: "*The necessary preconditions to establish a claim as a secondary party are:*

[123] **Wild v Southend University Hospital NHS Foundation Trust** [2014] EWHC 4053 (QB)

[124] **Mcloughlin v O'Brian** [1983] AC 410

[125] **Alcock v Chief Constable of South Yorkshire** [1992] 1 A.C. 310

[126] **Mcloughlin v O'Brian** [1983] AC 410

[127] **Alcock v Chief Constable of South Yorkshire** [1992] 1 A.C. 310

a. *A sufficient closeness both in terms of love and affection to the person injured or killed and being in sight or sound of the directly injurious event giving rise to the tortious liability;*

b. *The induction of psychiatric illness by shock, that is "the sudden appreciation by sight or sound of a horrifying event which violently agitated the mind*".

The Defendant at trial did not seek to dispute that both mother and grandmother had sufficiently close personal relationships in terms of love and affection with RE to give rise to a tortious liability in the event of RE suffering injury and accepted that both had witnessed the injurious event directly. It was also conceded that both were sufficiently close in terms of relationship to RE to be considered as secondary victims in any event. The sole remaining issue before the Court was whether the "*injurious event*" was sufficiently horrifying to establish a claim.

In reaching his decision, Goss J placed reliance on the considered the case of **Liverpool Women's Hospital NHS Foundation Trust v Ronayne** [2015] EWCA Civ 588[128] which previously had established that visitors to a hospital to a certain degree are "*conditioned as to what to expect, and in the ordinary way it is also likely that due warning will be given by medical staff of an impending encounter likely to prove distressing*" and therefore, in order to found a case in liability, the events would have to be "*something which is exceptional in nature.*" (paragraphs 21 and 41 of the Judgment.) In **Ronayne**[129] the Claimant had suffered psychiatric injury from the shock of seeing of his seriously ill wife's appearance in hospital. She had undergone a hysterectomy and a few days after discharge she became unwell and was admitted to A&E. Shortly before she underwent emergency surgery for septicaemia Mr Ronayne saw his wife connected

[128] **Liverpool Women's Hospital NHS Foundation Trust v Ronayne** [2015] EWCA Civ 588

[129] **Liverpool Women's Hospital NHS Foundation Trust v Ronayne** [2015] EWCA Civ 588

to various machines including drips and monitors. After surgery he saw her unconscious, connected to a ventilator, and being administered four types of antibiotic intravenously. He developed a psychiatric injury as a result of this.

The Court of Appeal found that the event was neither sudden nor sufficiently shocking and that his psychiatric illness was not caused by that event. In the case of **RE (A Minor)**[130], it was the viewing of the apparently dead and lifeless baby, coupled with the attempts to resuscitate that were found to fall outside of the standard events of childbirth, and therefore, couldn't be said to be "*part*" of the demands and experiences of child birth, and on this basis, Goss J found that both LE and DE satisfied the strict conditions required to be compensated as secondary victims. In dealing with the case of DE the evidence before the Court placed the grandmother square in the middle of the unfolding events. She was present throughout the birth and witnessed the aftermath and had believed that RE was dead. The control mechanisms in the opinion of Goss J were satisfied and the only matter to be determined was whether or not the event was sufficiently traumatic to be considered as sufficiently and objectively horrifying to establish a claim, which it was.

Goss J in his detailed Judgement on this specific issue held that this was not a situation whereby the events LE and DE were exposed to manifested gradually over time, but rapidly materialised. As such, it couldn't be said that there was "*a process of gradual realisation [and]… no conditioning for what came nor was there any warning of a materialising risk*". Applying the facts of this case to the framework set out in **Paul**[131], whilst at first blush, DE would not be able to bring a claim, she was present at all material times. Since at paragraph 95 of the Judgment, it is made clear that "*the right to recover damages for personal injury caused by witnessing a person's death or injury in an accident is affected by the length*

[130] **RE (A Minor) v Calderdale and Huddersfield NHS Foundation Trust** [2017] EWHC 824 (QB)

[131] **Paul v Royal Wolverhampton NHS Trust** [2024] UKSC 1

of time between the negligent act or omission and the accident", there are good arguments that **Re A**[132] could still be decided in the Claimant's favour[133].

Social media?

One point however that seems open for re-visitation (in the correct circumstance) is that whilst it is not sufficient for a Claimant to be informed, or to read about an event to recover compensation, there must be direct perception of the events. **Paul**[134] appears to acknowledge the fluidity of the concept of a Claimant's proximity to an actual accident. Emphasis is placed on the need to witness the accident itself (see paragraph 107 – 11 of the Judgment)

Whilst Paul is focused on clinical negligence clams, **Alcock** deals with a very different class of Claimants. The impact of technology and social media is yet to be expanded upon in common law. It is right to acknowledge that whilst the Claimants in **Alcock**[135] were family members and loved ones of victims of the Hillsborough disaster, and that many of their number had seen live television images of the events of the day and were later shown recordings, they only became aware that their loved ones had died when they were required to identify their bodies. The Judgment delivered in **Alcock**[136] identified the fact that television images broadcast of the disaster did not depict identifiable individuals but also that broadcasting ethics would prevent broadcasters from showing the suffering of recognisable individuals.

---

132 **RE (A Minor) v Calderdale and Huddersfield NHS Foundation Trust** [2017] EWHC 824 (QB)

133 **RE (A Minor) v Calderdale and Huddersfield NHS Foundation Trust** [2017] EWHC 824 (QB)

134 **Paul v Royal Wolverhampton NHS Trust** [2024] UKSC 1

135 **Alcock v Chief Constable of South Yorkshire** [1992] 1 A.C. 310

136 **Alcock v Chief Constable of South Yorkshire** [1992] 1 A.C. 310

Pausing there, the definition of who is a "*broadcaster*" in today's world, could encompass any person who for example, using a smart phone recorded and then uploaded any images or videos to the internet, principally social media where its proliferation would increase exponentially. By the nature of social media, this could well allow for the ready identification of individuals in such media. **Alcock**[137] makes it clear that when dealing with the impact of television footage the then Claimants did not fulfil the necessary criteria for secondary victims but, it was stressed that this was due to the fact that images didn't identify the suffering of individuals.

It does appear possible that this particular point could arise in the future and as the reach of use of social media and communication technology continues to advance, it may only be a matter of time before such a case reaches the upper Courts.

Reform?

It was sad, and frustrating that in applying the principals of **Alcock**[138] many claims failed for the reason of public policy. It is also vexing that **Paul**[139] has effectively excluded secondary claims in clinical negligence context.

Whilst the law continues to class certain types of relationships since **Alcock**[140] as lacking a sufficiently close tie of "*love and affection*" there does appear to be some movement on who could fall into this category following **Paul**[141]. Paragraph 141 and 142 of the Judgment sets out that whilst; "*a line must be drawn somewhere to keep the liability of negligent*

137 **Alcock v Chief Constable of South Yorkshire** [1992] 1 A.C. 310

138 **Alcock v Chief Constable of South Yorkshire** [1992] 1 A.C. 310

139 **Paul v Royal Wolverhampton NHS Trust** [2024] UKSC 1

140 **Alcock v Chief Constable of South Yorkshire** [1992] 1 A.C. 310

141 **Paul v Royal Wolverhampton NHS Trust** [2024] UKSC 1

actors for such secondary harm within reasonable bounds. Wherever the line is drawn, some people who suffer what may be serious illness in connection with the death or injury of another person will be left uncompensated… there is a rough and ready logic in limiting recovery by secondary victims to individuals who were present at the scene, witnessed the accident and have a close tie of love and affection with the primary victim. These limitations are justified, not by any theory that illness induced by direct perception is more inherently worthy of compensation than illness induced by other means; but rather by the need to restrict the class of eligible Claimants to those who are most closely and directly connected to the accident which the Defendant has negligently caused and to apply restrictions which are reasonably straightforward, certain and comprehensible to the ordinary person.

We have not been asked on these appeals to alter or abrogate the limits on the recovery of damages by secondary victims in accident cases established by the decision of the House of Lords in ***Alcock***".

Excluding genuinely injured Claimants and to requiring them to effectively deal with life altering psychiatric injuries predicated on a Defendant's negligence for reasons of public policy and what blood runs in their veins, remains a difficult and divisive issue.

A practical issue that appears to be ripe for consideration arises from secondary victim claims arising from workplace accidents. For example, let us take the example of 2 co-workers, who have been very close and firm friends for most their adult life. Let us assume that they have worked together for years building and running a business, sharing their success and failures equally. They have supported each other in times of trial and know each other's character nearly as well as they know themselves. It is a close platonic friendship, that when viewed in totality may well be closer than that of some blood relations.

One of them, in sight of the other suffers a horrific injury or is killed. The survivor is never in danger, so must be a secondary victim. The claim of the surviving secondary victim would be likely to fail due to the inability to demonstrate a sufficient tie of "*love and affection*" with the deceased due to how the Courts appear to apply the above principles. Further, considering the modern world and technology, in the context of an unfolding disaster such as a collapsing factory, or a sinking vessel, it is entirely possible for a person who holds sufficient ties of love and affection to a primary victim to learn of the unfolding disaster through technology and social media whilst many miles away and outside of the conventional sense of nearness. They may even be using a video call at the moment of injury, death or imperilment.

They may on learning of the disaster rush to the scene, but due to geography it may be hours till they arrive, all the while through technology they are continuously saturated and aware of the unfolding events through videos, pictures, and live accounts (albeit remotely). On their arrival at the scene of a disaster, or at a hospital, they then learn that their loved one has suffered serious injury or died, and they in turn suffer psychiatric injury as a result of this shock. It seems that **Paul**[142] may offer these persons a glimmer of hope, in that the law remains flexible.

The Courts over time have proved to be flexible and adaptive as to the concept of "*proximity in time and space*" in certain (and often meritorious) circumstances through an analysis of the factual circumstances in which a secondary victim finds themselves. While Lord Steyn in **White**[143] stated that "*it must be left to Parliament to undertake the task of radical law reform*" when dealing with such claims it may surprise practitioners that as far back as 1998, nearly three decades ago, the Law Commission in paper 249 ("*Liability for Psychiatric Illness*") foresaw the above problems and advised legal reform.

Powerfully (at paragraph 6.10), in relation to secondary victims, nothing short of legislative reform was advised. It was the Law Commission's opinion that "*there should be legislation laying down that a plaintiff, who suffers a reasonably foreseeable recognisable psychiatric illness as a result of the*

[142] **Paul v Royal Wolverhampton NHS Trust** [2024] UKSC 1

[143] **White v Chief Constable of South Yorkshire** [1999] 2 A.C. 455

death, injury or imperilment of a person with whom he or she has a close tie of love and affection, should be entitled to recover damages from the negligent Defendant in respect of that illness, regardless of the plaintiff's closeness (in time and space) to the accident or its aftermath or the means by which the plaintiff learns of it".

The report expressed the view that; "*the imposition of all three [**Alcock**] proximity requirements is unduly restrictive, and that it is the last two limitations that have resulted in the most arbitrary decisions. How many hours after the accident the mother of an injured child manages to reach the hospital should not be the decisive factor in deciding whether the Defendant may be liable for the mother's consequential psychiatric illness... Provided that the requirement for a close tie of love and affection between the plaintiff and the immediate victim is retained, the main 1oodgates objection of the possibility of many claims arising from a single event is limited*".

History has shown us that the Law often only develops in a reactionary manner and it takes either a great injustice, or a great tragedy to bring this about. Whilst in any disaster, the most important objectives are ensuring it never occurs again, and holding those responsible to account, the scope of the law in addressing a negligent party's liability to potential Claimants must not be artificially restrained so as to render a genuinely injured Claimant as nothing more than collateral damage for reasons of public policy.

For the reasons, the claims which flow from the Grenfell disaster may well define this area of law for the next generation. They are likely to provide the sort of facts from which the Court can grapple with this issues, and seek to define and recast how the Courts should approach this area in today's modern world.

CHAPTER NINE

STRESS AT WORK CLAIMS: AN OVERVIEW

Before we consider stress at work claims it's important to understand just how prevalent cases of stress at work are, but also what exactly they are. Stress at work cases are instances where an employee suffers from a recognisable psychiatric condition (commonly depression and anxiety) as a result of their employer's conduct. This spectrum of injury can extend to instances of hurt, or injured feelings.

Prevalence

Whilst research offers differing figures, it is clear that the issue of work-related stress is a serious and increasingly common issue faced by the workforce of Great Britain. From the point of view of the employer, stress is costly, especially for small firms where cover for sick employees may be difficult to arrange at short notice, or in cases of long-term illness impossible and uneconomic to accommodate. Stress additionally (before it leads to the manifestation of a psychiatric illness) can, and almost certainly will reduce the effectiveness of employees and lead to higher rates of absence.

The HSE studies

The issue was identified as a significant one by the HSE since 2005, where amongst other conclusions, it was shown that statistically work related stress accounted for over a third of all new incidences of ill health in the work place (work-related stress, depression or anxiety) and lead to an average of 30.6 for each incident, being roughly a total of 13.5 million working days being lost a year, costing employers in excess of £530 million.

In a detailed study completed by the HSE on the 3rd November 2023 (some 19 years later), this had risen to a 875,000 cases of work-related stress, depression or anxiety in 2022/23 alone, not counting long running issues and illness. Mental health issues accounted for approximately 12.7% of all sickness absences in the UK workforce, and work-related stress, anxiety, or depression accounted for 49% of all new or long-standing health conditions in 2022/23. In real terms that's around 6.6 million working days being lost in 2022/23 alone due to this issue and statistically it now affects, 2.5% of the workforce. In this period the estimated annual costs of workplace injury and illness was estimated to be £20.7 billion implying the cost to the economy could be as high as £10 billion.

There is an understandable but inadvisable tendency for employers to "*muddle along*" and treat a stressed employee as an irritation they can do without. An employer may well be too busy, or otherwise not able to dedicate the time that such an issue deserves. Employers need to understand that making proper time, managing the situation in a humane way and where necessary taking advice will not only act to ensure that the matter is sensibly handled, but will reduce their legal exposure. In short, money spent getting it right will be much cheaper than the aftermath of getting it wrong.

The cause?

Between 2000 and 2016, the Chartered Institute of Personnel and Development (CIPD) published an annual absence management survey which explored trends, policy and practice in the UK. In 2016, this survey found that stress and mental ill health were among the most common causes of long-term absence. It established that:

a. The most common cause of stress remained workload, followed by non-work relationships, management style and personal health issues;

b. While public sector and non-profit organisations that ranked stress among their top five causes of absence were particularly likely to be making efforts to address it, nearly two-fifths of private sector organisations that similarly ranked stress were not doing so;

c. The most common methods used to address stress were staff surveys, risk assessments or stress audits, as well as flexible working options or other steps to improve work-life balance;

d. Most organisations took some action to promote good mental health, with many providing training for line managers to more effectively identify and manage stress in their teams. Provision of employee assistance programmes (EAPs) and counselling, as well as involvement of occupational health specialists, were common in larger organisations;

e. Presenteeism (people coming to work when unwell) was growing in prominence, particularly in organisations where long working hours were the norm. As in previous years, this was associated with stress-related absence and mental health problems.

The CIPD reported in April 2019 that mental ill health was increasingly prevalent as a cause of both short and long-term illness and remained one of the most common causes of long-term absence which seemed to not be headed as it should, especially considering the breadth of the study. In the above-mentioned 3rd November 2023 study, the HSE identified the may cause of stress at work to be that workers and employees;

a. Are not able to cope with the demands of their jobs;

b. Are unable to control the way they do their work;

c. Do not receive enough information and support;

d. Are having trouble with relationships at work, or are being bullied;

e. Don't fully understand their role and responsibilities

f. Are not engaged when a business is undergoing change

Considering the economic downturn and the impact that this has had on individuals, namely their perceived and actual lack of job security as well as their workloads increasing as a result of budget reductions, there is scope for an expected further increase if not explosion in stress at work claims. While mental health issues at large continue to attract a great deal of stigma it is clear that, based on the available statistics, instances where an individual's employment is affected by "*stress at work*" are far more prevalent in the modern workplace than many would wish to acknowledge.

For theses reason, I would consider stress at work to be this working generations Asbestos.

Venue of Trial

Due to the clear link to the employment relationship inherent in any action for stress at work, a practical issue in deciding where to bring a stress at work claim will be that of limitation and costs. Pre-Jackson reforms and the introduction of QOCS, the threat of a Claimant who failed at trial having to bear a successful Defendant's costs created a real deterrent to a Claimant being able to pursue a claim in the County Courts. On the contrary the standard rule in the Employment Tribunals was that an unsuccessful Claimant would not face an order for costs.

The changes to costs rules in the Employment Tribunal (Enterprise and Regulatory Reform Act 2013) and the Jackson reforms however have altered this landscape and it appears may have inadvertently made the County Courts the easiest option to pursue what traditionally has been viewed as a difficult cause of action by creating a more highly favourable costs climate for Claimants. When you consider the complexities of Stress claims, how QOCS practically applies and the effect of costs budgeting being that parties can have some certainty as to the commercial value of the claim that there is now a genuine conundrum faced by Defendants in resisting such claims created by the opposition of the principal of resisting such a claim, as opposed to the commercial cost of resisting such a claim.

Time limits

In cases brought in the Courts the usual three-year personal injury limitation period will apply from the date of injury. While this may seem a large period of time, it can sometimes prove a problem as in many cases there exist a series of events stretching over often large periods of time. If a Claimant is to recover compensation for the earliest incidents there are clear occasions where "*date of knowledge*" and section 33 Limitation Act 1980 arguments will be required.

In the Employment Tribunal, the time limit for proceedings is usually three months minus one day (as per section 123 Equality Act 2010). The time limit for unfair dismissal claims is usually easy to calculate, although if a Claimant is late in bringing proceedings, it can be more difficult depending on the circumstances to bring the claim out of time.

For discrimination claims, time usually runs 3 months less one duty from the last act of discrimination complained of. It is possible to argue a "*series*" of events ending with a last straw (such as a dismissal) which is within three months of the commencement of proceedings. The real issue is that claims involving stress in the Employment Tribunal will often involve an aspect of disability discrimination (with the stress related condition being viewed as the disability, and also practically, involve a Claimant who is too badly injured to present a claim within this time limit, and it may well be over the three month limitation period before they feel well enough, and able to speak to a lawyer, let alone commence proceedings.

Recoverability of damages for "Stress" in the Tribunal

In Court proceedings, a Claimant will need to establish that he suffers from a recognised psychiatric condition whereas in an Employment Tribunal there is the opportunity to claim an award for injury to feelings arising from discrimination in certain circumstances as set out below (**Vento** Guidelines).

The two are very distinct, notably as a personal injury claim will legally, have a greater ambit to allow a Claimant to pursue a claim for consequential losses arising from a psychiatric injury as opposed to an injury to feelings. However, and assuming there is a cause of action in both forums but there is a doubt as to whether the client has suffered "*psychiatric injury*" (as opposed to "injured feelings") the Employment Tribunal would appear to be the preferred and safer forum.

A Claimant in the Employment Tribunal who suffers injury to feelings such that it results in the onset of psychiatric illness may recover compensation for personal injury in the Employment Tribunal (**Sherriff v Klyne Tugs Lowestoft Ltd** [1999] ICR 1170[144]). However it is not easy, nor in some cases even possible to distinguish where injury to feelings stops and injury to mental health begins, creating the very real risk of double recovery. The Tribunals have done their best to deal with this situation and in **HM Prison Services v Salmon** [2001] IRLR 425[145] the EAT suggested that in such cases the correct approach would be for a Tribunal to make a single award for injury to feelings and to include an element of psychiatric harm, but in course of doing so, it was essential for the Tribunal to make clear exactly what it was doing Further, damages for personal injury are recoverable for any harm caused by the discriminatory act and not simply harm which was reasonably foreseeable (**Essa v Laing Ltd** [2003] ICR 1110, EAT).

---

144 **Sherriff v Klyne Tugs Lowestoft Ltd** [1999] ICR 1170

145 **HM Prison Services v Salmon** [2001] IRLR 425

Courts vs Tribunals?

The Jackson reforms in stress cases provided a real opportunity for stress claims to be pursued especially when we turn to the consideration of costs. Considering that a potential Claimant's claim for future losses achievable in the Courts are likely to be significantly higher than those likely to be awarded in an Employment Tribunal (who typically will not award beyond 18 – 24 months of future loss), the change seems to funnel such Claimants into new, but more favourable territory providing that they can successfully establish liability. However, there are often greater difficulties in establishing a claim in negligence as opposed to under the Equality Act 2010, and careful consideration should be given at the onset as to the appropriate, and most favourable forum.

Abuse of process

As set out above, when dealing with Stress at Work cases one of the first issues that needs to be considered is in which forum (County or High Court as opposed to the Employment Tribunal) should a Claimant bring their claim? In cases where a Claimant has suffered psychiatric injury, issues that can arise with such an injury, such as an inability to engage with legal advisors, can naturally direct a Claimant to pursuing a claim for personal injury in the County or High Court as opposed to seeking remedies in the Employment Tribunal due to limitation issues.

However, what happens when an Employment Tribunal claim comes to an end but the Claimant seeks to bring County or High Court proceedings? A Claimant who may well have proceeded initially as a litigant in person in the Employment Tribunal can find themselves being precluded from being able to bring the later action due to it being classed as an abuse of process. Whilst most Confidentiality Agreements entered into upon the settlement of Employment Tribunal claims include clauses that limit future actions, but exclude future personal injury claims, it should always be remembered that an award for injury to feelings can be construed as falling into the class of damages for personal injury (**Sheriff** v **Klyne Tugs (Lowestoft) Ltd** [1999] I.C.R. 1170[146]) creating a situation whereby the same claim is effectively brought for a second time, just by a different mechanism (**Lennon v Birmingham City Council** [2001] EWCA Civ 435[147]). This can be especially hazardous considering part 44.15 (a) CPR which allows a Defendant to side-step the QOCS protection provided by part 44.14 CPR and recover its costs directly from a Claimant where a claim is struck out as being an abuse of process.

However, practitioners should be acutely aware of the effects of the Employment Tribunals (Constitution and Rules of Procedure) Regulations 2013/1237) and the effects of part 44.15 CPR. It is not a case of a Claimant being able to have two bites at the cherry, but rather giving finality to litigation.

The decisions of both **Manda v USB AG** (Central London County Court), 16th June 2016[148] and **Akay v Newcastle University** [2020] EWHC 1669 (QB)[149] provides guidance as to the issues such a scenario creates, and the application of the principles and analysis of "*res judicata*" as set out by Lord Sumption in **Virgin Atlantic Airways Ltd v Premium Aircraft Interiors UK Ltd** [2013] UKSC 46, [2014] A.C. 160[150].

Both claims involved Claimants who had presented one set of proceedings in the emp0lymenbt Tribunal, and after those cases concluding (without any agreement in either matter to preserve a cause of action in negligence), they issued fresh claim in the County Court. Both claims were struck out as an abuse of process

---

146 **Sheriff v Klyne Tugs (Lowestoft) Ltd** [1999] I.C.R. 1170

147 **Lennon v Birmingham City Council** [2001] EWCA Civ 435

148 **Manda v USB AG** (Central London County Court), 16th June 2016

149 **Akay v Newcastle University** [2020] EWHC 1669 (QB)

150 **Virgin Atlantic Airways Ltd v Premium Aircraft Interiors UK Ltd** [2013] UKSC 46, [2014] A.C. 160

HHJ Hand QC struck out Mr **Manda's**[151] claim on the grounds of "*res judicata*" and an abuse of process for two main reasons. Firstly, he held that the principle underlying the concept of "*res judicata*" was that there should be finality in litigation. Every case fell to be decided by applying the analysis and categories of "*res judicata*" as described by Lord Sumption in **Virgin Atlantic Airways Ltd**[152], namely that;

a. The bar to re-litigation or further litigation should be absolute when an attempt is made to raise points in subsequent proceedings, "*which had to be and were decided [in the earlier proceedings] in order to establish the existence or non-existence of a cause of action*";

b. Re-litigation or further litigation should also be barred when an attempt is made to raise points in subsequent proceedings which are "*essential to the existence or non-existence of a cause of action*" even where those points were not decided in earlier proceedings based on the same cause of action because they had not been raised if "*they could with reasonable diligence and should in all the circumstance have been raised*";

c. What has been known as issue estoppel prevents the raising in subsequent proceedings of points which;

    i. Were not raised in the earlier proceedings; or

    ii. Were raised unsuccessfully;

    iii. But with an exception of "*special circumstances where this would cause injustice*".

---

151 **Manda v USB AG** (Central London County Court), 16th June 2016

152 **Virgin Atlantic Airways Ltd v Premium Aircraft Interiors UK Ltd** [2013] UKSC 46, [2014] A.C. 160

d. Where "*the point was not raised, the bar will usually be absolute if it could with reasonable diligence and should in all the circumstances have been raised*".

When applying these principals to the case of Mr Manda, the reality was that Mr Manda was attempting to re-litigate the same points, just in a new forum. Mr Manda argued that the County Court proceedings were based on an entirely different cause of action with a different conceptual structure (negligence) but forgot that when a case in the Employment Tribunal is dismissed or withdrawn this action should be taken as to represent an adjudication of the case on its merits (Regulation 51 and 52 Employment Tribunals (Constitution and Rules of Procedure) Regulations 2013/1237). Whilst HHJ Hand QC accepted that the disability discrimination claim ended differently to the other causes of action (in that it failed because it had been inadequately pleaded and its demise might be seen as procedural rather than substantive) there was no significant distinction between the manner of its disposal and the other causes of action.

It is noted in paragraph 70 of the Judgment that: "*I do not accept the argument that there is any significant distinction between the manner of disposal of the disability discrimination claim and manner of disposal of the other causes of action raised before the Employment Tribunal. In my Judgment... The Employment Tribunal had jurisdiction in respect of the allegations of disability discrimination, including the jurisdiction to award compensation, which could include compensation for personal injury, in respect of any such discrimination.*"

HHJ Hand QC concluded at paragraph 74 of the Judgment that; "*The attempt to revive [this claim] ... under the guise of a claim in tort, as opposed to one in contract, to my mind falls within the absolute bar to resurrection identified by Lord Sumption in paragraphs 20, 21 and 22 of his Judgment in Virgin Atlantic .... [the Claimant's] arguments that there is a distinction between compensation arising from a statutory tort and compensation arising from breach of duty in the common law tort of negligence, as well as -flying in the face of the analysis of the Court of Appeal in Sheriff, ignores the fact that the statutory tort of unfair dismissal in the context of so- called "constructive dismissal" depends upon the establishing of a breach of duty in contract, which is exactly the same as the breach of duty in the common law tort of negligence*".

Lavander J in **Akay**[153] was rather more direct at paragraphs 50 – 51 with "*This is an unsatisfactory way of presenting an appeal. If it was to be alleged that the judge failed to take a relevant matter into account, then that matter ought to have been identified in the grounds of appeal. A ground of appeal such as ground 5 which asserts that, "The learned Judge should have … weighed in the balance arguments in the … Appellant's favour" cannot be used as a Trojan horse in order to smuggle in to the appeal all of the arguments deployed at the hearing below. For instance, in paragraph 67(xiii) of his skeleton argument [the Claimant] contended that the judge's construction of the Compromise Agreement was wrong. If that was to be alleged on appeal, then it should have been the subject of an express ground of appeal.*

Moreover, [the Claimants] contention that the Judge ought to have expressly considered all sixteen of these matters falls foul of the proposition that a judge is not obliged in his judgment to address every argument advanced before him. In any event, however, there is no merit in any of these sixteen points."

153 **Akay v Newcastle University** [2020] EWHC 1669 (QB)

CHAPTER TEN

THE HATTON GUIDELINES

Claims based on the concept of stress at work gained prominence following the case of **Walker v Northumberland County Council** [1995] 1 All ER 737[154]. The case itself was by today's standards unremarkable but at the time, was unusual being the first of its kind.

It involved a claim for the development of a psychiatric illness suffered by an employee of middle management status within the Defendant's social services department. The claim was advanced on the basis that the system of work in place imposed excessive stress and provided no means for identifying and investigating stressful aspects of work as they arose. It was accepted that the Defendant failed to respond to pleas for assistance despite knowing that the Claimant had previously suffered a breakdown attributable to stress caused by the volume of work and lack of assistance. It was highlighted that the earlier breakdown had rendered it reasonably foreseeable that the Claimant may well suffer a further breakdown unless appropriate precautions were taken, and safeguards put in place. The claim in respect of the first period of illness failed with the Court deciding that it was not reasonably foreseeable that the Claimant's workload would have given rise to a material risk of mental illness.

Coleman J famously provides that: "*the question is whether it ought to have been foreseen that… [the Claimant] was exposed to a risk of mental illness materially higher than that which would ordinarily affect a social services manager in his position with a really heavy workload. For if the foreseeable risk were not materially greater than that there would not, as a matter of reasonable conduct, be any basis upon which the… [Defendant's] duty to act arose.*"

---

[154] **Walker v Northumberland County Council** [1995] 1 All ER 737

In finding for the Claimant, **Walker**[155] became the first claim whereby a Claimant succeeded in a claim for psychiatric injuries.

Hatton v Sutherland

Following this development, within a decade the Court of Appeal provided the definitive guidelines on which to this day, all stress at work cases predicated in negligence are still based and applied as a starting point when assessing stress at work claims. Whilst the subsequent case law has sought to clarify respective aspects of the criteria, they have not changed. These defining principals were created by Hale LJ in **Hatton v Sutherland** [2002] EWCA Civ 76[156]. 16 Points were set down which can in turn be subdivided and considered.

Overarching principal

1. There are no special control mechanisms applying to claims for psychiatric (or physical) illness or injury arising from the stress of doing the work the employee is required to do. The ordinary principles of employer's liability apply.

Foreseeability of injury

2. The threshold question is whether this kind of harm to this particular employee was reasonably foreseeable. This has two components;

    a. An injury to health (as distinct from occupational stress) which;

    b. Is attributable to stress at work (as distinct from other factors).

155 **Walker v Northumberland County Council** [1995] 1 All ER 737

156 **Hatton v Sutherland** [2002] EWCA Civ 76

3. Foreseeability depends upon what the employer knows (or ought reasonably to know) about the individual employee. Because of the nature of mental disorder, it is harder to foresee than physical injury, but may be easier to foresee in a known individual than in the population at large). An employer is usually entitled to assume that the employee can withstand the normal pressures of the job unless he knows of some particular problem or vulnerability.

4. The test is the same whatever the employment: there are no occupations which should be regarded as intrinsically dangerous to mental health.

5. Factors likely to be relevant in answering the threshold question include;

    a. The nature and extent of the work done by the employee. Is the workload much more than is normal for the particular job? Is the work particularly intellectually or emotionally demanding for this employee? Are demands being made of this employee unreason- able when compared with the demands made of others in the same or comparable jobs? Or are there signs that others doing this job are suffering harmful levels of stress? Is there an abnormal level of sickness or absenteeism in the same job or the same department?

    b. Signs from the employee of impending harm to health. Has he a particular problem or vulnerability? Has he already suffered from illness attributable to stress at work? Have there recently been frequent or prolonged absences which are uncharacteristic of him? Is there reason to think that these are attributable to stress at work, for example because of complaints or warnings from him or others?

6. The employer is generally entitled to take what he is told by his employee at face value, unless he has good reason to think to the contrary. He does not generally have to make searching enquiries of the employee or seek permission to make further enquiries of his medical advisers.

7. To trigger a duty to take steps, the indications of impending harm to health arising from stress at work must be plain enough for any reason – able employer to realise that he should do something about it.

Breach of duty

8. The employer is only in breach of duty if he has failed to take the steps which are reasonable in the circumstances, bearing in mind the magnitude of the risk of harm occurring, the gravity of the harm which may occur, the costs and practicability of preventing it, and the justifications for running the risk.

9. The size and scope of the employer's operation, its resources and the demands it faces are relevant in deciding what is reasonable; these include the interests of other employees and the need to treat them fairly, for example, in any redistribution of duties.

10. An employer can only reasonably be expected to take steps which are likely to do some good: the Court is likely to need expert evidence on this

11. An employer who offers a confidential advice service, with referral to appropriate counselling or treatment services, is unlikely to be found in breach of duty.

12. If the only reasonable and effective step would have been to dismiss or demote the employee, the employer will not be in breach of duty in allowing a willing employee to continue in the job.

13. In all cases, therefore, it is necessary to identify the steps which the employer both could and should have taken before finding him in breach of his duty of care.

Causation

14. The Claimant must show that that breach of duty has caused or materially contributed to the harm suffered. It is not enough to show that occupational stress has caused the harm.

Apportionment

15. Where the harm suffered has more than one cause, the employer should only pay for that proportion of the harm suffered which is attributable to his wrongdoing, unless the harm is truly indivisible. It is for the Defendant to raise the question of apportionment.

16. The assessment of damages will take account of any pre-existing disorder or vulnerability and of the chance that the Claimant would have succumbed to a stress related disorder in any event.

Practically, as a practitioner when dealing with a case relating to stress at work, it is very useful to try and break down the claim factually into these four components. It is important to keep at the forefront of your mind that a Claimant has to succeed on all four, and due to this, and the nature of proving a case for psychiatric injury, the hurdles before a Claimant are high.

CHAPTER ELEVEN

STRESS AT WORK CLAIMS AND FORESEEABLE HARM

The central issue in a claim for stress at work will be the foreseeability of harm, and it is on this that commonly the bulk of such arguments revolve. Guidelines 2 – 7 of **Hatton v Sutherland** [2002] EWCA Civ 76[157] and also indicate what a Claimant needs to establish, in a checklist style.

Guidelines 2 – 7

Guideline 2

"*The threshold question is whether this kind of harm to this particular employee was reasonably foreseeable. This has two components;*

a. *An injury to health (as distinct from occupational stress) which;*

b. *Is attributable to stress at work (as distinct from other factors)*".

For a Claimant's injury to be foreseeable, it must be foreseen as arising from their work. Having work that is stressful is not going to be enough, there needs to be present evidence which shows that this source of stress created the actual risk of injury.

Guideline 3

"*Foreseeability depends upon what the employer knows (or ought reasonably to know) about the individual employee. Because of the nature of mental disorder, it is harder to foresee than physical injury, but may be easier to*

[157] **Hatton v Sutherland** [2002] EWCA Civ 76

foresee in a known individual than in the population at large). An employer is usually entitled to assume that the employee can withstand the normal pressures of the job unless he knows of some particular problem or vulnerability".

In practical terms, the issue can be addressed by considering the following;

a. What evidence exists to show that the Claimant has informed their employer that there work (as opposed to other matters) is making them unwell psychiatrically?

   From the work that the Claimant is doing, what fact specific risks and issues can an employer reasonable be said to aware of? On this point it can be helpful to consider;

   i. What risk assessments are in place dealing with the nature of the work performed by the Claimant;

   ii. What hours and volume of work does the Claimant's contract of employment expect them to be doing?

   iii. How many employees should be employed to deal with the work undertaken by the Claimant?

b. Are there any development which evidence a change in the factual circumstances of a Claimant's role that the employer would be reasonably aware of

   i. For example, a Claimant who works in a team of 2 people covering a specific field of work is required to take on the work of the 2 other employees when they unexpectedly resign or retire;

   ii. Or an employee who works in a team of 2 people managing 90 cases, sees an unexpected increase in their workload to 270 cases due to the growth of an employer's business.

c. Is there anything specific or unique about the Claimant's role that is different, and presents a specific risk not found in general employment and is reasonably known to the employer. For example;

   i. The police officer who has to review graphic imagery of child abuse;

   ii. The prison officer who is required to deal with the self-harm and suicide of inmates;

   iii. The crime scene investigator who attends and catalogue the scenes or murders and unexpected deaths;

   iv. The care home worker who in caring for unwell elderly patients is exposed to the distressing consequences of progressive dementia, poor physical health and unexpected injury and death in their patients.

<u>Guideline 4</u>

"The test is the same whatever the employment: there are no occupations which should be regarded as intrinsically dangerous to mental health".

The touchstone is not the work that was being done but what was known about the affected it had on the Claimant. The reasonable steps taken to bring any issues to their employer's attention is what is important when it comes to the evidence at trial.

<u>Guideline 5</u>

"Factors likely to be relevant in answering the threshold question include;

a. *"The nature and extent of the work done by the employee. Is the workload much more than is normal for the particular job? Is the work particularly intellectually or emotionally demanding for this employee? Are demands being made of this employee unreason- able when compared with the demands made of others in the same or comparable jobs? Or are there signs that others doing this job are suffering harmful levels of stress? Is there an abnormal level of sickness or absenteeism in the same job or the same department?*

b. *Signs from the employee of impending harm to health. Has he a particular problem or vulnerability? Has he already suffered from illness attributable to stress at work? Have there recently been frequent or prolonged absences which are uncharacteristic of him? Is there reason to think that these are attributable to stress at work, for example because of complaints or warnings from him or others?"*

This is a more complex guideline as shown by its content, and intersects with guideline 3. In addition to the above, it is advisable to consider the following;

a. When the work is looked at broadly, what risk assessments have been completed dealing with the risk it poses?

b. Consider if there are emails from a Claimant complaining about their work related stress levels and the negative impact it is taking on their Claimant's health;

c. Consider if there are other sources where this may have been written down, for example text messages, WhatsApp or other forms of electronic communications. Be aware that the style of communication may be likely to need explanation;

d. Is there any evidence of a Claimant in appraisal meetings or other formal reviews raising issues to do with their stress levels and its negative impact upon their health;

e. Have any grievances or complaints been made by the Claimant in regards to their work related stress levels;

f. Has the Claimant been referred to, or sought referral to their employer's occupational health department to have any stress related issues assessed and addressed?

g. Have there been any previous issues of work related stress reported by the Claimant or, have they identified the source of any unreasonable levels of stress in their work;

h. Is there any evidence of the Claimant suffering from a previous stress related absence, as opposed to absences that are not stress related

    i. For example do any sick notes relating to a Claimant's absence cite a psychiatric reasons for their absence?

    ii. If such absences are not stress related, are they for reasons which would cause a reasonable employer to consider that the Claimant was at a heightened risk of suffering from a stress related injury;

i. Consider if any disciplinary actions have been taken against a Claimant previously that evidence through a fact finding investigation underlying work related stress issues;

j. Is there any evidence which shows that the Claimant is not able to fulfil the expectations of their role. If so, has any root cause been identified and what assistance and support has been provided;

k. Are there any appraisal documents or minutes of recorded development meetings, is there any reference to work related stress related issues, or complaints being raised by a Claimant about how their work is causing them an unreasonable level of work related stress;

l. Have any of the Claimant's colleagues doing a similar level of work suffered from stress related absences?

m. What level of absenteeism does the employer face as an organisation and what are its causes? This can involve a wider disclosure exercise than may be initially envisaged when the employer is a large organisation.

Guideline 6

"*The employer is generally entitled to take what he is told by his employee at face value, unless he has good reason to think to the contrary. He does not generally have to make searching enquiries of the employee or seek permission to make further enquiries of his medical advisers.*"

Guideline 6 can give rise to difficult factual issues when considered against guidelines 3 and 5. Practically;

a. Are there any records where the Claimant has made it reasonably clear that they are not suffering from unreasonable work related stress levels. For example;

    i. The executive who in appraisals, talks of how they are able to manage their heavy work load;

    ii. The junior employee who actively seeks to take on more responsibility and work to progress their career;

    iii. The nurse who in frequent 1-2-1 meetings doesn't raise any issues with work related stress;

    iv. The employee who when asked by their employer if they are managing their work, replies that there is no issue.

b. Consider what witness evidence that is likely to be provided by an employer when dealing with conversations about work related stress. Is the Claimant going to face a near insurmountable evidential hurdle?

c. Following any return to work meetings after a period of absence, has the Claimant identified a work related source as the reasons for the absence;

d. Objectively, are there any clear and obvious signs of an impending work related stress injury present in the Claimant's case. For example;

   i. In the case of a longstanding employee who the employer knows well, has their appearance or demeanour changed significantly?

   ii. In the case of a longstanding employee who the employer knows are they displaying behaviours or attitudes that are out of character for them?

   iii. Does the employee seem stressed, tired or unwell.

<u>Guideline 7</u>

"*To trigger a duty to take steps, the indications of impending harm to health arising from stress at work must be plain enough for any reasonable employer to realise that he should do something about it.*"

Guideline 7 in may regards acts as a summary of those that come before it. The use of the language "*plain enough*" is helpful, since it grounds the question of the foreseeability squarely on an objective assessment of the evidence. A Court is not going to look at evidence in isolation when addressing the issue, but consider the entirety of the facts it finds proven. Certain elements of evidence may hold more weight, but ultimately the

Court is entitled to reach conclusions as to the foreseeability of evidence that it considered just and correct.

The law

Hatton[158] provides useful and fairly common-sense advice when dealing with the foreseeability of harm stating that; "*Foreseeability depends upon what the employer knows (or ought reasonably to know) about the individual employee. Because of the nature of mental disorder, it is harder to foresee than physical injury, but may be easier to foresee in a known individual than in the population at large.... An employer is usually entitled to assume that the employee can withstand the normal pressures of the job unless he knows of some particular problem or vulnerability.*

Stress cases in practice when it comes to success or failure turn on if the injury sustained by the employee was reasonably foreseeable by the employer. Each case will depend on the particular facts, including whether the employer had been put on notice that the employee concerned was particularly vulnerable or struggling to cope. The question for the Court in each case as per **Hatton**[159] is "*whether a harmful reaction to the [breach of duty complained of] is reasonably foreseeable in the individual employee concerned.*"

The Court of Appeal in **Hatton**[160] referred to the observation of Simon Brown LJ in **Garrett v London Borough of Camden** [2001] EWCA Civ 395[161], that "*Many, alas, suffer breakdowns and depressive illnesses and a significant proportion could doubtless ascribe some at least of their problems to the strains and stresses of their work situation: be it simple overworking, the tensions of difficult relationships, career prospect worries, fears or feelings of discrimination or harassment, to take just some examples. Unless, however,*

158 **Hatton v Sutherland** [2002] EWCA Civ 76

159 **Hatton v Sutherland** [2002] EWCA Civ 76

160 **Hatton v Sutherland** [2002] EWCA Civ 76

161 **Garrett v London Borough of Camden** [2001] EWCA Civ 395

there was a real risk of breakdown which the Claimant's employers ought reasonably to have foreseen and which they ought properly to have averted, there can be no liability"

The above is a helpful reminder of the issues one experiences in such claims, and further, the standard of proof which is going to be applied. Also heard in conjunction with **Hatton**, was the case of **Barber v Somerset County Council** [2004] UKHL 13[162] which found its way up from the Court of Appeal to the House of Lords.

To place the case into a factual context, the Claimant was the head of a school mathematics department who had previously established negligence against his employer for a claim based on stress at work. The Claimant had fallen ill for three weeks and in this period, sick notes and a sickness declaration form which referred to stress and depression as being the cause of his illness were provided to his employer. When he returned to work, he was treated unsympathetically and his workload remained as heavy as before. It was said in the House of Lords that the managers of his school ought to have taken the initiative in making inquiries on his return to work and reduced his workload to ease his return. His condition should have been monitored and, if it did not improve, some more drastic action should have been taken. His employer was held to be liable for injuries, those injuries having been foreseeable with lord Walker providing at paragraph 67 of the Judgment that the; "*...employer's duty to take some action arose in June and July 1996, when Mr Barber saw separately each member of the school's senior management team. It continued so long as nothing was done to help Mr Barber. The Court of Appeal evidently considered that Mr Barber was insufficiently forceful in what he said at these interviews, and that he should have described his troubles and his symptoms in much more detail. But he was already suffering from depression, and neither Mrs Hayward nor Mrs Newton was a sympathetic listener. What the Court of Appeal failed to give adequate weight to was the fact that Mr Barber, an experienced and conscientious teacher, had*

[162] **Barber v Somerset County Council** [2004] UKHL 13

been off work for three weeks (not two weeks, as the Court of Appeal thought at para 160 of the appendix) with no physical ailment or injury. His absence was certified by his doctor to be due to stress and depression. The senior management team should have made inquiries about his problems and seen what they could do to ease them, in consultation with officials at the county council's education department, instead of brushing him off unsympathetically (as Mrs Hayward and Mrs Newton did) or sympathising but simply telling him to prioritise his work (as Mr Gill did)".

Subsequently, in **Hartman v South Essex Mental Health and Community Care NHS Trust** [2005] EWCA Civ 6[163] the application of **Hatton**[164] and **Barber**[165] was considered in six appeals heard consecutively. Each case involved a claim for damages for psychiatric injury arising out of stress at work. Whilst the individual cases turned on their particular facts, close attention paid to the trial Judges findings of fact, as the basis upon which issues of foreseeability were determined. The judgment is lengthy, but what can be distilled from it is that when dealing with the issues of foreseeability, the following three principles require application.

a. First, Liability for psychiatric injury caused by stress at work was in general no different in principle from liability for physical injury;

b. Second, for an employer's breach of duty that gave rise to the liability, it does not follow that because a Claimant suffered stress at work and that the employer was in some way in breach of duty in allowing this to occur, that the Claimant will be able to establish a claim in negligence. The risk of any breakdown ought

163 **Hartman v South Essex Mental Health and Community Care NHS Trust** [2005] EWCA Civ 6

164 **Hatton v Sutherland** [2002] EWCA Civ 76

165 **Barber v Somerset County Council** [2004] UKHL 13

to be one which the Claimant's employers ought reasonably to have foreseen;

c. Third, it was emphasised that whilst the general principles relating to stress at work cases were to be found in **Hatton**[166], they needed care in their application to the facts of the case under consideration.

Practically, every case turns on its own facts, but the threshold a Claimant needs to reach for an injury to be foreseeable is a high one, as set out in **Hartman**[167].

How does a stress related injury become foreseeable?

With the above in mind, how does a Claimant satisfy a Court of that a psychiatric injury was in fact, foreseeable? As seen from the above all of the facts of a claim need to be considered, weighed and assessed in answering the question.

Practically as set it above, it is useful to identify situations in which a Claimant has written to their employer or superiors setting out the work related stress issues they have been enduring, as it creates a clear evidential paper trail (physical or electronic) whereby what was being communicated contemporaneously can be easily ascertained and collated.

In cases where this evidence doesn't exist, a Claimant is likely to struggle. While the reason for a Claimant not making such a disclosure, such as not wanting to either appear inept, weak, or jeopardise their employment a Court is concerned with what evidence it has before it, and what findings of fact can be made. This difficult becomes especially acute in situations where a Claimant is only able to say that they raised such issues

166 **Hatton v Sutherland** [2002] EWCA Civ 76

167 **Hartman v South Essex Mental Health and Community Care NHS Trust** [2005] EWCA Civ 6

with employer orally. It is quite straightforward for a Defendant to deny such interactions, and thus argue that the Claimant's injuries cannot have been foreseeable.

Occupational health records

One potential way to avoid such an issue arising is of course to consider the employee's mental health records. There still exists some protection for employers between knowledge which is known to the employer if it was gained is in a confidential manner. The Court of Appeal in **Hartman**[168] held it was not right to attribute to the employer knowledge of confidential information which an employee had disclosed to the company's physician. Hence, where the employee disclosed an earlier nervous breakdown in a health-screening questionnaire and the Occupational Health Department had passed her fit for work, the employer would not be deemed to be aware of her past medical history. The issue of foresight remains at its core, about clearly bringing these matters to the notice of a Defendant.

This principal was reiterated by the High Court in **Piepenbrock v The London School of Economics** [2018] EWHC 2572 (QB)[169]. In this case the Claimant failed to satisfy the Court that the Defendant was on notice of any vulnerability to injury of the nature sustained. The Judgment is detailed, and Davies J at Paragraph 250 of the Judgments held that she did not "*accept that the nature of the breaches were of themselves sufficient to create a foreseeable risk of psychiatric injury. Further, there is nothing in the Claimant's conduct prior to his reaction on the night of 12 December which provides any evidential basis for finding that the Defendant should have foreseen such a reaction, still less the development of the depressive illness. On the contrary, the Claimant was travelling to India for what appears to*

[168] **Hartman v South Essex Mental Health and Community Care NHS Trust** [2005] EWCA Civ 6

[169] **Piepenbrock v The London School of Economics** [2018] EWHC 2572 (QB)

have been a successful trip. He was communicating with one of the Heads of Department regarding his future work, he was getting on with the job. I find that the severity of the Claimant's reaction on 12 December was a reflection of his personality. The Defendant had no relevant information as to the Claimant's personality or past medical history which would have rendered the development of the Claimant's illness reasonably foreseeable".

Although the Court accepted that "*stress*" was reasonably foreseeable from the events in question (allegations of inappropriate conduct towards a teaching assistant), the Court concluded that the Defendant had no evidence or information which could have rendered the development and extent of the Claimant's depressive illness foreseeable. The Claimant's allegation that he had notified the Defendant of previous problems prior to commencing employment was not accepted, but as made clear art paragraph 244, "*even on the Claimant's account, there was nothing to put the Defendant on notice of any vulnerability...*"

Un-communicated mental health problems

As stated above, when considering the stigma which mental health issues attract, employees may not always be as forthcoming as employers would wish, and understandably employers may well be unwilling to pry. Demonstrating this point in **Bonser v RJB** [2004] IRLR 164[170] the Court of Appeal reversed the trial Judge's finding that it was foreseeable the Claimant would suffer a nervous breakdown in the face of facts where the Claimant employee had taken 5 months off with depression in her previous employment. She had started this job with a reference stating that she "*would not be particularly good in a highly stressful environment but she is good at dealing with IT users, training and communication*".

The trial Judge had found that severe pressures were put on her team and it should have been apparent she could not cope as she broke down in tears in front of her line manager and said she could not cope and thought

[170] **Bonser v RJB** [2004] IRLR 164

her holiday was under threat. There was a finding of fact in this matter that the Claimant's employer did not know of her pre-existing emotional vulnerability and on this basis (perhaps due to her previous employer's tact) that the claim failed.

In a similar vein in **Sayers v Cambridgeshire CC** [2007] IRLR 29[171], two of the Claimant's fellow employees were aware she was taking anti-depressant medication (not an uncommon thing one may think in a workplace considering the friendships that develop therein). The High Court held this knowledge of fellow employees could not be equated with knowledge by the employers. Knowledge which is not communicated to higher management could not be taken to be knowledge, actual or imputed for the purpose of determining whether the indications were plain enough for the employers to realise that they should have intervened. Further in **Sayers**[172] at no stage were the employers made aware that the Claimant was suffering from or had any history of depressive symptoms which made her vulnerable to a recurrence or psychiatric injury. Nor were they aware that the Claimant was suffering from any depressive episodes before and during the course of her employment.

Factually these two cases highlight the reality of the workplace and the very human issues and manner in which issues can be and are communicated and shared. Where an employee suffers from stress related symptoms, but there is nothing unusual in absences taken, and he or she deliberately avoids references being made to his or her medical conditions, an employee will struggle to establish liability. Whilst the idea of a Claimant always adopting a policy of full and complete disclosure with his or her employee may well be unattractive to them, it certainly can assist in any litigation. Considering these points as first port of call is certainly advised.

171 **Sayers v Cambridgeshire CC** [2007] IRLR 29

172 **Sayers v Cambridgeshire CC** [2007] IRLR 29

Previous stress related absences

When a Claimant has been signed off sick from work, it is to be expected that their employer will require them to provide a sick note from their general practitioner indicating the cause of their absence. Such notes may well indicate that the reason for the Claimant's absences, are stress related, or even identify a recognisable psychiatric condition as being the cause.

In these circumstances whilst it may be difficult to argue that a proceedings breakdown was foreseeable per se, any breakdown that follows is more likely to be deemed foreseeable. On this point the case of **Young v Post Office** [2002] EWCA Civ 661[173] provides a helpful example of how the clear communication of such issues by a Claimant to their employer can overcome these issues.

In **Young**[174] the Post Office appealed against a finding that it had breached its duty of care to its employee, Mr Young. Mr Young was employed in 1973 and in 1994 started suffering from stress at work. He had a nervous breakdown in 1997 and was off work for four months. The Post Office agreed that in order to enable Mr Young to return to work he would be allowed to work at his own pace and on flexible hours and that he would be regularly visited by management to check on his progress. The last step did not take place and after seven weeks Mr Young was back to full time work doing his old job. He was unable to cope and suffered another breakdown, taking voluntary early retirement in May 1998. His claim for damages was successful, the Judge finding that given Mr Young's psychiatric history the Post Office had had a duty of care to him which it had breached by failing to implement the agreed measures, and that it had not been up to Mr Young to inform The Post Office that he was having difficulties.

173 **Young v Post Office** [2002] EWCA Civ 661

174 **Young v Post Office** [2002] EWCA Civ 661

As to the issue of foreseeability, Lord Justice May at paragraphs 20 – 23 held that "*The appellants were well aware that Mr Young was psychiatrically vulnerable, because he had just been off work for four months due to a stress–related illness. The managers ought to have known, as apparently they did not, that Mr Young was going to be sent on a course and that Mr Legg had a pre–booked holiday. The appellants' own witnesses accepted in evidence that what happened was inappropriate and had they known the full facts they would have acted differently….*

Mr Young had already suffered from psychiatric illness resulting from occupational stress. His employers knew this. After May 1997 it was, in my view, plainly foreseeable that there might be a recurrence if appropriate steps were not taken when he returned to work. The employers owed him a duty to take such steps".

Paragraph 26 creates a helpful ratio for similar cases, requiring that "*… in many circumstances an employer may not be expected to know that an employee who does not speak up is vulnerable, an employee who is known to be vulnerable is not necessarily to be regarded as responsible for a recurrent psychiatric illness if he fails to tell his employer that his job is again becoming too much for him. A finding of contributory negligence in a case of psychiatric illness, although no doubt theoretically possible in other circumstances, does not in my view sit happily with the facts of this case. I know of no case in which a Claimant such as Mr Young, vulnerable to psychiatric illness which he successfully holds to his employers, has been held to be contributorily negligent, and counsel was unable to draw our attention to any such case. I would reject this ground of appeal*".

Cries for help

A cry for help is not a legal term, but rather a common expression to be applied to the factual situation in which a Claimant asks for help and in doing so, makes it reasonably clear and plain that help and support is required to prevent them suffering injury. Such cases are highly fact dependent, and it is helpful to consider the leading judgements where such matters arose.

First, in **Dickins v O2 Plc** [2008] EWCA Civ 1144[175], the appellant employer O2 Plc appealed against a decision that it was liable to the respondent employee Ms Dickins for psychiatric injury negligently caused by excessive stress in the course of her employment with O2 Plc.

Ms Dickins had been employed by O2 plc for several years and promoted to a position for which she did not have the necessary qualifications, although appropriate training and support had been promised he her. Ms Dickins did not this receive help and soon became exhausted and "*at the end of her tether*". She asked to move to a less stressful job, but was told that there were no vacancies at the time. Ms Dickins continued to struggle with her job and requested six months off as she felt she lacked physical and mental energy and did not know how long she could carry on before taking sick leave. She did not contact the in-house counselling service that her manager recommended, since she was already undergoing private counselling. Ms Dickins asked again for a six-month break and her manager agreed to refer her to the occupational health department, but that was not done. She was later signed off as unfit for work on account of anxiety and depression, and never returned. Her employment was later terminated and she brought an action for damages.

The Court held that it was clear that Ms Dickins had been under extreme stress, that she should have been granted time off when she first requested it, and that an immediate referral to occupational health should have been made. It also held that the failure to do so had deprived Ms Dickins of the chance of not plummeting to the depths of illness that she later reached. O2 Plc appealed on 3 points, in dealing with the issue of foreseeability it was argued that Ms Dickins had not gone far enough to put O2 plc on clear notice that unless something was done it was foreseeable that she would suffer psychiatric harm. O2 Plc also argued that the Court had erred in finding that all previous incidents in which Mr Dickins complained of stress amounted to sufficient notice

175 **Dickins v O2 Plc** [2008] EWCA Civ 1144

The appeal was dismissed this point on the basis that Ms Dickins condition should have been plain to her managers, so it was clear that O2 Plc had received a clear indication of her impending illness. The Court was entitled to take the whole background into account when considering O2 Plc's reaction to Mr Dickins request for time off. Therefore, what Claimants can rely on is an expectation that a Court will look at not only the time notifications are made to employers, but also the manner of the language used to make such a communication. At paragraphs 25 of the Judgment of Lady Justice Smith, it was recited that "*It was clearly that meeting that was crucial, when the respondent spelled out the seriousness of her condition and said in terms that she did not know how long she could go on. The background history was important in that these problems had not come out of the blue. The fact that the respondent had been mentioning difficulties over a period of time was the more significant because she was usually a conscientious, hardworking and reliable employee. The judge was entitled to take the whole of the background into account*"

But what of cases where an employee breaks down in tears in front of an employer blaming work related stress as the cause, or demonstrates other stress related symptoms? This can be a surprisingly common feature encountered when dealing with cases of this nature, and practically, serves as the clearest indicator that is "*plain enough*" to warn of the risk of impending injury. In the case of **Intel Corporation v Daw** [2007] IRLR 355[176] the Claimant had previously suffered from two long periods of postnatal depression which she was quite open about with her employer, She had fully recovered and prior to the events that gave rise to this case, was doing well.

Matters changed when two connected factors contributed to, and led to her subsequent work related stress and breakdown;

176 **Intel Corporation v Daw** [2007] IRLR 355

a. First, the reporting lines in her job were confused and there was a problem of priorities between the demands made on her by different managers;

b. Second, she was provided with insufficient assistance and had to work excessive hours. She had complained about both these problems. Her manager found her in tears and asked her to write down her problems. Her written response included reference to the fact she couldn't sustain the level of work she was doing, she was "*stressed out evidenced by [her] violent mood swings – bad sign.... been here before twice...demoralising me and I want out*". Her appraisals had referred to mood swings.

Ms Daw (as alluded to above) had been employed by the Defendant for around 13 years before her injury in June 2001. She was initially employed as a finance assistant, during which time she had had two periods off work with post-natal depression. After her return to work following the birth of her second child, she had progressed to payroll analyst. Intel Corporation was a very large international company that frequently acquired other companies and Ms Daw worked on payroll integration, which was accepted to be a sensitive and complex job. Shortly after assuming her new role, a reorganisation took place which in turn led to an increase in her work and an increase in the number of managers to whom she was accountable (some of whom were unaware of her previous post-natal depression). Ms Daw made at least 14 written and verbal representations to her managers that there were insufficient resources to deal with the workload for which she had responsibility and that she was having to work excessive hours to complete the work.

The Claimant was also found on at least on occasion to be tearful, and clearly struggling. Pill LJ at paragraphs 42 and 43 of the Court of Appeals Judgment provided that; "...*The judge was fully entitled to hold that it was a failure of management which created the stresses and led to the breakdown. The judge was entitled to hold that by early March injury to the Claimant's health was reasonably foreseeable. The indications of impending harm to health were plain enough for the Defendants to realise that immediate action was required .... The judge was entitled to find that, in the context of frequent complaints by the Claimant of "overwork and conflicting pressures upon her", urgent action was required of the Defendants immediately upon receipt of the early March 2001 memorandum*".

In **Hiles v South Gloucestershire NHS Primary Care Trust** [2006] EWHC 3418 (QB)[177] the Claimant had been employed as a health visitor with responsibility for children. When she commenced employment she was told by her then manager that her workload should not exceed responsibility for 200 children. A new manager was subsequently appointed and coincidentally her workload increased to responsibility for 230-240 children. This was shown to be due to a combination of natural causes, and a severe staff shortage. This caused the Claimant unreasonable levels of occupational stress. The Claimant underwent a performance review with her manager and in this meeting, claimed at to have explained that difficulties she was having in managing her workload and broke down in tears. Her manager promised to keep the effect which her work-related stress was having on her under review, but her workload increased again leading to the Claimant suffering a psychiatric breakdown.

The High Court concluded at paragraph 41 that it was "*abundantly clear that Mrs Hiles suffered stress at work in the course of 2002 and as the year progressed became increasingly ill as a result of that stress, until in November she became unfit for work. From May 2002 her line manager ... appreciated that Mrs Hiles was at risk of becoming overstressed and as a result unwell, unless her situation was kept under review so that action might be taken to prevent that happening, and unless she received appropriate support. Despite that, Mrs Hiles' position was not kept under review, and she did not receive the promised special support. On the contrary her workload was increased by reducing the strength of her team; and formal and informal reports that she could not cope with the workload were met with no more than advice about*

177 **Hiles v South Gloucestershire NHS Primary Care Trust** [2006] EWHC 3418 (QB)

the need to prioritise. It was Mrs Phillips herself who foresaw that Mrs Hiles might become unwell if she did not receive special help, yet signs that she was in fact becoming ill went unnoticed: the penny did not drop. Mrs Phillips freely admitted that stress levels were such that it was foreseeable that any one of her Health Visitors might go off sick, and indeed that she herself foresaw just such an eventuality. I do not think it makes any difference that Mrs Phillips did not realise that Mrs Hiles was probably more vulnerable to illness than her colleagues (as I found her to have been); but in any event it is my view that Mrs Phillips should have realised this, having been alerted to Mrs Hiles' emotional state on the occasion of the IPR in May 2002, and being directly involved in Mrs Hiles' inability to face work on her return from holiday in September 2002".

<u>The nature of the Claimant</u>

Having considered cases where a Claimant shows that they were at risk of injury, what about cases where a Claimant appears particularly robust or intentionally conceals the issues they are facing.

In **King v Medical Services International** <u>[2012] EWHC 970 (QB)</u>[178] the High Court reached a different conclusion that those above, due to facts relating to how the Claimant conducted herself and presented herself robustly at work. The Claimant had worked as an executive manager in a hospital who alleged that she had suffered a serious psychiatric breakdown due to being harassed and bullied by the Defendants then a chief executive officer. She relied on a series of incidents as having had the cumulative effect of causing her harassment and work related stress.

Her claim failed as the evidence identified that that she would have complained of being at risk of injury has she considered the same to be the case. The High Court concluded that "*the Claimant was the Executive Manager, used to exercising authority over others and speaking her mind*

[178] **King v Medical Services International** <u>[2012] EWHC 970 (QB)</u>

when called upon to do so. I am satisfied that as a manager she was perceived as robust. In present day industry CEOs often work under considerable pressure. Tough decisions have to be made and executives have to fight their corner. Executives are expected to withstand the demands and criticisms of their CEOs. The Claimant acknowledges this when she refers to the various incidents as individually not of sufficient gravity to have an impact on "an experienced manager such as myself." Mr Anderson would have expected the Claimant to have protected herself. He said "she was a tough cookie. She would have coped with it"".

A similar outcome was reached in **Daniel v Secretary of State for the Home Department** [2014] EWHC 2578 (QB)[179] the Claimant's claim (which was advanced on three grounds) was dismissed for a single reason; she had not taken the opportunity to make her employers aware of the stress she was under. She unfortunately enjoyed a stressful and difficult relationship with a senior co work, and it was well known that the two disagreed about the direction of projects and the funding they should receive.

The fact that she did not want to seem weak in the "*war*" between her and Professor Gabra, while understandable, was not relevant to this point. Furthermore there were no outward indicators of her stress to have put the Defendant on notice.

Sir Robert Nelson giving the Judgment of the High Court held found there were no outward indications of her stress, as set out in paragraphs 181 and 184 of the judgement, "*she did not wish to be seen as weak… and to remain at all times professional in her conduct and approach*". Effectively, her stoic nature whist commendable was to the detriment of her health and also to the success of her claim. Had she made her concerns known at an early stage and the outcome of the claim could have been very different. This seems to be hinted at by Sir Robert Nelson

[179] **Daniel v Secretary of State for the Home Department** [2014] EWHC 2578 (QB)

at paragraph 195 who stated that;_"*whilst she did not exhibit signs of this or make it known to the Defendant in such a manner as to give rise to a duty, it was, I am satisfied having an effect upon her. Secondly, although she was not overworked, the pressures of a hardworking long hour's job together with her perception of bullying combined to create the stress which, in my judgment was a factor in her psychiatric breakdown because of her particular vulnerability*".

The same trend was reinforced in **Easton v B&Q** [2015] EWHC 880 (QB)[180], where the Claimant who desire to appear robust and not endanger his prospects of promotion, did not raise in a clear and plain manner with his employer the work related issues and difficulties he experienced. Davis J made a finding of fact that Mr Easton did not complain about the effect of the changes because he wanted to impress senior management, While Davis J was satisfied that running the store was a real challenge, it was Mr Easton's desire to maintain his profile as a high performing manager that he said nothing to his management.

Allegations as to working hours

But what of cases where there is no complaint of a threat to health by an employee who has no previous history of psychiatric illness but appears to be indicating that one could materialise, is there an argument that injury is not foreseeable? The answer appears to be that it will depend on the facts of the case as set out by the two below examples.

In the case of **Hone v Six Continents Retail** [2006] IRLR 49[181], the Judge had concluded that the fact that the employee had been asking for an assistant manager from early on in the employment relationship, that he had complained about excessive hours, that he was very tired, that he had put in returns showing that he was working 90 hours a week on a seven-day week basis were sufficiently plain indications of impending

---

180 **Easton v B&Q** [2015] EWHC 880 (QB)

181 **Hone v Six Continents Retail** [2006] IRLR 49

harm for a reasonable employer to realise that they should do something about it.

The Claimants claim to be working 90 hours a week, which was not made for any financial benefit and was dismissed by the employers as "*nonsense*", indicated either that he was working hours greatly in excess of anything that could reasonably have been expected, or that he was making irrational claims and, in effect, making a cry for help.

All those matters were taken in conjunction with the employers' knowledge that the section 4 Working Time Regulations 1998 imposed a requirement of no more than 48 hours per week without consent (which the Claimant had refused to give). The Court of Appeal held that the employer was liable.

This result sits somewhat oddly however with **Sayers**[182], in which the trial Judge rejected a contention that a breach of obligation under section 4 Working Time Regulations 1998 (i.e. to take all reasonable steps to ensure the 48-hour limit is complied with) gave rise to common law cause of action for breach of statutory duty.

The foreseeable harm must be imminent

Considering these principals, there exists almost a no-man's land between cases of clear-cut foreseeable stress at work, and cases where such symptoms may occur at a later date. In such cases when considering liability, the Courts will often prefer the employer, ironically discouraging pre-emptive action.

In the case of **Pratley v Surrey County Council** [2003] IRLR 794[183], the Claimant who had been employed by the local authority as a care manager, appealed against a decision that the local authority was not liable in negligence for her stress-induced psychiatric illness. By way of

182 **Sayers v Cambridgeshire CC** [2007] IRLR 29

183 **Pratley v Surrey County Council** [2003] IRLR 794

background the Claimant's role involved considerable pressure because of the demanding nature of the work and lack of funding. The Claimant claimed that the local authority had failed to take the necessary steps to lighten her workload or to reduce her stress, which had been both apparent and complained about.

The trial Judge found that the system of working imposed upon the Claimant involved a foreseeable risk of injury to her in the long term, but not a foreseeable risk of imminent injury, and her claim accordingly failed. When heard in the Court of Appeal, Mance LJ stated that "*There is a potentially relevant distinction between a risk of psychiatric injury arising from continuing overload in the future, and a risk of collapse in the short term arising from disappointment of a "cherished idea" developed as a result of a conversation about possible problems if there was continuing work overload over a further period. The harm in each case is psychiatric injury, but not only does it occur by quite different mechanisms, more importantly it occurs at quite different times. It follows that the judge was right to consider whether the risk of imminent collapse was foreseeable, which he held was not.*"

CHAPTER TWELVE

STRESS AT WORK AND THE BREACH OF DUTY OF CARE

Once the risk of psychiatric harm is deemed foreseeable, an employer is then placed under an obligation to act in such a manner as to minimise the danger posed to their employee.

Breach of a Defendant's duty of care is often not as difficult to establish in claims relating to stress at work once the foreseeability of imminent injury is established for reasons which should be obvious. However, the alleged breach must be seen to;

a. Have been causative of the Claimant's injury;

b. Have been within the Defendant's control;

c. Have been a reasonable response.

For example, the completion of a risk assessment can be helpful, but if the cause of injury is that of the reduction of work, it is unlikely that the risk assessment itself would have prevented the injury. It is more likely than not that such a risk assessment would have identified the need for a reduction in workload and give rise to liability but an overall view needs to be taken when assessing such breaches.

Failings can, and still occur even in situations where an employer clearly knows of the existence of an employee's vulnerability to psychiatric injury and has put in place appropriate measures to avoid such injury occurring but fails to implement them promptly or appropriately. This format of breach is one of the more common examples such claim practical experience.

As in the previous chapter, the **Hatton v Sutherland** [2002] EWCA Civ 76[184] guidelines remain the starting point.

Guidelines 8 – 13

Guideline 8

"*The employer is only in breach of duty if he has failed to take the steps which are reasonable in the circumstances, bearing in mind the magnitude of the risk of harm occurring, the gravity of the harm which may occur, the costs and practicability of preventing it, and the justifications for running the risk*".

In most cases of stress at work, the steps needed will be obvious and basic. They can include;

a. Reducing a Claimant's workload;

b. Carrying out a risk assessme3nt to understand the sources of their work related stress;

c. Providing a Claimant with support, or other means to reduce and combat their work related stress.

Guideline 9

"*The size and scope of the employer's operation, its resources and the demands it faces are relevant in deciding what is reasonable; these include the interests of other employees and the need to treat them fairly, for example, in any redistribution of duties*".

Guidelines 9 provides a balancing exercise and is always highly evidence based. Particular attention should be given in witness statements to competing issues and how a Claimant was managed.

[184] **Hatton v Sutherland** [2002] EWCA Civ 76

Guideline 10

"*An employer can only reasonably be expected to take steps which are likely to do some good: the Court is likely to need expert evidence on this*".

Guideline 10 is an important guideline, in that it focuses the mind of the practitioner on not just establishing if a breach of duty of care occurred, but what the likely effect would have been had the breach been avoided. In this sense guidelines 10 straddles the questions of pure breach of duty and causation, and brings into consideration the reasonableness and proportionality of the response required.

Guideline 11

"*An employer who offers a confidential advice service, with referral to appropriate counselling or treatment services, is unlikely to be found in breach of duty*".

On its bare construction, guidelines11 appeared to provide an absolute defence for an employee facing a claim of occupational stress. Its force has been reduced, with an increases factual focus as required in the above guidelines 10, on what differed it would have made to the outcome, if a Claimant had used it. The situation is of course, rather different where a Claimant can evidence that they have made use of such a service, and none the less gone on to suffer a recognisable psychiatric injury.

Guideline 12

"*If the only reasonable and effective step would have been to dismiss or demote the employee, the employer will not be in breach of duty in allowing a willing employee to continue in the job*".

Guideline 12 rarely arises in claims of occupational stress, but provides a helpful safeguard in claims where such rare facts arises.

Guideline 13

"*In all cases, therefore, it is necessary to identify the steps which the employer both could and should have taken before finding him in breach of his duty of care*".

In most occupational stress cases, especially where foreseeability is denied, a Claimant will be able to identify a series of breaches.

Considering the below sub-headings, some of the Judgements referred to relate to cases of physical injury. Due to Courts considering when assessing if there has been a breach of a Defendant's duty of care the need to prevent injury (be it physical of psychiatric, as per **Page v Smith** [1996] A.C. 155) they are a helpful source of jurisprudence and authority to support both a Claimant's and Defendant's case in occupational stress claims, and are put forward on this basis.

Support services

The Court of Appeal in **Hatton**[185] suggested that an employer who offered a confidential advice service, with referral to appropriate counselling or treatment services, was unlikely to be found in breach of duty. At that time the Court took the view that "*Schemes now being developed and encouraged which recognise and respond to the peculiar problems presented both to employees and employers. The key is to offer help on a completely confidential basis. The employee can then be encouraged to recognise the signs and seek that help without fearing its effects upon his job or prospects; the employer need not make intrusive inquiries or over-react to such problems as he does detect; responsibility for accessing the service can be left with the people who are best equipped to know what the problems are, the employee, his family and friends; and if reasonable help is offered either directly or through referral to other services, then all that reasonably could be done has been done. Obviously, not all employers have the resources to put such systems in place, but an employer who does have a system along those*

[185] **Hatton v Sutherland** [2002] EWCA Civ 76

lines is unlikely to be found in breach of his duty of care towards his employees"

In **Hartman v South Essex Mental Health & Community Care NHS Trust** [2005] EWCA Civ 6[186], the Court of Appeal reiterated the position set out in **Hatton**[187] namely that if an employer has an occupational health system or counselling service, that should not be taken to indicate that the employer has foreseen psychiatric injury but, rather, makes it less likely that the employer will be in breach of its duty if such injury does occur.

Whilst a sensible suggestion, the concept of having a policy in place which by virtue of its presence should absolve a Defendant of any breach of duty of care, has not found favour with the Courts. For example in **Intel Corporation (UK) Ltd v Daw** [2007] EWCA Civ 70[188], the Court of Appeal identified that counselling services were not a panacea by which employers could discharge their duty of care in all cases. Whether the provision of such services would assist an employer to discharge its duty of care would depend on their relevance to the facts of the case and helpfully set out that; "*Whether in any given case the counselling service provided will be enough to discharge the reasonable employer's duty must depend on the facts of each case. ... [Mrs Daw] cannot reasonably be criticised for not using it ... A short term counselling service could not have done anything to ameliorate that risk or help Mrs Daw cope with it. It could not reduce her workload. The most it could have done was to advise her to see her doctor. It does not seem to me that on the facts of this case the service provided was a sufficient discharge of the Defendant's duty.*"

---

186 **Hartman v South Essex Mental Health & Community Care NHS Trust** [2005] EWCA Civ 6

187 **Hatton v Sutherland** [2002] EWCA Civ 76

188 **Intel Corporation (UK) Ltd v Daw** [2007] EWCA Civ 70

In **Dickins v O2 plc** [2008] EWCA Civ 1144[189], the Court of Appeal held that referring Ms Dickins to the Defendant's counselling services, as was done, was insufficient to avoid liability. It found that the Court in **Hatton**[190] had made it clear that the advantage of a confidential service was to permit employees to take advice when they were unwilling to admit to line management that they were not coping with their work for fear of damaging their reputations. However, the Claimant had told her manager that she was "*at the end of her tether*" and in this context, where the impending severity of foreseeable injury was plain, making a referral was not enough.

In **Dickins**[191], and **Daw**[192], that point raised by both Defendants and was only able to be overcome by the respective Claimants due to the specific facts of their respective claims. In **Dickins**[193], the Court of Appeal held that it was entitled to infer that O2 Plc should have referred Ms Dickins to occupational health and given her a break as requested, which was in and of itself, a breach of duty. Ms Dickins' impending illness should have been clear to O2 Plc, so it should have been clear that a reference to occupational health would have set in motion a proper professional consideration of Ms Dickins' problems by a specialist doctor, while allowing Ms Dickins time away from work which would have removed the pressure upon her. Factually it was also relevant to note that Ms Dickins was already receiving counselling and had made it clear to O2 Plc that she was suffering because of the stress at work. In a somewhat fiery part of the Judgement at paragraph 28, lady justice Smith provided that "*In Daw v Intel Corporation [2007] ICR 1318, the Court of Appeal observed that the reference to counselling services in Hatton did not make such services a panacea by which employers can discharge their duty of care*

---

189 **Dickins v O2 plc** [2008] EWCA Civ 1144

190 **Hatton v Sutherland** [2002] EWCA Civ 76

191 **Dickins v O2 plc** [2008] EWCA Civ 1144

192 **Intel Corporation (UK) Ltd v Daw** [2007] EWCA Civ 70

193 **Dickins v O2 plc** [2008] EWCA Civ 1144

in all cases. In that case, the judge had been entitled to hold the employer in breach notwithstanding that it provided a counselling service. The employee's problems could only be dealt with by management intervention. The same is true here. Mr Gardiner's reliance on the summary in paragraph 43(11) serves to demonstrate how dangerous it is to apply guidance given by the Court as though it were a statutory provision".

In the case of **Daw**[194], at paragraph 43 of the Judgement of Pill LJ the Court of Appeal differentiates between the likely outcome of such a services provision "*There will be cases in which an employee may be expected to take refuge in counselling services. The problems of this capable and loyal employee could, however, as the judge found, be dealt with only by management reducing her workload. The judge was entitled to find that, in the context of frequent complaints by the Claimant of "overwork and conflicting pressures upon her", urgent action was required of the Defendants immediately upon receipt of the early March 2001 memorandum*".

Whilst the provision of such a service is a useful defence for a Defendant, it does not seem that the Courts adopt the same initial hard line indicated in **Hatton**[195] as to the provisions of such services. Also, a Claimant who takes advantage of outside counselling services as in **Dickins**[196], appears able to seek to argue that they would have had no effect. The mere suggestion that a Claimant should have used a Defendant's counselling service does not appear to be adequate per se to defeat any allegation of breach of duty, nor does the presence of such a service automatically discharge a Defendant's duty to a Claimant.

194 **Intel Corporation (UK) Ltd v Daw** [2007] EWCA Civ 70

195 **Hatton v Sutherland** [2002] EWCA Civ 76

196 **Dickins v O2 plc** [2008] EWCA Civ 1144

Occupational health departments

The knowledge of an employer's employee or agent, such as an occupational health adviser, may be inferred to be that of the Defendant, but factually we still need to consider if this was confidential and if the employee had consented to it being provided to the employer. In **Gallop v Newport City Council** [2013] EWCA Civ 1583[197] the Defendants occupational health adviser regularly informed an employer that an employee was suffering from stress but considered that the employee was not disabled for the purposes of the Equality Act 2010. The EAT held that the employer did not have imputed knowledge of the employee's disability since the knowledge imputed to the employer was that the employee was not disabled, not that he was disabled. However, this was overturned by the Court of Appeal. The Court held that the task for the employment tribunal had been to decide whether the employer had actual or constructive knowledge of the facts concerning the employee's disability.

In **Donelien v Liberata UK Ltd** [2018] EWCA Civ 129[198], the Defendant did not acquire constructive knowledge of an employee's disability where it had taken reasonable steps to ascertain whether the employee was disabled. The employer had not just "*rubber stamped*" an occupational health report that stated that the employee was not disabled: it had asked further questions of its occupational health advisers, held "*return to work*" meetings with the employee and considered correspondence received from her GP. The Court of Appeal held that, viewed as a whole, the employer's actions were sufficient to avoid having constructive knowledge of the employee's disability.

Occupational Health departments, and the evidence that they record is for all intrinsic purposes one of the primary courses of supportive evidence, or lack thereof in claims for stress at work. After all, it is

---

[197] **Gallop v Newport City Council** [2013] EWCA Civ 1583

[198] **Donelien v Liberata UK Ltd** [2018] EWCA Civ 129

reasonable for a Court to conclude that an employer who creates a department, and employs people to manage risks to its employees' health, will need to take seriously what risks they report as being present.

Is an employer ever under a duty to dismiss an employee?

Rarely, there are cases where the only step and employer can take to protect a Claimant is to dismiss them. **Hatton**[199] makes it clear that if this is the only reasonable step an employer could take was to dismiss or demote the employee, the employer would not be in breach of duty in allowing a willing employee to continue in their job. However, and here the friction and need for flexibility becomes apparent, the House of Lords in **Barber v Somerset County Council** [2004] UKHL 13[200] took a differing stance, providing that "*There must be situations where, just as an adult cannot be required to undergo medical treatment against their will, an employee should be entitled to continue working at high pressure, even though there is a risk that they will damage their mental or physical health. For example, a university teacher employed to do research should be permitted to choose to work all hours of the day and night, at possible or even obvious risk to their health, in the hope of making a breakthrough in deciphering an ancient language or unravelling some secret in genetics...*

*...in other cases, it could be said that where an employee is liable to develop some illness if they carry out the job that they have been employed to do, the employer owes a duty of care not to continue to employ them to perform that job. However, such a duty would have to mesh with the provisions of the relevant employment contract regulating sickness absences and ill-health retirement. More importantly, at least where the risk was small, the common law has taken the view that the employee can decide whether to run it (**Withers v Perry Chain Co Ltd** [1961] 1 WLR 1314)*".

[199] **Hatton v Sutherland** [2002] EWCA Civ 76

[200] **Barber v Somerset County Council** [2004] UKHL 13

Considering this point, in the matter of **Vahidi v Fairstead House School Trust Ltd** [2005] EWCA Civ 765[201]. In this matter the Claimant had claimed that the Defendant had caused her to suffer severe clinical depression. She had been employed by the Defendant as a reception class teacher and assistant head until her dismissal for ill health. The Claimant claimed that, owing to a government scheme resulting in changes to the school's teaching methods, she had suffered stress, and that the Defendant had failed to provide her with sufficient support in order for her to return to work after a period of absence. Her claim was dismissed on the basis that the evidence showed that her mental condition had collapsed under the strain arising from her attempts, albeit with reasonable support, to make fundamental changes to her teaching methods, with which she had been unable to cope. The Court concluded on the evidence before it that her following instances of severe depressive illness were not caused by any breach of duty on the part of the Defendant since. Notably, the Claimant argued that the judge had been wrong to dismiss the claim since there was evidence to show that the Defendant had failed to support her adequately and most other steps, should have sent her home.

The Court of Appeal dismissed the appeal, finding for the Defendant. The Court of Appeal identified that there was evidence to support the Courts findings that the Claimant's mental condition had collapsed under the strain arising from her attempts to make fundamental changes to her teaching methods, with which she had been unable to cope. The evidence showed that the Defendant had put into place support mechanisms. It was notable that the Defendants staff at the school were anxious for her to return to work, and it was difficult to see what more could have been done without the Defendant becoming being intrusive or unsupportive. It was concluded that there was no merit in the Claimant's submission that the Defendant should have sent her home; such an action would be bound to have been seen as a hostile act since it

---

[201] **Vahidi v Fairstead House School Trust Ltd** [2005] EWCA Civ 765

would have indicated a lack of confidence in her and been just the sort of conduct that might have brought on a relapse.

A duty to remove a Claimant from a role that poses a risk

In **Coxall v Goodyear Great Britain Ltd** [2002] EWCA Civ 1010[202] the Court of Appeal held that the question of whether an employer was under a duty to remove an employee from work that exposed them to the risk of physical danger depended on the magnitude of the risk.

The Claimant in this case had predisposition to asthma, and was employed at the Defendant's tyre factory in the paint section. the Claimant has informed the Defendant of the risks, and told the Defendants occupational health department had decided that the Claimant should not work with paint. No steps were taken by the Defendant, and the Claimant collapsed due to occupational asthma caused by the fumes of the paint. The Court of Appeal found for the Claimant, with Brown LJ conclusion at paragraphs 35 and 36 of the Judgment that "*The law's dilemma in a case like this arises when an employer has done all that is reasonably practicable to protect his employee from harm in the work he reasonably requires him to do, but the employee has some personal idiosyncrasy which puts him at risk while performing work which can be safely performed by virtually all his fellow employees. If the employer simply has no alternative work reasonably available, what is he to do? He cannot reasonably be required to continue to employ and pay the employee for doing no work. If the employee, with full knowledge of the risks he runs, tells his employer, following a discussion of the available alternatives, that he nevertheless prefers to run those risks rather than have no work at all, is the employer nevertheless compelled to dismiss him on the grounds that he would otherwise be held liable for negligently endangering his employee's health? ... Mr Coxall's dilemma is that he was found to be peculiarly sensitive to industrial asthma in work which carried with it no measurable risk to the*

[202] **Coxall v Goodyear Great Britain Ltd** [2002] EWCA Civ 1010

rest of the workforce, provided that they made use of the protective equipment issued to them.

... the whole spirit of the common law in this country is concerned to protect the freedom of the individual... It may be that, as our law now ... an employee may not elect to stay at work in these circumstances if to do so meant that he would run a very significant risk of being exposed to harm of a considerable magnitude, but these are vague concepts which would need to be tightened up when a Court is invited to consider particular factual situations. For greater clarity we will have to await occasions where the relevant points arise for decision and when the issues on both sides of the argument are fully and thoroughly canvassed".

Claims arising from excessive workload

As an employer is permitted to assume that an employee can withstand with the "*normal pressures*" of the job and take employees' actions at "*face value*" there are immediate difficulties in claims arising from overworking.

A helpful illustration of this is where an employee returns from a period of sick leave sue to stress. Unless there are statements to the contrary from the employee, the assumption that they are fit to return to work often appears sound. However, if the employee makes it clear that they are still suffering from the impact of stress then it is helpful for employers to consider if reasonable adjustments should be made. These could include;

a. Reduction in workload;

b. Carrying out risk assessments;

c. Implementing health and safety surveillance;

d. Altered working hours;

e. Redistributing work; and

f. Providing support possibly through a counselling service.

One of the problems with overworking cases for employers is that the quantity of work an employee needs to deal with is often quantifiable. It is also not uncommon that where an employee has returned from a stress related absence flowing form stress, that throwing them straight back into the deep end of work is likely to put them in the same position as caused them to become unwell.

There are a plethora of cases which can assist on this point, but in reality, they are illustrative. There is no substitute for careful and objective consideration of the factual aspects of a claim.

The Court of Appeal in **Johnstone v Bloomsbury Health Authority** [1992] QB 333[203] agreed that an action for damages could succeed where the employee was able to show that it was reasonably foreseeable that the employer's conduct in requiring the employee to work excessive hours would damage their health. Factually, the case of Johnstone has immediate application to such claims and provides a helpful illustration of how such cases arise. Dr Johnstone was required to work 40 hours per week plus a further 48 hours a week on call under his contract of employment, meaning that sometimes he was required to work over 100 hours per week without adequate sleep, causing him to suffer stress and exhaustion. While the case was settled, the acceptance by the majority of the Court that working excessive working hours might be foreseen to cause injury to health was important for both employers and employees.

The Court of Appeal held that "*There is no difference between the duty to provide a safe system of working and the duty to take reasonable care for the safety of the employee. The former is merely an ingredient in the latter duty. Moreover, I cannot see, in the example I have just given, that it makes any difference that instead of the overtime being "as required" the workman is contracted to work up to 88 hours a week. If these were the hours of a contract*

[203] **Johnstone v Bloomsbury Health Authority** [1992] QB 333

of a heavy goods driver, and he fell asleep at the wheel through exhaustion and suffered injury I entertain no doubt that, subject to any defence of contributory negligence, the employee would have a good claim against his employer for operating an unsafe system of work. There is no obligation on the employer to require the man to drive for 88 hours in the week, and if by so doing he exposes him to foreseeable risk of injury he will be liable.

It must be remembered that the duty of care is owed to the individual employee and different employees may have different stamina. If the Defendants in this case knew or ought to have known that by requiring him to work the hours they did, they exposed him to risk of injury to his health, then they should not have required him to work in excess of those hours that he safely could have done".

In **Jones v Sandwell Metropolitan Borough Council** [2002] EWCA Civ 76[204] (one of the conjoined cases in **Hatton**[205]), Mrs Jones initially claimed that she if ten worked a 60-hour week, but never less than 48 hours. The Court of Appeal set out at paragraph 66 and 67 that what the Court needed to focus on was if it was "*sufficiently foreseeable that … to be a breach of duty for the employers to carry on placing unreasonable demands upon her and not to follow through their own decision that something should be done about it…*

Once it is concluded that the combination of the way in which she was being treated and her formal complaints about it made injury to her health foreseeable, it is not difficult to identify what might have been done to prevent the injury which in fact occurred. The judge was entitled to conclude that failure to do this caused her breakdown. There was no challenge to the quantification of damages in this case. We have not therefore been able to consider whether any of the matters discussed earlier in this judgment might have led to any modification of the award. Our conclusion on liability should

---

[204] **Jones v Sandwell Metropolitan Borough Council** [2002] EWCA Civ 76

[205] **Hatton v Sutherland** [2002] EWCA Civ 76

not be taken as any indication of our view on the appropriate measure of damages in this or any other such case".

Further, and whilst covered in an earlier chapter **Hone v Six Continents Retail** [2006] IRLR 49[206] show that the Claimant's complaint about his about excessive hours, (90 hours a week) over a seven-day week basis were sufficiently plain indications of impending harm for a reasonable employer to realise that they should do something about it. They needed to take steps to reduce this, and due to the facts of the claim, breach of duty followed the finding of foresight.

The Management of Health and Safety at Work Regulations 1999

In workplace stress cases, the Courts accept that the Management of Health and Safety at Work Regulations 1999 have application. This most commonly arises in three separate example of a duty of care being breached, namely;

a. A failure to assess and manage risks created by an employee's work (regulation 3, Management of Health and Safety at Work Regulations 1999);

b. A failure to implement appropriate preventative and protective measures (regulations 4 and 5 Management of Health and Safety at Work Regulations 1999);

c. A failure to implement health and safety surveillance and have in place health and safety assistance (regulations 6 and 7 Management of Health and Safety at Work Regulations 1999); and

[206] **Hone v Six Continents Retail** [2006] IRLR 49

d. A failure to ensure that staff are both capable and trained to carry out their roles (regulation 13, Management of Health and Safety at Work Regulations 1999);

Risk assessments will often when the issue of foreseeability of harm is considered, present as the main area of focus in stress at work claims since risk assessments once completed, are likely to identify the steps which need to be taken to avoid a breach duty when dealing with clams for occupational stress, but also establish that an injury attributable to this stress (if this is assessed) has been foreseen.

It is also advisable that practitioners present cases with a focus on what the risk assessment would have identified on the balance of probabilities, and what a reasonable employer would have done in response to it. This can be an especially potent line of argument in cases where a Claimant has already suffered one absence due to work related stress, and a risk assessment is carried out to help manage their safe return to work (as in **Young v Post Office** [2002] EWCA Civ 661[207])

Following the advent of the Enterprise and Regulatory Reform Act 2013 and the removal of civil liability for breach of the Management of Health and Safety at Work Regulations 1999 liability, a breach of the regulations remains a strong indicator of negligence, when a Court comes to assess if an employer has acted practical and reasonably.

This has been made more than tolerably clear in **Goldscheider v Royal Opera House Covent Garden Foundation** [2019] EWCA Civ 711[208], **Cockerill v CXK Ltd** [2018] EWHC 115 (QB)[209] where at paragraph 106 of the Judgment the High Court at paragraphs 18 sets out "*In removing the Claimant's cause of action for breach of statutory duty, the 2013*

207 **Young v Post Office** [2002] EWCA Civ 661

208 **Goldscheider v Royal Opera House Covent Garden Foundation** [2019] EWCA Civ 711

209 **Cockerill v CXK Ltd** [2018] EWHC 115 (QB)

Act did not repeal the duties themselves. Those duties continue to bind employers in law. So they continue to be relevant to the question of what an employer ought reasonably to do". Recently in **Chadwick v RH Ovenden Ltd & Hamilton** [2022] EWHC 1701 (QB)[210], where the High Court repeated the same sentiment with "*those statutory duties continue to exist but that this is a claim in negligence and that a breach of regulation no longer automatically provides a civil remedy*" and weas applied in **Lewin v Gray** [2023] EWHC 112 (KB)[211].

When considering the issue of breach of the regulations within the context of work related stress, the practitioner should remember that;

a. Guidance in managing work related stress has been readily available since 1995 when the HSE advised that stress should be treated like any other occupational health risk. The HSE directed that an employer's Risk Assessment should include the risks of psychological as well as physical injury;

b. From March 2019 employers were advised to carry out the risk assessment process by following the principles laid out in the HSE's publications "*Making the Stress Management Standards Work*" and "*Real Solutions, Real People.*"

c. Further guidance concerning the management of occupational stress was published by the HSE entitled "*Tackling work related stress using the management standards approach*" in March 2019.

Risk assessments in the context of work related stress

The mere foreseeability of a risk does not give rise to breach of duty however, if it can be met by an employer and their employees taking practical and effective steps to avoid it. If a significant risk cannot be reduced to safe levels, then the employer must warn employees and

210 **Chadwick v RH Ovenden Ltd & Hamilton** [2022] EWHC 1701 (QB)

211 **Lewin v Gray** [2023] EWHC 112 (KB)

prospective employees that is exists, as shown in **White v Holbrook Precision Castings Ltd** [1985] I.R.L.R. 215 at where, Lawton LJ held "*If a job has risks to health and safety which are not common knowledge but of which an employer knows or ought to know and against which he cannot guard by taking precautions, then he should tell anyone to whom he is offering the job what those risks are if, on the information available to him, knowledge of those risks would be likely to affect the decision of a sensible, level-headed prospective employee about accepting the offer.*"

In **Kennedy v Cordia (Services) LLP** [2016] UKSC 6[212] the Supreme Court emphasised that it had become generally accepted at paragraph 110 of the Judgment that "*it has become generally recognised that a reasonably prudent employer will conduct a risk assessment in connection with its operations so that it can take suitable precautions to avoid injury to its employees. In many circumstances, as in those of the present case, a statutory duty to conduct such an assessment has been imposed. The requirement to carry out such an assessment, whether statutory or not, forms the context in which the employer has to take precautions in the exercise of reasonable care for the safety of its employees. That is because the whole point of a risk assessment is to identify whether the particular operation gives rise to any risk to safety and, if so, what is the extent of that risk, and what can and should be done to minimise or eradicate the risk*".

The Supreme Court concluded at paragraphs 111 that "*It follows that the employer's duty is no longer confined to taking such precautions as are commonly taken or, as Lord Dunedin put it, such other precautions as are so obviously wanted that it would be folly in anyone to neglect to provide them. A negligent omission can result from a failure to seek out knowledge of risks which are not in themselves obvious*".

[212] **Kennedy v Cordia (Services) LLP** [2016] UKSC 6

In the case of **Cockerill v CXK Ltd** [2018] EWHC 1155 (QB)[213] the High Court applied the ratio of **Kennedy**[214] to different facts. In this matter, that Claimant who was visiting unfamiliar premises fell down a second seven-inch doorstep from the lobby down into a kitchen area, and hurt her ankle. Her claim failed. As to the question of risk assessments, the Court concluded at set out at paragraph 63 that the Defendant "*needed to have taken reasonable care to see that visitors would be reasonably safe in entering the premises across the lobby/kitchen step. The Avenue was, it was clear to see, a period building in busy community use. It had been competently risk-assessed for those purposes. The step, with the kitchen door open, stood in plain view. It was reasonably clearly marked out on its lip with hazard warning tape. It was reasonably clearly lit. It was unimpeded*".

Considering the failure to complete any risk assessment, paragraph 81 of the Judgment is a practical and helpful example of how the Court may deal with similar situations, and provides "*I cannot find a reason why, if [the Defendant] had undertaken its own [risk assessment], it would have assessed the step any differently… or that it would, or reasonably should, have taken any measure in relation to the step beyond those already taken… I cannot see what more there was to know about the kitchen step, the risk it posed to visitors, or the measures available to give them reasonable protection from that risk…. To the best of everyone's knowledge, there was no history of particular concerns about the step in question… Marking them with hazard tape gives employees, all else being equal, the best reasonable chance of avoiding problems with them*".

The High Court decision of **Chell v Tarmac Cement & Lime Ltd** [2020] EWHC 2613 (QB)[215] when considering the scope and nature of the risk needs to be assessed, accepted that it was not reasonable to expect the employer to extend its risk assessment to cover "*horse-play, ill-discipline and malice*" in claim where the Claimant was injured following a practical

[213] **Cockerill v CXK Ltd** [2018] EWHC 1155 (QB)

[214] **Kennedy v Cordia (Services) LLP** [2016] UKSC 6

[215] **Chell v Tarmac Cement & Lime Ltd** [2020] EWHC 2613 (QB)

joke. At paragraph 31 of the Judgment, Spencer J held that "*the learned judge was entitled to find that there was not a reasonably foreseeable risk of injury from a deliberate act on the part of any employee of the Defendant to the Claimant. This finding was underpinned by the learned judge's findings of fact and is therefore essentially unassailable. He submits that the learned judge was entitled to conclude that the Defendant's health and safety procedures were adequate, that increased supervision to prevent horseplay or ill-discipline was not a reasonable step for an employer to take and that a risk assessment would not have prevented the incident. So far as the suggestion that the Defendant should have reassured Mr Heath (and Mr Starr) that the security of their jobs was not at risk, Mr Lyons submits that this was not a point taken below, nor was there any evidence that this would have prevented the incident in question, nor could any such duty arise given the finding that the index incident was not reasonably foreseeable*".

For the practitioner dealing with a case of this nature, what is important to establish is that the failure to conduct a risk assessment has been causative of the Claimant's injury (as in **Harris v Bartram's Haulage and Storage Ltd** [2020] EWHC 900 (QB)[216]). It has been, and remains an established principle as laid down in **Clifford v Charles H Challen & Son Ltd** [1951] 1 K.B. 495[217] that if a Defendant knows of a risk and is aware that reasonable steps are not taken to prevent the risk of injury to a Claimant, then the claim is likely to succeed.

Competing issues and the duty of care

Employers will often have to manage a number of completing interests when it comes to managing the danger work related stress poses to a Claimant.

One area of litigation that has begun to develop involved situations where a Defendant fails to act out of fear of reprisals. In **Connor v Surrey**

216 **Harris v Bartrams Haulage and Storage Ltd** [2020] EWHC 900 (QB)

217 **Clifford v Charles H Challen & Son Ltd** [1951] 1 K.B. 495

County Council [2010] EWCA Civ 286[218] Claimant who was the head teacher and member of her school's governing body, experienced problems starting in 2003 due to the actions of a new governor, and his associates, who criticised the Claimant and the school for insufficient engagement with the Muslim community. Tensions escalated, resulting in the new governor's removal in May 2005, but he subsequently filed a complaint of institutional racism and was involved in circulating a malicious petition of no confidence in the Claimant.

The Defendant was slow to respond, but in July 2005, commissioned an independent inquiry into the complaint. By October 2005, the governing body was replaced with an interim executive board (IEB) under the School Standards and Framework Act 1998. The judge found that by May 2005, the local authority had a duty of care to the Claimant, which required replacing the governing body with an IEB. The judge also held that initiating the inquiry into the complaint had been a breach of that duty.

The Court of Appel held at paragraphs 70 – 72 that; "*The council were frightened to stand up to the aggressive confidence of Mr Martin, the bullying tactics of Mr Saleem, and the support they had from others. They feared the charge of racism and, no doubt, of prejudice against Islam. The council's capitulation to these sombre pressures was lamentable. The consequence was a serious neglect of their duty to the Claimant who was in the firing-line of these assaults, and was also the council's employee. In my judgment the deputy judge's findings of fact as to the council's breach of duty are well justified.*

72. The deputy judge stated, at para 239, that what had to be foreseeable was not simply stress but specific psychiatric injury. The complaint is that he should have grappled with the question whether there were actual signs of impending psychiatric injury demanding action on the employer's part, and not merely some future risk or possibility... On the facts there was a welter of

[218] **Connor v Surrey County Council** [2010] EWCA Civ 286

evidence that from at least late 2004 into 2005 the Claimant's mental health was imminently at risk. We did not call on Mr Taylor on this point".

Where the employer unaware of pre-existing vulnerability

Whilst mentioned in the previous chapter, let us consider again **Bonser v UK Coal Mining Ltd** [2003] EWCA Civ 1296[219]. In this matter the Court of Appeal considered a claim by the Claimant who had joined the Defendants after 20 years in the coal industry, during which time she had been signed off work for five weeks with depression. When she was offered a job by, her reference stated that she "*would not be particularly good in a highly stressful environment but she is good at dealing with IT users, training and communication*". The Claimant had burst into tears at work after being asked to complete an additional project which she feared might jeopardise a planned holiday. The trial judge took the view that a reasonable man would have thought that if things continued in this way that the Claimant would "*crack up*". However, the Court of Appeal disagreed, holding that this had not been enough to establish that it was reasonably foreseeable that overwork would result in her suffering from psychiatric illness "*This was a sad case because here we have a very hard working, conscientious lady who was, in a sense, the victim of her own good conscience. She did what was required of her but she did not manifest by her conduct, or by complaint, anything which in my judgment sufficiently put her employer on notice that she was vulnerable to imminent risk of injury to her health. The only visible sign was of her being tearful and upset on that single occasion ... That degree of understandable upset and distress alone does not, however, in my judgment, impose upon a reasonable employer a need to take steps to avert an imminent psychiatric breakdown*"

Instead, the incident should have informed the Defendant that Ms Bonser might become vulnerable to the stress of overwork but not to a psychiatric breakdown. The distinction may seem fine, but when such

[219] **Bonser v UK Coal Mining Ltd** [2003] EWCA Civ 1296

cases are determined at trial, it is important to ensure that a claim is on the right side of this divide.

In **Sayers v Cambridgeshire County Council** [2007] IRLR 29[220], two of Ms Sayers' colleagues were aware that she was taking anti-depressants. The High Court held that this could not be equated to the council having that knowledge "*knowledge of an individual which is not communicated to the higher management but is treated as information held confidentially by that employee cannot be knowledge, actual or imputed, of the council for the purpose of determining whether the indications are plain enough for the council, as a reasonable employer, to realise that it should do something about it*". Again, due to these issues as in **Bonser**[221]., there was no need to take immediate action, and therefore there could be no breach of duty.

Second breakdown cases

It should be clear by now that foreseeability is claims of stress at work is an issue. This hurdle is reduced and ameliorated where there is a second breakdown. Afterall, if the employee becomes unwell due to stress, their individual vulnerability to stress on balance, should be apparent to an employer where it flows form their work. This principle is aptly demonstrated by **Walker v Northumberland County Council** [1995] IRLR 35 (QB)[222]. Mr Walker, who was a social worker, suffered a nervous breakdown as a result of his excessive workload. On his return to work, he asked for, and was promised, additional assistance but it was not provided. He suffered a second breakdown and was dismissed on the grounds of ill-health.

The High Court found that the council was not liable for the first breakdown as it had not been reasonably foreseeable. However, once the Claimant had returned to work, his employer was on notice that there

220 **Sayers v Cambridgeshire County Council** [2007] IRLR 29

221 **Bonser v UK Coal Mining Ltd** [2003] EWCA Civ 1296

222 **Walker v Northumberland County Council** [1995] IRLR 35 (QB)

was a risk of a repetition of a breakdown if he was exposed to the same workload without adequate support. In relation to the standard expected of an employer, the Court held that the duty must be measured against the yardstick of reasonable conduct on the part of the employer. As a safety net, reasonableness was identified as always depending on;

a. The nature of the relationship between the parties;

b. The magnitude of the risk of injury that is reasonably foreseeable;

c. The seriousness of the consequences and the cost and practicability of preventing the risk.

Due to this the Court of Appeal held the Defendant liable for the Claimant's second breakdown.

Another strong example of this arises from the case of **Young v Post Office** [2002] EWCA Civ 661[223]. In this matter the Post Office appealed against a finding that it had breached its duty of care to its employee, Mr Young. Mr Young was employed in 1973 and in 1994 started suffering from stress at work. He had a nervous breakdown in 1997 and was off work for four months. The Post Office agreed that in order to enable Mr Young to return to work he would be allowed to work at his own pace and on flexible hours and that he would be regularly visited by management to check on his progress. The last step did not take place and after seven weeks Mr Young was back to full time work doing his old job. He was unable to cope and suffered another breakdown, taking voluntary early retirement in May 1998. His claim for damages was successful, the Judge finding that given Mr Young's psychiatric history the Post Office had had a duty of care to him which it had breached by failing to implement the agreed measures, and that it had not been up to Mr Young to inform The Post Office that he was having difficulties.

[223] **Young v Post Office** [2002] EWCA Civ 661

On appeal, The Post Office argued that the psychiatric illness might have occurred in any event, that it had taken reasonable steps to care for Mr Young and that Mr Young's failure to speak up amounted to contributory negligence. The Court of Appeal dismissed the appeal and held that the Judge had been right to find that The Post Office owed a duty of care given its knowledge that Mr Young's psychiatric problems were work-related. It was The Post Office's failure to fully implement the agreed measures for Mr Young's return to work which on the facts of the case were sufficiently serious to amount to a breach of that duty. Of further concern to employers, no finding of contributory negligence was made despite Mr Young continuing to suffer in silence. Lord Justice Mays Judgment at paragraph 26 still holds strong and is a useful practical yardstick "... *in many circumstances an employer may not be expected to know that an employee who does not speak up is vulnerable, an employee who is known to be vulnerable is not necessarily to be regarded as responsible for a recurrent psychiatric illness if he fails to tell his employer that his job is again becoming too much for him. A finding of contributory negligence in a case of psychiatric illness, although no doubt theoretically possible in other circumstances, does not in my view sit happily with the facts of this case. I know of no case in which a Claimant such as Mr Young, vulnerable to psychiatric illness which he successfully holds to his employers, has been held to be contributorily negligent, and counsel was unable to draw our attention to any such case. I would reject this ground of appeal*".

Young[224] represents a case in which a clear-cut duty is established and accepted by the Defendant as existing. It also has the benefit of, due to the previous issues with Mr Young's health, that his vulnerability to psychiatric injury was foreseeable.

Claims arising from mishandled disciplinary procedures

An interesting area of stress at work litigation is how the Court approaches the mishandling of disciplinary process. As a starting point,

[224] **Young v Post Office** [2002] EWCA Civ 661

the Court of Appeal in **Gogay v Hertfordshire County Council** [2000] EWCA Civ 228[225], held that an employer's mishandling of a disciplinary procedure could give rise to a common law claim on the basis of negligence as well as breach of the implied term of trust and confidence. As established in **Yapp v Foreign and Commonwealth Office** [2014] EWCA Civ 1512[226] the Court of Appeal at paragraph 119 of the Judgment identify that in claims for breach of the common law duty of care, it was immaterial that the duty arose in contract as well as tort. Both should be treated as being governed by tortious rules. These points were further applied in by the High Court decision of **Marsh v MoJ** [2017] EWHC 1040 (QB)[227]. When considering such claims a practitioner is advised to assess;

a. Contractually how long should such a process take?

b. What has the Claimant done to make the link between the delay and risk of psychiatric harm?

c. What steps did the Defendant fail to take?

d. What difference would those steps have realistically made?

e. When did psychiatric harm manifest?

Claims arising from traumatic roles

Whilst the Court of Appeal in **Hatton**[228] identify that no job was inherently susceptible to stress such that it was reasonably foreseeable that simply doing the job could lead to psychiatric injury, this point appears to be in need of some revision. When we consider for examples of police

---

225 **Gogay v Hertfordshire County Council** [2000] EWCA Civ 228

226 **Yapp v Foreign and Commonwealth Office** [2014] EWCA Civ 1512

227 **Marsh v MoJ** [2017] EWHC 1040 (QB)

228 **Hatton v Sutherland** [2002] EWCA Civ 76

officers who must review graphic imagery, to say that these roles don't carry any risk is not sustainable.

If a certain type of work can be classed as "*inherently stressful*", then typically the risk of injury will be foreseen, and the Defendant under a proactive duty to steps to prevent harm the Claimant. In **Melville v The Home Office** [2005] EWCA Civ 6[229], the Claimant was employed by the Home Office as a prison health care officer. His duties included recovery of the bodies of prisoners who had committed suicide. He did this several times. However, after an occasion on which he had to help cut down a body, remove a ligature and attempt revival, he suffered from nightmares and flashbacks and developed what was subsequently diagnosed as a stress-related illness. The Claimant was signed off sick and retired on the grounds of ill-health some months later.

The County Court determined the question of foreseeability as a preliminary issue and held that, in the circumstances, it had been reasonably foreseeable that Mr Melville might suffer psychiatric damage. The Court of Appeal rejected the Defendant's argument on appeal that the Judge had erred by deciding that psychiatric harm was foreseeable if it could be predicted as a general risk to a group of employees. It noted that the Home Office recognised that people who were called on to deal with certain traumatic incidents in prisons, such as suicides, might sustain injury to their health and that they should receive support from the prison care team following such an incident. This meant that the Home Office had foreseen that employees who were exposed to particular traumatic incidents might suffer psychiatric injury.

Contributory negligence and ex turpi causa

But what of situations where a breach occurs due to a Claimant's own conduct? Well logically a Defendant is very likely to not be found to be in case of a clear and traditional case of contributory negligence, partially

---

[229] **Melville v The Home Office** [2005] EWCA Civ 6

to blame on a percentage basis to be assessed by the Court, in the usual manner. However, in stress cases this is actually rare (as in **Young**[230] for example).

But what of where a Claimant's injury arises from an illegal act? Whilst this may seem an extreme example, it is not as uncommon as one may suppose in practise to encounter employees who may well find themselves suffering injuries arising from just such acts, for example a police officer misusing the power of his office and being disciplined subsequently and suffering a stress related illness as a result.

It is not very often that trials are held in secret in England and Wales, but we have the benefit of the Judgment in **AB v Chief Constable of X** [2015] EWHC 13 (QB)[231] which deals with not only a stress at work claim held in private, but the case is of assistance since it explores the defence of illegality in stress claims.

While a full transcript of the decision of **AB**[232] is not available, we are aware of the following facts. The claim took place between the 8th – 16th December 2013 and was heard by Males J in the High Court. The Claimant was a former undercover police officer and the Defendant is the Chief Constable of the force of which he was a member. The Claimant was deployed to another region (outside the area covered by the collaborative unit) as an undercover officer tasked with the obtaining of intelligence in relation to a serious organised criminal group. It was common ground that during the period of his deployment undercover on this operation the Claimant misused cocaine on more than one occasion. He did not make any report at the time that he had done so. The bedrock of the Claimant's claims was that that the Defendant

230 **Young v Post Office** [2002] EWCA Civ 661

231 **AB v Chief Constable of X** [2015] EWHC 13 (QB

232 **AB v Chief Constable of X** [2015] EWHC 13 (QB

breached its duty of care in failing to provide him with appropriate support during the period undercover.

The Defendant denied breach of duty and further denied that the matters complained of by the Claimant (not being accepted to amount to a breach) had any causative relevance. The Defendant contended that any psychiatric injury which the Claimant had suffered was attributable to his own misconduct in abusing cocaine and the effect of this on him when this was discovered. Further the Defendant argued that the Claimant was barred by public policy from recovering damages, because the effect of success in this claim would be that the Claimant would be recovering damages for the consequences of his own illegal acts and serious misconduct in abusing cocaine.

It was agreed by the parties' psychiatric experts that the Claimant suffered from a chronic adjustment disorder but Males J found that there was no objective evidence of any symptoms of such a disorder before the Claimant was confronted with his misconduct by more senior officers. The Claimant's case was dismissed for a number of reasons.

Firstly, it was the use of cocaine which led to the investigatory meeting, which was found to have caused the psychiatric injury complained of. In this sense, the Court found that there was no pre-existing psychiatric injury or symptoms prior to the notification of such a meeting to the Claimant (paragraphs 16 – 17 of the Judgment).

Secondly, there was a complex and full system in place to protect AB from breaches of duty of care, frustratingly for the purposes of analysis contained in a confidential annex A with Males J commenting that "*the real question is whether these measures were properly implemented. For the reasons given in the Confidential Annexe I conclude that they were*" (paragraph 30 of the Judgment). Males J went on to reject the evidence called on behalf of the Claimant that his psychiatric disorder arose as a result of his undercover work for an extended period, and that it was compounded by lack of appropriate support and supervision. It is appropriate to note that it was accepted that due to the stressful nature of the Claimant's work, psychiatric injury was foreseeable paragraph 29 of the Judgment).

However, and of the most interest, it was added that even if the Claimant could prove that the Defendant was in breach of duty by failing properly to care for his welfare or to supervise and monitor his mental health, it would remain the case that the cause of his psychiatric injury was the fact that he was confronted with his own misconduct and its consequences. Effectively the Claimant's injury was caused by his own criminal act (the taking of cocaine) and in this sense, the doctrine of "*ex turpi causa*" would apply, and the Claimant's case fail.

By way of background on this point, **Gray v Thames Trains Ltd** [2009] UKHL 33[233] sets out how the principal applies. In this matter Mr Gray suffered head injuries in the Ladbroke Grove rail crash, which was caused by the Defendant's negligence, and later, under the effect of the psychiatric disorder stabbed to death a drunken pedestrian. Mr Gray pleaded guilty to manslaughter on the ground of diminished responsibility. He brought a claim to recover his loss of earnings incurred during the period he was detained, general damages for his detention, conviction and damage to reputation and an indemnity against any claim brought against him by the deceased's dependants.

The claim failed. Lord Hoffmann identified two rules of public policy. Firstly that "*the punishment inflicted by a criminal Court is personal to the offender, and that the civil Courts will not entertain an action by the offender to recover an indemnity against the consequences of that punishment*" (paragraph 31). Secondly that "*you cannot recover for damage which is the consequence of your own criminal act*" (paragraphs 51 and 52).

[233] **Gray v Thames Trains Ltd** [2009] UKHL 33

CHAPTER THIRTEEN

STRESS AT WORK CLAIMS AND BULLYING

As a first point, and as colleague continues to inform me, "*there is no such thing as a tort of Bullying*". I agree. It is nothing more than a concept of negligence and the same principal of **Hatton**[234] apply to these claims. Until Parliament legislates on this particular issue the area will need to be approached on a fact-by-fact basis. In this sense, I use the term bullying to reflect its normal meaning within the workplace.

The most common causes of action in claims of bullying will be;

a. A claim in common law negligence;

b. A claim under the Harassment Act 1997;

c. A claim for the tort of intentional harm.

The current test for Bullying in negligence

On the basis of **Daniel v Secretary of State for the Home Department** [2014] EWHC 2578 (QB)[235] a Claimant needs to evidence that their injury has been caused by conduct which is;

a. Genuinely offensive; and

b. Unacceptable;

---

234 **Hatton v Sutherland** [2002] EWCA Civ 76

235 **Daniel v Secretary of State for the Home Department** [2014] EWHC 2578 (QB)

c. Examples of which may be;

   i. Intimidating,

   ii. Malicious; or

   iii. Insulting behaviour;

   iv. Intended to undermine, humiliate or denigrate.

Factually the test is both assessed on a subjective and objective basis. When considering evidence in such claims, it is rare practically that there will be a clear email train which can been said to be bullying. Therefore it is important to obtain witness evidence not only from a Claimant, but witnesses who can support their account of the alleged bullying.

It is also important to remember that a Claimant's case based on bullying doesn't have to be based on an employer failing to stop acts of bullying taking place, but on the basis of an employer's vicarious liability for the action of the employee who is bullying the Claimant. In this context there can be both direct acts of bullying, and indirect acts of bullying.

Common law negligence and Bullying

It was not until the case of **Daniel v Secretary of State for the Home Department** [2014] EWHC 2578 (QB)[236] that tortious bullying was clearly, for my mind defined. The Courts have struggled to define what bullying should be classed as, no doubt due to concerns of floodgate litigation and straying into the province or parliament.

To illustrate the confusion, prior to this point the Courts have held that In **H v Isle of Wight Council** (unreported), 23 February 2001, (High

[236] **Daniel v Secretary of State for the Home Department** [2014] EWHC 2578 (QB)

Court)[237], Wright J held that "*The criterion of what does or does not amount to bullying in any given circumstances is not to be judged solely by the subjective perception of the victim himself ... but involves an objective assessment of the observed behaviour, taken in conjunction with any apparent vulnerability in the target of the behaviour complained of.*"

Around two years later, in **Barlow v Broxbourne** [2003] EWHC 50 (QB)[238], the High Court held that the behaviour complained about needed to amount to bullying or harassment "*in the ordinary connotation of those terms*"

Around three years later in **Green v DB Group Services (UK) Ltd** [2006] EWHC 1898 (QB)[239], the High Court found that Ms Green had been subjected to "*a relentless campaign of mean and spiteful behaviour designed to cause her distress. ... [T]he behaviour amounted to a deliberate and concerted campaign of bullying within the ordinary meaning of that term.*"

Finally, some 4 years later in **Mullen v Accenture Services Ltd** [2010] EWHC 2336 (QB)[240], the High Court found that the circumstances of Green provided an instructive example of what may constitute bullying within the ordinary meaning of the term and was "*a useful yardstick*". This included;

a. Being humiliated him in front of other members of staff;

b. Regularly being shouted and swore at;

c. Placed under immense pressure to solve any problems; and

237 **H v Isle of Wight Council** (unreported), 23 February 2001, (High Court)

238 **Barlow v Broxbourne** [2003] EWHC 50 (QB)

239 **Green v DB Group Services (UK) Ltd** [2006] EWHC 1898 (QB)

240 **Mullen v Accenture Services Ltd** [2010] EWHC 2336 (QB)

d. Never satisfied by anything the Claimant did.

As can be seen, there really was no clear and definitive guidance. To a certain degree this was not harmful as all cases turn on their own facts, but nonetheless it was needed and has been helpful.

The polemic of Daniel

The case of **Daniel**[241] is important practically, and acts as polemic of the issues inherent in the cases based on bullying. The facts of the claim were complex but can be summarised as follows. The Claimant alleged that in the course of her employment with the Defendant she suffered occupational stress that developed into a psychiatric condition causing her in turn to suffer serious and continuing mental illness. It was agreed by the parties that the Claimant had a pre-existing history of bipolar disorder with a very high rate of recurrence and that this condition was unknown to the Defendant. The Claimant's employment required her to lead, manage and develop her employer's research strategies in the field of cancer treatment within the NHS. Professor Gabra, the Claimant's superior (the individual whom the Claimant pinpointed as the catalyst of her breakdown), headed the development of a broad programme of cancer research. The research did not just include approved NHS studies but also commercial studies too. Professor Gabra wanted research resources pooled together in a manner he phrased as "*working without walls*". The Claimant fundamentally disagreed with the concept of this, primarily because she passionately believed that the use of NHS resources on private commercial trials was morally wrong.

Between 2004 and 2006 a series of emails were sent between the Claimant and Professor Gabra. These were contentious and at times "*forceful and blunt*" but were found to have never been oppressive or openly aggressive. Additionally, the Claimant felt that she had not received the resources or staff she required and was being undermined

241 **Daniel v Secretary of State for the Home Department** [2014] EWHC 2578 (QB)

by Professor Gabra, who was diverting resources to other areas. On the 25th September 2006 the Claimant reported Professor Gabra for bullying to the Defendant. This was the first time the Claimant had raised any issues of bullying. It emerged in evidence that she had not raised her concerns for fear of appearing weak. Following her complaint, on the 4th December 2006 Professor Gabra sent an email to the Claimant containing an apology stating "*I have absolutely no personality issues with you whatsoever... On the point of you feeling upset that I belittled you let me say that if you did feel that way it was not my intention and I am unreservedly sorry if that was what came over.*" Matters continued until in January 2007 the Claimant was diagnosed with depression precipitated by stress at work. The Claimant was signed off sick for 2 weeks on the 15th January 2007. Following her return to work she suffered a number of relapses culminating in her admission to a private psychiatric hospital on the 14th April 2007 (she subsequently discharged herself). The Claimant battled on but after returning to work on the 13th June 2007 (where no written risk assessment was undertaken), and following a number of relapses she took ill health retirement in March 2009.

The Claimant's claim (which was advanced on three grounds) was dismissed for a single reason; she had not taken the opportunity to make her employers aware of the stress she was under. The fact that she did not want to seem weak in the "*war*" between her and Professor Gabra, while understandable, was not relevant to this point. Furthermore there were no outward indicators of her stress to have put the Defendant on notice. Daniel is an innovatively pleaded case within the stress at work context in that the bullying of which the Claimant complained was used as the bedrock of her claim rather than more traditional facts, such as a Claimant being overworked.

While the Claimant was unsuccessful, **Daniel**[242] does indicate that if bullying was found to have taken place, resulting in a psychiatric injury

[242] **Daniel v Secretary of State for the Home Department** [2014] EWHC 2578 (QB)

and this was communicated to the employer, then a claim could be brought using bullying as the bedrock of the claim. This in itself is an interesting variation.

The first point which flows from the Judgment is how a Court should approach the issue of defining bullying? While there is no definition of bullying as far as claims for stress at work go, guidance is found firstly in **Waters v Commissioner of Police** [2000] 4 AER 934[243] where Lord Hutton stated, "*It is not every course of victimisation or bullying by fellow employees which would give rise to a cause of action against the employer, and an employee may have to accept some degree of unpleasantness from fellow workers*".

Secondly, in **H v Isle of Wight Council** (QBD 23.2.01)[244] Mr Justice Wright held that "*the criterion for what does or does not amount to bullying in any given circumstances is not to be judged solely by the subjective perception of the victim himself, but involves an objective assessment of the observed behaviour taken in conjunction with any apparent vulnerability in the target of the behaviour complained off*". Distilling the key aspects of these decisions, and with reference to harassment, Sir Robert Nelson at paragraph 146 of the judgement set out that "*for bullying to be established the conduct must be genuinely offensive and unacceptable, examples of which may be intimidating, malicious or insulting behaviour intended to undermine, humiliate or denigrate*".

The issue in the Claimant's case was that all of the perceived bullying she suffered sprang from the notion of "*working without walls*", something she was fundamentally opposed to. Sir Robert Nelson found at paragraph 160 of the Judgement that while some of Professor Gabra's communications were "*forceful and blunt*", they were not bullying. It was on this factual basis that Sir Robert Nelson could not find that the exchanges between the two could be classed as bullying, and perceptively

---

243 **Waters v Commissioner of Police** [2000] 4 AER 934

244 **H v Isle of Wight Council** (QBD 23.2.01)

at paragraph 169 noted "*it may however have been the Claimant's perception that the more she found the tide turning against her, as it undoubtedly was on the issue of pooled resources, the more she found the situation oppressive and perceived Professor Gabra's conduct in the dispute between them as bullying*". In layman's terms, it was all in her head.

The question arises however, what if the Defendant had been aware of the Claimant's perceptions and the effect it was having on her at an early stage? This would arguably have given rise to a duty of care, but also a foreseeable risk of harm – despite the Claimant's perception of bullying being tainted by her fundamental belief as to "*working without walls*".

The decision in **Daniel**[245] may have been very different if the Claimant had raised her concerns earlier and if Professor Gabra had not dealt with the matter as he did by his apology. The point remains though that utilising the stress suffered through an employee's exposure to bullying is a valid vehicle through which to advance a claim. The Claimant's claim that her injury was foreseeable failed on the basis that there were no outward indications of her stress, as set out in paragraphs 181 and 184 of the judgement, "*she did not wish to be seen as weak... and to remain at all times professional in her conduct and approach*". Effectively, her stoic nature whist commendable was to the detriment of her health and also to the success of her claim.

Had she made her concerns known at an early stage and had the behaviour of Professor Gabra continued, the outcome of the claim could have been very different (**Sayers v Cambridgeshire CC** [2007] IRLR 29[246]). Arguments could have been advanced that the conduct complained of had to be viewed within the context of what was known regarding the Claimant's reactions and risk of harm to her as a result. This seems to be hinted at by Sir Robert Nelson at paragraph 195 who

---

245 **Daniel v Secretary of State for the Home Department** [2014] EWHC 2578 (QB)

246 **Sayers v Cambridgeshire CC** [2007] IRLR 29

said that "*whilst she did not exhibit signs of this or make it known to the Defendant in such a manner as to give rise to a duty, it was, I am satisfied having an effect upon her. Secondly, although she was not overworked, the pressures of a hardworking long hour's job together with her perception of bullying combined to create the stress which, in my judgment was a factor in her psychiatric breakdown because of her particular vulnerability*".

It seems that the answer of how to approach the issue of foreseeability in bullying cases, from an evidential basis, is to look for unequivocal complaints regarding stress from Claimants, and in the absence of such, behavioural changes or emotional outbursts which would indicate a stress related condition. This would result in a situation akin to **Intel Corporation v Daw** [2007] IRLR 355[247] and result in the claim being far more likely to be successful.

The protection from Harassment Act 1997

There is an apparent intersect between the law in relation to the Protection from Harassment Act 1997 and bullying which seems to imply that the gap between the two is blurring. The use of the words "*intimidating malicious, insulting*" and that is "*intended to undermine, humiliate or denigrate*" does appear to have synergy with the Protection from Harassment Act 1999.

The test

While covered later, that to establish liability under the Protection from Harassment Act 1997 there must be;

a. Conduct which occurs on at least two occasions;

b. Which is targeted at the Claimant;

[247] **Intel Corporation v Daw** [2007] IRLR 355

c. Which is calculated in an objective sense to cause alarm or distress; and

d. Which is objectively judged to be oppressive and unreasonable.

There is no requirement for a Claimant to establish foresight of injury. Stepping back from this and in the context of bullying, let us consider the legislation. Section 4 of the Protection from Harassment Act 1997 provides that: *(1) A person whose course of conduct causes another to fear, on at least two occasions, that violence will be used against him is guilty of an offence if he knows or ought to know that his course of conduct will cause the other so to fear on each of those occasions.*

Section 7 (2) of the Protection from Harassment Act 1997 provides in addition that *(2) References to harassing a person include alarming the person or causing the person distress.*

The use of the words in **Daniels**[248] as set out above do seem to be directly correlated to the use of the word "*alarm*". If anything, alarm is likely to a component of the reaction to any such conduct as envisaged in **Daniels**[249].

The laws development in cases of bullying

In the case of **Rayment v Ministry of Defence High Court** [2010] EWHC 218 (QB)[250] the Claimant, Ms Rayment was a volunteer member of the Territorial Army from 1987 to 2003. During her time with the TA, she received driver training which qualified her to drive vehicles ranging from cars to HGVs. In 2003 she got a job working at

---

248 **Daniel v Secretary of State for the Home Department** [2014] EWHC 2578 (QB)

249 **Daniel v Secretary of State for the Home Department** [2014] EWHC 2578 (QB)

250 **Rayment v Ministry of Defence High Court** [2010] EWHC 218 (QB)

the Honourable Artillery Company in City Road, London and in early 2004 won promotion and became the driver for the Commanding Officer of the HAC. For various reasons Ms Rayment did not get on well in this job. She fell ill and took time off work. Correctly or otherwise, she came to believe there was a real sense of hostility directed towards her by those who worked at the HAC. She complained to her CO that; *"I have been discriminated and harassed in my working environment with varying degrees of verbal and non-verbal abuse, resulting in feelings of isolation and anxiety"*

She was eventually discharged and then brought an action for damages in the High Court alleging breach of the Protection from Harassment Act 1997 and/or negligence and claimed she had been subjected to bullying, victimisation and harassment in the form of persistent, offensive, abusive, intimidating, bullying, humiliating and insulting behaviour. Davis J found that to establish liability under the Protection from Harassment Act 1997 (as set out above) there must be:

a. Conduct which occurs on at least two occasions;

b. Which is targeted at the Claimant;

c. Which is calculated in an objective sense to cause alarm or distress; and

d. Which is objectively judged to be oppressive and unreasonable.

The Court found that, from a long catalogue of allegations, there were three incidents which satisfied the "*oppressive and unreasonable*" test.

Whilst the Courts ultimately have the last say in defining whether or not they believe that the behaviour complained of crosses the relevant threshold as in **Majrowski v Guy's and St. Thomas' NHS Trust** [2006] UKHL 34[251] by Baroness Hale who held that it must be "*Left to the*

[251] **Majrowski v Guy's and St. Thomas' NHS Trust** [2006] UKHL 34

wisdom of the Courts to draw sensible lines between the ordinary banter and badinage of life and genuinely offensive and unacceptable behaviour." It does seem we are moving to helpful set of definitions which can be applied in their strict meaning.

In case of **Veakins v Kier Islington Ltd** [2009] EWCA Civ 1288[252], the Court of Appeal held that the Claimant had in the context of her employment been harassed by virtue of the act. The nature of the conduct complained of in question was a very generalised set of allegations made by the Claimant, namely that her supervisor did not like her and picked on her. Her claim was unsuccessful in the lower Courts but the Court of Appeal allowed the Claimant's appeal. Giving the Judgment of the Court Maurice Kay LJ noted that the primary test to be drawn from **Majrowski**[253] was whether or not the conduct was "*oppressive and unacceptable*" *although* the Court would need to bear in mind that the conduct must be "*of an order which would sustain criminal liability*".

The context of criminal liability is considered later in this text. However an important point to remember is that whilst this many well hold true for a claim under the Protection from Harassment Act 1997 the standard in the common law appears to be far lower, and therefore easier to satisfy.

To demonstrate the flexibility of the Protection from Harassment Act 1997, we need only consider the case of. **Iqbal v Dean Mason Solicitors** [2011] EWCA Civ 123[254]. The claim concerned a series of three letters sent between solicitors, which were said to amount to a deliberate attack on the Claimant's professional and personal integrity, and constitute harassment under the Protection from Harassment Act 1997 An application to strike out the claim was made and granted. The Claimant then appealed to the Court of Appeal.

[252] **Veakins v Kier Islington Ltd** [2009] EWCA Civ 1288

[253] **Majrowski v Guy's and St. Thomas' NHS Trust** [2006] UKHL 34

[254] **Iqbal v Dean Mason Solicitors** [2011] EWCA Civ 123

In hearing the matter the Court of Appeal concluded that firstly, the three letters, when viewed in light of each other arguably amounted to a deliberate attack on the Claimant's professional and personal integrity. Secondly, that this on the Claimant's case had been done in an attempt to pressurise him, into declining to continue to act for a client.

The Court went on set out at paragraph 42 of the Judgement the following; "*..in my judgment, each of these letters does, when considered side by side, arguably evidence a campaign of harassment against Mr Iqbal. They are arguably capable of causing alarm or distress. They are arguably unreasonable, or oppressive and unreasonable, or oppressive and unacceptable, or genuinely offensive and unacceptable. Arguably, they go beyond annoyances or irritations, and beyond the ordinary banter and badinage of life. Arguably, the conduct alleged is of a gravity which could be characterised as criminal. A professional man's integrity is the lifeblood of his vocation. If it is deliberately and wrongly attacked, whether out of personal self-interest or malice, a potential claim lies under the Act*".

When considering the totality of the conduct complained of, paragraph 45 of the Judgment sets out that the Protection from Harassment Act 1997 is "*concerned with courses of conduct which amount to harassment, rather than with individual instances of harassment. Of course, it is the individual instances which will make up the course of conduct, but it still remains the position that it is the course of conduct which has to have the quality of amounting to harassment, rather than individual instances of conduct. That is so both as a matter of the language of the statute, and as a matter of common sense.... That course of conduct has to amount to harassment, both objectively and in terms of the required mens rea (see section 1(1)(b)). In the case of a single person victim, there have to be "at least two occasions in relation to that person" (section 7(3)(a)), but it is not said that that those two occasions must individually, ie standing each by itself, amount to harassment. The reason why the statute is drafted in this way is not hard to understand. Take the typical case of stalking, or of malicious phone calls. When a defendant, D, walks past a claimant C's door, or calls C's telephone but puts the phone down without speaking, the single act by itself is neutral, or may be. But if that act is repeated on a number of occasions, the course of conduct may well amount to harassment. That conclusion can only be arrived at by looking at the individual acts complained of as a whole. The course of conduct cannot be reduced to or deconstructed into the individual acts, taken solely one by one. So it is with a course of communications such as letters. A first letter, by itself, may appear innocent and may even cause no alarm, or at most a slight unease. However, in the light of subsequent letters, that first letter may be seen as part of a campaign of harassment*".

The Judgement is one that is often overlooked, but is an important one to be aware of in the context of stress at work claims arising from interactions with other professionals.

The tort of intentional harm

Whilst discussed again later in this text, the torts components was revised in case of **Rhodes v OPO** [2015] UKSC 32[255] where the supreme Court held the tort was comprised of three limbs

a. Firstly, that the act complained of had to be done with the aim of intentionally causing physical or psychological harm (or wilfully infringing the right to personal safety). This would require words or conduct directed towards the Claimant for which there was no justification or reasonable excuse;

b. Secondly, there was a required mental element on the part of the tortfeasor, namely that there was an intention to cause physical harm or severe mental or emotional distress;

c. Thirdly, physical or psychiatric harm would have to flow as a consequence of these actions, mere upset or grief would not be enough.

[255] **Rhodes v OPO** [2015] UKSC 32

When we consider claims of bullying, this tort when the difficulty of the common law approach under **Hatton**[256] is considered, appears to be the underutilised tonic to such claims.

Whilst this tort historic and rarely used, it appears perfectly places to address the real issues in claims of bullying, namely motive, action and effect. There is little prejudice to a Claimant articulating their claims in bullying in the alternative in this manner.

Data and Privacy based claims of bullying

Considering cases of bullying are by their very nature personal attacks on a Claimant, they increasingly feature issues involving how a Claimant's private of sensitive information is used. This can give rise to claims under;

a. UK GDPR and the Data Protection Act 2018; and

b. The tort of the misuse of private information.

UK GDPR and the Data Protection Act 2018

UK GDPR and the Data Protection Act serve to regulate how organisations collect, store, and process personal data of individuals. The law applies if the data controller, processor, or subject is based in the UK and encompasses almost all personal data, except for data processed by individuals for purely personal or household activities.

Article 5 of UK GDPR outlines seven key principles governing personal data processing, which if breached, can give rise to a claim. these are to ensure that a data subjects' data is;

a. Processed lawfully, fairly and in a transparent manner in relation to the data subject ('lawfulness, fairness and transparency');

256 **Hatton v Sutherland** [2002] EWCA Civ 76

b. Collected for specified, explicit and legitimate purposes and not further processed in a manner that is incompatible with those purposes ('purpose limitation');

c. That the data stored is adequate, relevant and limited to what is necessary in relation to the purposes for which it is being processed are processed ('data minimisation');

d. Accurate and, where necessary, kept up to date. Every reasonable step must be taken to ensure that personal data that are inaccurate, having regard to the purposes for which they are processed, are erased or rectified without delay ('accuracy');

e. Kept in a form which permits identification of data subjects for no longer than is necessary for the purposes for which the personal data are processed ('storage limitation');

f. Processed in a manner that ensures appropriate security of the personal data, including protection against unauthorised or unlawful processing and against accidental loss, destruction or damage, using appropriate technical or organisational measures ('integrity and confidentiality').

The misuse of private information

Since the Judgment of **Vidal-Hall v Google Inc** [2015] EWCA Civ 311[257] the tort of misuse of private information has been formally recognised. Its development has been influenced by the incorporation of the ECHR by the Human Rights Act 1998 and, in particular, the Convention right to respect for private life, contained in article 8.

Considering the legal framework as established in **Campbell v MGN Ltd** [2004] UKHL 22, where private information is concerned the modern approach adopted and applied by the Courts is to reflect on the privacy

[257] **Vidal-Hall v Google Inc** [2015] EWCA Civ 311

issues raised, and to do so in line with article 8 ECHR and the rights afforded to the Claimant therein. In doing so a two stage test is applied;

a. Stage one – reasonable expectation of privacy:

   i. Assess whether the Claimant objectively has a reasonable expectation of privacy in the relevant information;

   ii. Is there a reasonable expectation of privacy?.

b. Stage two – balancing exercise;

   i. If so, assess whether that expectation is outweighed by the Defendant's right to freedom of expression or other competing rights (as far as any apply);

   ii. This involves a balancing exercise between the Claimant's Article 8 right to privacy and the Defendant's competing rights (if any), most commonly a Defendant publisher's Article 10 right to freedom of expression.

   iii. Is the Defendant's interference with the Claimant's Article 8 rights justified?

The test for what is private information is not information which is trivial. It is important and of such significance that it bring into question an individual's rights under the ECHR. There is also, when one looks at the test, due to the nature of such cases and the serious consequences of misuse, a presumption that the private information in question will have been misused or at the very least, used. In cases of bullying, the use can often be readily identified, and little more needs to be said.

In **Murray v Express Newspapers Plc** [2008] EWCA Civ 446[258] Sir Anthony Clarke MR at paragraphs 35 – 36 of the Judgement identified

[258] **Murray v Express Newspapers Plc** [2008] EWCA Civ 446

that the question of if a Court should determine there existed a reasonable expectation of privacy, was an objective one. The Court needed to consider all the circumstances of the case, including "*the attributes of the Claimant, the nature of the activity in which the Claimant was engaged, the place at which it was happening, the nature and purpose of the intrusion, the absence of consent and whether it was known or could be inferred, the effect on the Claimant and the circumstances in which and the purposes for which the information came into the hands of the publisher.*" The test provides, and requires, a Court to consider.

a. What a reasonable person of ordinary sensibilities would feel if they were placed in the same position as the Claimant and faced with the same publicity'

b. Whether there is a reasonable expectation of privacy is a broad question, which takes account of all the circumstances of the case. These include:

   i. The attributes of Claimant;

   ii. The nature of the activity in which the Claimant was engaged;

   iii. The place at which it was happening;

   iv. The nature and purpose of the intrusion;

   v. The absence of consent and whether it was known or could be inferred; and

   vi. The effect on the Claimant, and the circumstances in which and the purposes for which the information came into the hands of the publisher.

Threats to publish?

The requirement that information is used, not just held onto or stored and essential for any claim by way of either UK GDPR/DPA 2018 or as a misuse of private information. This can create friction as to if a threat to publish can arise in a claim for bullying. It is likely that as far as common law duty stands, such a claim may have prospects of success, but as far as the above 2 causes of action stand, it's likely the claim will face significant hurdles.

As set out in **Warren v DSG Retail Ltd** [2021] EWHC 2168 (QB)[259] Saini J held that:

a. While "*misuse*" of private information could include unintentional use, it still required "*use*," that is, a positive action;

b. There had to be an "*interference*" by the Defendant, which fell to be justified;

c. The Defendant's failure to provide sufficient security for the Claimant's data was not sufficient to amount to misuse;

d. Misuse of private information did not impose a data security duty.

Paragraph 27 of the Judgement concludes "*I accept that a 'misuse' may include unintentional use, but it still requires a 'use': that is, a positive action. In the language of Article 8 ECHR (the basis for the MPI tort), there must be an 'interference' by the Defendant, which falls to be justified. I have not overlooked the Claimant's argument that the conduct of DSG was "tantamount to publication." Although it was attractively presented, I do not find it persuasive. If a burglar enters my home through an open window (carelessly left open by me) and steals my son's bank statements, it makes little sense to describe this as a "misuse of private information" by me.*

[259] **Warren v DSG Retail Ltd** [2021] EWHC 2168 (QB)

Recharacterizing my failure to lock the window as "publication" of the statements is wholly artificial. It is an unconvincing attempt to shoehorn the facts of the data breach into the tort of MPI." Further, as per **Farley v Paymaster (1836) Limited (trading as Equiniti)** [2024] EWHC 383 (KB)[260] where Nicklin J set out that for a claim to be viable claim (be it as a misuse of private information and/or data protection), the Claimant must establish that there was a real prospect of demonstrating that their data processed had been opened and read by a third party. As set at paragraphs 143 – 145; "*In my judgment, to have a viable claim for misuse of private information and/or data protection, each Claimant must show that s/he has a real prospect of demonstrating that the ABS was opened and read by a third party. Without that, the relevant Claimant would have no real prospect of demonstrating that there had been "misuse", an essential element of the tort of misuse of private information…*

I reject the submission that these Claimants can advance a claim on the basis that, until returned, their personal information/data was "in danger" or "at risk". The general law of tort does not generally allow recovery for the apprehension that a tort might have been committed; a person crossing a road cannot recover damages (whether for distress or otherwise) for almost being struck by a passing lorry or for a defamatory letter that was never actually received by its intended recipient. To be entitled to any remedy, a claimant must demonstrate that s/he is the victim of a tortious wrong. A near miss, even if it causes significant distress, is not sufficient. Without the contents of the ABS coming to the attention of a third party there is no viable claim for misuse of private information. In simple terms, there has been no interference with the Article 8 rights of the relevant Claimant because the privacy of the information contained in the ABS has not been compromised at any stage".

---

260 **Farley v Paymaster (1836) Limited (trading as Equiniti)** [2024] EWHC 383 (KB)

CHAPTER FOURTEEN

BREACH OF CONTRACT IN STRESS AT WORK CLAIMS

There is an implied term between an employer and employee that they must not, without reasonable cause, act in a manner that is calculated and likely to destroy or seriously damage the relationship of trust and confidence between them. Any breach of this term will be repudiatory, entitling the affected party to treat the contract as terminated. In an employment context, the employee becomes entitled to claim for constructive dismissal.

Considering the manner in which stress at work claims arise, it is foreseeable that Claimants may well be assisted by an argument made on this basis. Lord Steyn stated in **Malik v Bank of Credit and Commerce International SA (In Liquidation)** [1997] I.R.L.R. 462 HL[261] "*The major importance of the implied duty of trust and confidence lies in its impact on the obligations of the employer… and the implied obligation as formulated is apt to cover the great diversity of situations in which a balance has to be struck between an employer's interest in managing his business as he sees fit and the employee's interest in not being unfairly and improperly exploited…*

… In assessing whether there has been a breach, it seems clear that what is significant is the impact of the employer's behaviour on the employee rather than what the employer intended. Moreover, the impact will be assessed objectively…

[261] **Malik v Bank of Credit and Commerce International SA (In Liquidation)** [1997] I.R.L.R. 462 HL

… The employer will not, without reasonable and proper cause, conduct itself in a manner calculated or likely to destroy or seriously damage the relationship of confidence and trust between employer and employee."

Drawing the line?

In light of these principles, at first blush there may well appear to be a wide range of facts into which such claims arising from a stress at work situation can be brought. The difficulty has become where to draw the line between which remedy should be sought and the venue in which it must be pursued, be that in the Employment Tribunal or the Courts.

In **Johnson v Unisys Ltd** [2001] UKHL 13[262] the House of Lords held that an employee could not use the implied term of trust and confidence to claim damages for psychological injury if the damage was caused by the manner in which he was dismissed.

The House of Lords did contrast that situation with one where the damage was caused by a breach of the implied term during the continuance of the relationship, in which event damages for such injury could be recovered.

The House of Lords made clear that an employee is not entitled to attempt to circumvent the statutory unfair dismissal regime and bring a claim at common law for damages where it is alleged that his dismissal breached the implied term of trust and confidence. Such a claim falls within what has become known as the "*Johnson*" exclusion area, namely the realm which should be adjudicated in the Employment Tribunals and not the ordinary Courts.

In **Eastwood v Magnox Electric plc** [2004] UKHL 35[263] the House of Lords sought to clarify where the boundaries of the "*Johnson exclusion zone*" are to be drawn. In the first case, two employees (E and W) were

[262] **Johnson v Unisys Ltd** [2001] UKHL 13

[263] **Eastwood v Magnox Electric plc** [2004] UKHL 35

dismissed by their employer in what they claimed was bad faith. Both pursued claims for unfair dismissal in the Employment Tribunal. The claims were settled. Both then commenced proceedings in the County Court alleging negligence and breach of the implied term of mutual trust and confidence in their employment contracts and claiming damages for personal injuries in the form of psychiatric injuries caused by deliberate misconduct in the disciplinary processes used against them.

These claims were dismissed by the Judge who, applying **Johnson**, held that the common law implied term of trust and confidence could not be used in the area of unfair dismissal that included the operation of disciplinary machinery. This decision was upheld by the Court of Appeal.

In the second case, the employment tribunal found that the employee (M) had been unfairly dismissed after suspension and disciplinary proceedings. M brought proceedings in the High Court alleging that he had sustained psychiatric illness by reason of his employer's failure to investigate the allegations against him and to conduct the disciplinary proceedings properly. The Judge struck out the claim, relying on **Johnson**[264] as extended in the case of **Eastwood v Magnox**[265]. The Court of Appeal allowed M's appeal on the basis that there should be a trial to determine where, on the facts, the line should be drawn between the dismissal and the conduct prior to that which caused injury compensable in damages at common law.

The House of Lords nonetheless disagreed with the Court of Appeal, holding that these events were separable and distinct from the claim relating to the dismissal itself.

It was held that **Johnson**[266] showed that breach of the implied term of trust and confidence could not be relied on as a foundation for a claim at

---

264 **Johnson v Unisys Ltd** [2001] UKHL 13

265 **Eastwood v Magnox Electric plc** [2004] UKHL 35

266 **Johnson v Unisys Ltd** [2001] UKHL 13

common law arising from unfair dismissal because Parliament had established a statutory code for unfair dismissal. The statutory code provided remedies for infringement of the statutory right not to be dismissed unfairly. An employee's remedy for unfair dismissal, whether actual or constructive, was therefore, the remedy provided by statute.

If before a dismissal (whether actual or constructive) an employee had acquired a cause of action at law, for breach of contract or otherwise, that cause of action remained unimpaired by his subsequent unfair dismissal and the statutory rights which arose in such a situation. In law such a cause of action existed independently of the dismissal.

In the ordinary course (suspension apart) an employer's failure to act fairly in the steps leading to dismissal did not of itself cause the employee financial loss. The loss arose when the employee was dismissed and it arose by reason of his dismissal. Accordingly any resultant claim for loss fell squarely within the **Johnson**[267] exclusion area.

However, on the facts of the case before the House of Lords, that was not the case and financial loss flowed directly from the employer's failure to act fairly when taking steps leading to dismissal. Financial loss flowing from suspension was an instance. Another instance was cases such as these where an employee suffered financial loss from psychiatric or other illness caused by his unfair treatment pre any dismissal. In such cases, the employee had a common law cause of action that preceded, and was independent of, his subsequent dismissal.

In respect of his subsequent dismissal, a Claimant in such circumstances might of course present a claim to an employment tribunal. If he brought proceedings both in Court and before a tribunal, he could not recover any overlapping heads of loss twice over. It followed that the employer's appeal in M's case should be dismissed and the appeals of E and W allowed. In the case of all three, the assumed facts constituted causes of

[267] **Johnson v Unisys Ltd** [2001] UKHL 13

action that accrued before the dismissals and they disclosed reasonable causes of action that should proceed to trial.

The implications of this decision in the stress at work context are potentially far-reaching. It appears that when considering the **Johnson** exclusion zone, the line which must be drawn will be done so firmly in the employee's favour so that any event that can be separated from the dismissal may give rise to a cause of action.

Potentially, Respondents should be aware that the incorrect implementation of a contractual disciplinary procedure could give rise to such a claim. Suspension could also do so if there were no proper grounds for such suspension. However, considering the reality of these situations, in the main no actual financial loss will flow from such actions and any potential claim will most likely be made where the primary loss consists of psychiatric injury

More recently in, **GAB Robins (UK) Ltd v Triggs** [2008] EWCA Civ 17[268], the Court of Appeal considered the issue of whether loss of earnings was recoverable in a constructive dismissal case based on a breach of trust and confidence, where the employer caused stress and depression to the employee which preceded the date of dismissal leading to a loss of earnings claim.

It was contended by the employer, on the basis of **Eastwood v Magnox**[269] that the Claimant's loss of earnings was not in consequence of her dismissal but because of pre-dismissal incapacity. The Court of Appeal first held that it was correct that the employee had been constructively dismissed because the acts relied upon by the employee (overwork and bullying) amounted cumulatively to a breach of the implied term of trust and confidence as at the time she went on sick leave.

268 **GAB Robins (UK) Ltd v Triggs** [2008] EWCA Civ 17

269 **Eastwood v Magnox Electric plc** [2004] UKHL 35

Secondly, the Court of Appeal overturned the EAT's decision on remedy. The Court of Appeal held that loss sustained by a Claimant in consequence of a constructive unfair dismissal within section 123 Employment Rights Act 1996 did not include loss flowing from wrongs already inflicted upon her by her employer's prior conduct. Those losses, including any future lost income, were not caused by the dismissal. Damage caused by that conduct was not damage suffered in consequence of the dismissal.

However, the Claimant had an accrued right for a common law claim for the losses caused by the antecedent breaches of the implied term as to trust and confidence.

Foresight and Remoteness

The law when dealing with claims for psychiatric injury arising from a single act, despite the recent Court of Appeal Judgment in **Yapp v Foreign and Commonwealth Office** [2014] EWCA Civ 1512[270] remains fluid and turbulent, and one in which liability can crystallise. Historically (and in most regards quite understandably) the Courts have taken a somewhat cautious approach to this area of law for a number of reasons but primarily in fear of creating floodgate litigation.

However, as our understanding of psychiatric injury continues to grow, alongside a fluctuating employment market and a marked dilution of the rights of employees to bring claims, the opportunity for the abuse of power by an employer has become a genuine cause for concern, specifically in the service industries of the UK's major cities.

In order to properly understand **Yapp**[271] and its significance, we have to go back to the base principals. An employer's potential liability for psychiatric injury occasioned by a single event during an employee's

270 **Yapp v Foreign and Commonwealth Office** [2014] EWCA Civ 1512

271 **Yapp v Foreign and Commonwealth Office** [2014] EWCA Civ 1512

employment was dealt with by the House of Lords in the case of **Johnson v Unisys Ltd** [2001] UKHL 13[272]. Here it was held that employees were not entitled to attempt to rely on statutory provisions pertaining to unfair dismissal in order to circumvent the statutory unfair dismissal regime, by bringing claims in common law alleging that that their dismissals breached the implied term of trust and confidence. These claims fell within what become known as the **Johnson** exclusion area, namely, they should be adjudicated on in the Employment Tribunals. Lord Hoffmann justified this on the basis that it would be contrary to parliamentary intention to develop a general common law right, whose substance would shadow the right not to be unfairly dismissed, but dispensing with the limitations that Parliament had imposed on the statutory right.

However, the House of Lords in **Eastwood v Magnox Electric plc** [2004] UKHL 35[273] held a that a distinction should be drawn between events leading up to the dismissal in respect of which a common law breach of contract claim may still be brought, and the dismissal itself for which the only remedy is an unfair dismissal claim. This principal was further refined by the Court of Appeal in the case of **Monks v Cann Hall Primary School** [2013] EWCA Civ 826[274] where a Claimant was allowed to bring a claim for damages for psychiatric injury resulting from the manner in which she was dismissed, having been publicly escorted from her workplace. The process of dismissal and the dismissal itself were held to be distinct, and if an employee could show that the facts relied upon occurred prior to any dismissal, a claim for psychiatric injury could be advanced.

272 **Johnson v Unisys Ltd** [2001] UKHL 13

273 **Eastwood v Magnox Electric plc** [2004] UKHL 35

274 **Monks v Cann Hall Primary School** [2013] EWCA Civ 826

The Court of Appeal in the case of **Yapp**[275] have again reassessed this area of law showing a clear acceptance that such claims are not only possible, but can succeed in the correct circumstances.

The facts of **Yapp**[276] were that in January 2007 Mr Yapp was appointed to the post of High Commissioner in Belize by the Foreign and Commonwealth Office (FCO). Ten months after commencing this post, the FCO received allegations in confidence that Mr Yapp had sexually harassed women at social events and had behaved in a manner likely to damage the reputation of the United Kingdom. It was also alleged that he had bullied and harassed staff members. In dealing with these allegations, the FCO withdrew Mr Yapp from his role on the basis of the first allegation (which was later found to be unsubstantiated) and he received a written warning in respect of the second allegation. Mr Yapp became depressed and remained unable to work for several years until his retirement in 2011. A claim was brought and Cranston J sitting in the High Court held that the decision to withdraw Mr Yapp amounted to a breach of contract, and a breach of the FCO's duty of care to Mr Yapp. It was also held that these breaches caused Mr Yapp to develop a depressive illness.

The FCO appealed and argued firstly that Cranston J had applied the wrong test to the question of whether Mr Yapp's withdrawal was fair, and secondly that even if Mr Yapp's illness was caused by the breach of contract or breach of duty of care, it was too remote to attract damages. The issue of whether not the FCO's conduct amounted to a specific breach of the common law duty of care owed to Mr Yapp was not explored, the respondent focusing on the issue of whether the decision was unfair and the issue of the remoteness.

The Court of Appeal decided that while the FCO enjoyed a broad discretion whether or not to immediately withdraw a post-holder for

---

[275] **Yapp v Foreign and Commonwealth Office** [2014] EWCA Civ 1512

[276] **Yapp v Foreign and Commonwealth Office** [2014] EWCA Civ 1512

operational reasons (precluding any effective and fair investigation) this was not inconsistent with the exercise of such discretion being unfair. It had been unnecessary for the FCO to act pre-emptively, without making any further inquiries or even putting the allegations to Mr Yapp. Cranston J had been entitled to find that if the FCO was going to take such a drastic step, it should have found a way of dealing with the issue of confidentiality (paragraphs 60-67 of the Judgement).

However, with regard to foreseeability and remoteness, Mr Yapp's psychiatric injuries were deemed to be too remote, and the appeal succeeded on this point. This point, it must be stressed, was decided by a Judge who on the facts, only took a different view than the Judge who heard the claim in the Court below. This was not a recasting or reinforcing of the principals of **Johnson** but an application on the facts of the claim before the Court of Appeal.

The current test in cases of breach of contract

The Judgment in **Yapp**[277] provides a useful summary of the law on remoteness and sets out the test to be applied in such cases (paragraph 119 of the Judgement), which can be summarised as follows.

Firstly, where considering the common law duty of care, and in particular whether it was reasonably foreseeable that an employer's acts or omissions would cause an employee psychiatric injury, such an injury would not usually be foreseeable unless there were indications of some problem or psychological vulnerability on the part of the employee (as in **Barber v Somerset County Council** [2004] UKHL 13[278]).

Secondly, where a Court is dealing with claims for breach of the common law duty of care, these claims were governed by the law of tort,

[277] **Yapp v Foreign and Commonwealth Office** [2014] EWCA Civ 1512

[278] **Barber v Somerset County Council** [2004] UKHL 13

(**Walker v Northumberland CC** [1995] 1 All E.R. 737[279]), and it was necessary to establish that psychiatric injury was reasonably foreseeable. If a Claimant could satisfy this point then the issue of remoteness could not arise.

Thirdly, these principals applied to cases of a one-off breach or act, in Mr Yapp's case as established in **Deadman v Bristol City Council** [2007] EWCA Civ 822[280]).

Fourthly, the Court of Appeal stressed that there was no hard and fast rule with all cases turning on their own facts.

Fifthly, when dealing with a claim based on breach of the implied duty of mutual trust and confidence, or of any express contractual term, the action was rooted in contract, and accordingly the contractual test of remoteness would be applicable.

The Court of Appeal accepted that an employer's conduct might be so devastating that it was foreseeable that a person of ordinary robustness might develop a depressive illness, but that it would be exceptional for an apparently robust employee, with no history of psychiatric fragility, to develop a depressive illness as a result of even a very serious setback at work. It was on this basis, and with some sympathy for Mr Yapp, that Underhill LJ found on the facts of the case there was no evidence of sufficient weight to render it foreseeable that the withdrawal of Mr Yapp from his post would have caused him to suffer a psychiatric injury. Factually, the FCO's actions had not been tantamount to dismissal, and Mr Yapp was told that if exonerated by the investigation, the FCO would try to find him another posting. The FCO was in essence attempting to follow due process, despite the unfairness of what had occurred. Therefore the psychiatric injury suffered by Mr Yapp was not

---

279 **Walker v Northumberland CC** [1995] 1 All E.R. 737

280 **Deadman v Bristol City Council** [2007] EWCA Civ 822

reasonably foreseeable and could not give rise to a claim for a breach of the common law duty of care.

Usefully for Claimants, the Court of Appeal has provided in the Judgement that claims for psychiatric injury as a result of a single breach of duty of care can succeed. Of note Underhill LJ, at paragraphs 122 – 123 of the Judgement reiterated that "*I have not found this issue easy, but in the end I have come to the conclusion that the Judge was wrong to find that it was reasonably foreseeable that the FCO's conduct in withdrawing the Claimant from his post without having had the opportunity to state his case might lead him to develop psychiatric illness.... it will in my view be exceptional that an apparently robust employee, with no history of any psychiatric ill-health, will develop a depressive illness as a result even of a very serious setback at work... But his decision was not one of primary fact, or indeed one of fact at all. Rather, it was a judgment... This Court is as well placed to make that judgment as he was; and, having reached a different conclusion I am, I think, obliged to give effect to it.*"

Underhill LJ stated that such cases are purely fact-dependent and must be approached in a bespoke format, with the decision reached by the Judge hearing the case relating to remoteness remaining the deciding factor. The inference to take from the Judgment is that assuming a Claimant can satisfy the issue of remoteness or even better foreseeability, then a Court is likely to be favourable to such claims. Practically this could involve supplying medical evidence asking for a period of leave before any action is taken, and expressly stating that any disciplinary process needs to be halted due to health reasons. In the bulk of such cases, a period of paid leave could be granted in which an employer could consider any allegations, and deal with them fairly. The refusal to do so then would be likely to reflect either unreasonable behaviour, or an intention to run the risk of injury that has been brought to its attention.

Whilst Mr Yapp was not successful with regards to his claim for psychiatric injury, it needs to be remembered that his claim for unfair dismissal succeeded. **Yapp**[281] sets out that claims of this nature can and will succeed where "*the employer was, or should have been, already aware of some relevant susceptibility or vulnerability on the part of the employee*" (paragraph 156 of the Judgement). This is actually quite an easy a step for a Claimant to begin to surmount when the requirements are considered. At trial, a potential issue may be whether or not (due to the speed with which such disciplinary proceedings moved) a Claimant may practically have lacked the time to clearly voice their concerns, or suggest alternatives. On this basis, early intervention which clearly communicates the risks faced by Claimants prior to such a dismissal, and seeks to delay proceedings on a fair and balanced basis would be likely to be viewed as strong evidence that the employer not only knew of the risk, but went a step further and ignored a reasonable suggestion which would have preserved both party's positions.

As the cases of **Monks**[282] and **Yapp**[283] both show, employers no matter their size will on occasion decide on a course of conduct which is not entirely reconcilable with the issue of fairness and their duty of care to an employee on the basis that it is necessary for the greater good of their interests. In this sense, their conduct is unlikely to change no matter what a Claimant says, but where a Claimant draws concerns about their health to their employee's attention, a claim for psychiatric injury would be likely to succeed. As Underhill LJ took pains to stress, all such claims turn on their own facts, and in this sense, there is a certain sense of justice to a well-informed Claimant seeking to use the bullish intentions of their employer against them, to generate a scenario where their claim must succeed.

---

281 **Yapp v Foreign and Commonwealth Office** [2014] EWCA Civ 1512

282 **Monks v Cann Hall Primary School** [2013] EWCA Civ 826

283 **Yapp v Foreign and Commonwealth Office** [2014] EWCA Civ 1512

Disciplinary processes

The term of mutual trust and confidence extends to any disciplinary process but how does a Court deal with a case where this contractual term, and its application, becomes the source of injury? In response to this, the fist of wat may well be a new line of authority is **Marsh v MoJ** [2017] EWHC 1040 (QB)[284].

In this matter, the Claimant was employed as a prison officer as a prison officer in a Female Prison. Due to a number of allegations Surrey Police began investigating the prison in 2009, following allegations of what were a serious and deep reaching level of complaints of corruption and sexual misconduct with female inmates. The Claimant was implicated in various allegations of sexual misconduct made by a serving prisoner from sexual assault to rape. Due to these allegations, the police in February 2010 executed a search warrant on the Claimant's home in February 2010, and the Defendant simultaneously suspended him from work.

However, in September 2010, the police indicated that he would not be charged. The Defendant instigated a disciplinary investigation into his conduct but suspended it in November 2010 because of ongoing criminal proceedings against other officers involved in these allegations on a larger scale. Chronologically, the Claimant remained suspended on full pay and the disciplinary investigation resumed in October 2011 and in June 2012, the Defendant dismissed the disciplinary complaint and invited the Claimant to return to work.

Sadly and perhaps understandably reflecting on what he had been through the Claimant began to suffer from depression and in May 2013 he was dismissed on ill health grounds. The Claimant's case was in part based on the argument that the Defendant, in breach of contract had failed to investigate the first complaint when it was made and had failed to remove the complainant from the prison. The Claimant also went on

[284] **Marsh v MoJ** [2017] EWHC 1040 (QB)

to argue that the Defendant had failed to complete the disciplinary process within a reasonable time, which prolonged his psychiatric injury.

The Claimant was successful. Of note, and whilst highly fact specific, Thirlwall LJ held that; "*the decision to postpone the investigation in November 2010 was a clear breach of the Defendant's duty of care to the Claimant and a breach of the Malik term of the contract. It led to the continued suspension (on the basis that nothing had changed) and to foreseeable injury*".

The case of **Marsh**[285]. warrants reading for the facts it turns up, but focusing on the immediately applicable, two practical points can be arrived at. Firstly, where a Defendant carries out a disciplinary process which runs for longer than is responsible, and secondly, they are aware, or should be aware that is exposes a Claimant to a risk of psychiatric injury, then liability could, and can crystalise.

285 **Marsh v MoJ** [2017] EWHC 1040 (QB)

CHAPTER FIFTEEN

CAUSATION AND APPORTIONMENT IN STRESS CLAIMS

Guidelines 14 – 16 of **Hatton v Sutherland** [2002] EWCA Civ 76[286] address the issues of causation and apportionment.

Guidelines 14 – 16

Guideline 14

"*The Claimant must show that that breach of duty has caused or materially contributed to the harm suffered. It is not enough to show that occupational stress has caused the harm*".

As already dealt with earlier in this text, it is important for focus to places on the actual brerach and its consequences, as opposed to other factors robust medical evidence, and detailed and comprehensive witness evidence is likely to assist.

Guideline 15

"*Where the harm suffered has more than one cause, the employer should only pay for that proportion of the harm suffered which is attributable to his wrongdoing, unless the harm is truly indivisible. It is for the Defendant to raise the question of apportionment*".

[286] **Hatton v Sutherland** [2002] EWCA Civ 76

Guideline 16

"*The assessment of damages will take account of any pre-existing disorder or vulnerability and of the chance that the Claimant would have succumbed to a stress related disorder in any event*".

Guidelines 15 and 16 need to be really considered together. Whilst they helpful set the parameters of what a Court needs to go when assessing damages, how the principals apply to the evidence in case can be difficult, contested and detail focused.

Causation

For a claim to succeed, the Claimant must establish a causal link between the breach of duty, ort duties complained of, and the injury alleged. The points already made in the previous chapters as to causation continue to apply.

In **Dickins v O2 plc** [2009] IRLR 58[287], the Court of Appeal considered an employer's response to an employee's inability to cope with the ordinary demands of roles she had been promoted into and the failure to provide training. In this case, the Court of Appeal concluded the psychiatric injury suffered by the Claimant had been both reasonably foreseeable and caused by her employer with "*the judge's task was to identify the breach of duty and to decide whether that breach had made a material contribution to the respondent's ill-health.*"

While the Judge in the County Court claim had not correctly identified that test, and there were other factors to consider (for example her vulnerable personality, her relationship with her partner and her IBS), it was plain from the Judge's findings of fact that and the psychiatric evidence that the Defendant's breach of duty had made a material contribution to her ill health.

287 **Dickins v O2 plc** [2009] IRLR 58

In contrast, in **MacLennan v Hartford Europe Ltd** [2012] EWHC 346 (QB)[288], in which an employee alleged that she had contracted chronic fatigue syndrome as a result of workplace stress, the Court held that the medical evidence failed to establish a causal link between the two, and the claim failed as a result.

These two cases established the need for a Claimant to establish that any psychiatric injury complained of was caused by the alleged breaches of any Defendant. Practically, this can create complex issues in such cases since it is possible that whilst a Claimant may well have suffered a psychiatric injury as a result of working practices, the injury inflicted may well be seen to have not been foreseeable.

It is entirely possible that this can be the only injury suffered by a Claimant and as a result, whilst a Claimant may have returned to work, with further time off work and losses flowing, that there is no "*fresh*" site of injury on which later acts of negligence can be annexed.

The interplay of the law and facts

The Judgment in **Bailey v Devon Partnership NHS Trust** [2014] 7 WLUK 450[289] raised a number of points regarding causation in these circumstances, as well as indicating an implied change in how a Court will approach the issue of breach of duty of care, but is also a strong reminder as to the difficulties caused by medical causation in stress claims.

In **Bailey**[290], Ms Bailey brought a claim for personal injury and consequential loss allegedly caused by occupational stress arising from her role as a Child and Adolescent Consultant Psychiatrist, a position which she had held since 2002. Ms Bailey's claim concerned two distinct

288 **MacLennan v Hartford Europe Ltd** [2012] EWHC 346 (QB),

289 **Bailey v Devon Partnership NHS Trust** [2014] 7 WLUK 450

290 **Bailey v Devon Partnership NHS Trust** [2014] 7 WLUK 450

periods of time. Firstly a 6-month period leading up to July 2008 where she suffered a breakdown and was admitted to hospital with heart problems. Of note, historically, she had suffered in the past from a severe depressive disorder. Ms Bailey argued that this had been caused by a significant increase in the demands of her job due to organisational change, a lack of support from her management, a lack of administrative support and extra responsibilities being placed on her.

The second period of time was concerned with when Ms Bailey returned to work in July 2009 following absence due to stress. While a phased return to work plan was agreed by the parties and included her working reduced hours and relinquishing some duties, Ms Bailey failed to cope and went on long-term sick leave in February 2010, retiring on the grounds of ill health in 2011. Judgment was given in favour of the Defendant on the basis that Ms Bailey could not establish causation with regards to her injuries for the following two reasons.

Firstly, HHJ Cotter Q.C. found that in line with **Barber**[291] the threshold at which Ms Bailey's employer should have foreseen indications of impending harm to her health were those that were plain enough for any reasonable employer to realise they should act to do something about it. HHJ Cotter Q.C. held that the Defendant was in breach of its duty to undertake a risk assessment and then implement its own policy for the assessment of stress but, that even if Ms Bailey had undergone such an assessment, the acute event of July 2008 would and could not have been foreseen and avoided. On this point it was noted in evidence that Ms Bailey had been hesitant about giving a full and accurate account regarding her health to her employer, including the fact that she was taking anti-depressant medication and had seen a psychotherapist. At paragraph 292 HHJ Cotter Q.C. held that "*as for causation of the first breakdown it was, as the experts have identified multi–factorial and in my*

[291] **Barber v Somerset County Council** [2004] UKHL 13

judgment even if the assessment had led to some immediate reduction in or alteration to her workload it would not have prevented the first breakdown".

Secondly, while there was a finding that the Defendant was in breach of its duty of care to Ms Bailey following her return to work in February 2009, it was held that whilst her first breakdown;

a. Caused significant and long-lasting damage to her health; and

b. That she was not fit to return to work when she did and that she failed to cope with the requirements of her job upon her return, and that reasonable further steps or adaptations to her work would not have prevented the outcome

While Claimants may feel dispirited for Ms Bailey who presented sound arguments as to breach of duty of care only to fail squarely on the issue of causation, there are positives which can be taken away from this case. Firstly, this case turned on its own unique set of facts. Ms Bailey worked in high-pressure job, had a detailed understanding of psychology but also appeared to actively be concealing her problems related to stress from her colleagues and superiors. In addition whilst the outward warning signs of stress were apparent, they were multifaceted. No hard and fast rule can be taken from the case to infer that similar cases must fail.

Secondly, the Judgment accepted, and certainly went as far to note that the Judiciary following over a decade of occupation stress cases appearing before the Courts may be beginning to alter their attitudes with regards to the issue of breach of duty of care. It was acknowledged by HHJ Cotter Q.C. in paragraph 280 of his Judgment that "*whilst the authorities have tended to focus on a threshold in relation to need for the employer to be put on notice of the risk of stress related illness to an individual employee, given the developments in the state of knowledge and information post early 2002, a duty to risk assess in relation to stress in a workplace can now arise at a much lower threshold than that set out by Hale LJ*".

HHJ Cotter Q.C. continued that "*such a risk assessment may well then (and this is a question of fact) put an employer on clear notice of the need to take adequate steps to prevent an employee or employees from injury. Such steps may include a more detailed personal assessment… which may then provide indications of impending harm to health arising from stress at work which are plain enough for any reasonable employer to realise that he should do something about it*".

Depending on how the Judgment is read, it seems that the previously high hurdles of breach of duty of care, and even foreseeability are in fact being lowered. There is noticeable judicial acceptance that occupational stress is a serious and crippling disease, and secondly that our more detailed and comprehensive understanding of occupational stress justifies that further, and in certain cases more thorough steps are taken by employers to combat the issue of occupational stress.

The irony of Ms Bailey's case is that it appears that had she **raised the issue of occupational stress to her employer at an early stage, it is likely on the findings of <u>HHJ Cotter Q.C</u> that she would have satisfied the issue of causation and foreseeability. Whilst the Defendant may have escaped liability on the grounds of causation, there is a strong** argument that this was due to the fact that Ms Bailey was conservative and nervous regarding disclosing the issues she had been experiencing to her employer.

Apportionment

One issue that troubles and continues to frustrate stress at work claims is how a Court approaches damages in cases where only certain breaches are established or smaller aspects of psychiatric damage established.

It is not unknown for a Defendant to accept an individual and often apparently inconsequential breach in the knowledge that they will be capable of arguing that the injures which flow from that incident, are not causative of the Claimant's injuries as a whole, or in manifest part.

Whilst the **Hatton**[292] guidelines had previously indicated that a Defendant should only be responsible for the component of injury attributable to stress, the case of **Dickins v O2 PLC** [2008] EWCA CIV 1144[293] appears to have in some way, reversed this point in favour of Claimants. Paragraphs 42 – 48 of the judgment provided that "*... Was this not a case of an indivisible injury (the respondent's seriously damaged state following her breakdown) with more than one cause? It was not possible to say that, but for the tort, the respondent would probably not have suffered the breakdown but it was possible to say that the tort had made a material contribution to it. If that is a correct analysis, should not the starting point have been that the respondent was entitled to recover in full?*

In Hatton, Hale LJ said that a Claimant could establish causation by showing that the tort had made a material contribution to the injury. She was presupposing that there were other non-tortious factors in play and that it would not be possible for the Claimant to succeed outright on causation by showing that, but for the tort, he would probably not have suffered the injury. That means that a Claimant can succeed on causation even though he cannot demonstrate what the causative potency of the tort was, save to say that it had some effect which went beyond the minimal. It seems to me that, if in one breath the judge holds that all that can be said about the effect of the tort is that it made an unspecified material contribution, it is illogical for him, in the next breath, to attempt to assess the percentage effect of the tort as a basis for apportionment of the whole of the damages. That is not to say that it is not important to have in mind in assessing damages the condition of the Claimant before any tortious act occurred. In particular it might be appropriate, where the judge holds that non-tortious factors have been in play, to discount particular heads of damage, for example, to reflect the risk that the Claimant might in any event have suffered a breakdown at some time in the future and would then have suffered some loss of earnings or incurred some expense.

---

292 **Hatton v Sutherland** [2002] EWCA Civ 76

293 **Dickins v O2 plc** [2008] EWCA Civ 1144

In my experience, apportionment of the whole of the damages is usually carried out only in cases where the injury is divisible. In such cases the seriousness of the medical condition in question is often related to the degree of exposure to the agent causing it; in other words the condition is 'dose-related'. The true nature of such cases is that the tort has caused only part of the overall injury. The only practicable way of assessing the right sum for the relevant part may be to assess the damages for the whole injury and to apportion them on the basis of an assessment of the tortious and non-tortious exposures. This is possible in cases such as dust exposure, noise-induced deafness and hand/arm vibration syndrome. In other cases, the true nature of the case may be that the tort has aggravated an existing condition or injury and it may be that the only practicable way of assessing the effect of the aggravation is by an across the board apportionment of the total loss. I am doubtful of the applicability of this type of approach to a case of psychiatric injury where there are multiple causes of the breakdown.

In Hatton, Hale LJ said that, where multiple causes were at work in a case of psychiatric injury, a sensible attempt at apportionment should be made….

I respectfully wish (obiter) to express my doubts as to the correctness of Hale LJ's approach to apportionment. My provisional view (given without the benefit of argument) is that, in a case which has had to be decided on the basis that the tort has made a material contribution but it is not scientifically possible to say how much that contribution is (apart from the assessment that it was more than de minimis) and where the injury to which that has lead is indivisible, it will be inappropriate simply to apportion the damages across the board. It may well be appropriate to bear in mind that the Claimant was psychiatrically vulnerable and might have suffered a breakdown at some time in the future even without the tort. There may then be a reduction in some heads of damage for future risks of non-tortious loss. But my provisional view is that there should not be any rule that the judge should apportion the damages across the board merely because one non-tortious cause has been in play".

The importance of this point in stress cases cannot be underestimated. It is more common than not for those who suffer from a stress related illness to have other psychiatric causative components to their illness. **Dickins**[294], stresses that the result is what matters, not necessarily the individual components that comprise it.

Apportionment

Once causation of injury is established, and unless a Court is able to find that the injury is indivisible, then the Court must seek to apportion the injury to the proven breaches. The question of apportionment in stress cases was revisited in **Brown v Richmond upon Thames LBC** [2012] EWCA Civ 1384[295]. In this matter, the appellant employee (Mr Brown) appealed against a decision in his claim for damages resulting from the negligence of his employer.

Mr Brown had been employed by Richmond upon Thames LBC for 38 years until his retirement on the grounds of ill health. There had been a lack of investment in Mr Brown's department and staff were lost and not replaced which had led to two prior incidents of work related stress. At an appraisal Mr Brown had revealed that he had been to his doctor with headaches and heart palpitations whereupon his employer had promised a referral to the occupational health unit but omitted to make one. The following year Mr Brown referred to the increase in workload and stress levels of the department and it was noted that Mr Brown had failed to take a significant amount of his annual leave entitlement.

Subsequently, Mr Brown's doctor wrote to his employer stating that Mr Brown's physical and mental health was being affected by his work environment. Richmond upon Thames LBC referred Mr Brown to its occupational health unit which considered him to be fit for work. The occupational health unit carried out a risk assessment and developed an action plan to minimise risks to his health but no action was taken in the next six months. He sadly suffered a breakdown and never returned to

---

294 **Dickins v O2 plc** [2008] EWCA Civ 1144

295 **Brown v Richmond upon Thames LBC** [2012] EWCA Civ 1384

work. Two months later his marriage broke down and his wife left him. A year later Mr Brown was declared permanently unfit to work and was retired.

At trial Mr Brown was awarded general damages of £25,000 (representing moderately severe psychiatric harm). Dealing with the issue of special damages it was determined that Mr Brown's claim for loss of earnings should be cut off after 12 months, after which the operative cause of Mr Brown's condition was his matrimonial breakdown. Following this decision, Mr Brown appealed on two grounds:

a. That the selection of the date of Richmond upon Thames LBC breach of its duty of care should have been much earlier, namely when Richmond upon Thames LBC had failed to refer B to its occupational health unit; and

b. The selection of the cut-off date of the claim for loss of earnings should have been to the end of B's working life.

The Appeal was only allowed in part. As to the first ground it was accepted that there was a substantial body of evidence, including that of Mr Brown's own expert, supporting the Judge's determination of the date at which the breach had occurred.

As to the second ground, the Judge appeared not to have given proper thought to the consequence of his decision on the cut-off date, which was that the matrimonial breakdown would have caused B to lose his job if there had been no breach of R's duty and no work stress related breakdown. Nor had he considered that the matrimonial breakdown had occurred when B was vulnerable by reason of the work related stress. Of note, the agreed expert evidence referred to the "*compounding effect*" of the marital breakdown. The case was remitted for further judicial consideration of the impact of the Claimant's marital breakdown on his damages for loss of earnings.

The Court of Appeal, considering consequential matters following a successful appeal, determined that remittal should be to the trial Judge (and that the appellant should have 50 per cent of his costs to reflect lack of success on some issues). Treacy LJ states at paragraph 42 of the Judgment that "...*It seems to me that for the Respondent to uphold the judge's decision, the judge would have had to have made a clear finding that the Appellant would have lost his job in any event as a result of mental damage caused by the breakdown of his marriage...*

The judge seems not to have asked himself what the position would have been if there had been no breach of duty in 2003 and no work stress related breakdown in June 2003. There is no finding that the effects of the marital breakdown were so severe that they would have led to dismissal in their own right.

There is also no apparent consideration of the fact that the marital breakdown took place at a time when the Appellant was undoubtedly vulnerable and suffering from the effects of the work related breakdown".

The key issue to emerge from this particular Judgment firstly is the level of forensic investigation and, to some degree, the speculation that is required in dealing with the issue of causation and consequential loss. While the breakdown of anyone's relationship as a result of occupational stress may be a foreseeable and tragic consequence, the question of how personal relationship issues and the impact such breakdowns can have on an individual remains unaddressed and a matter which is likely to be determined on an individual basis in each instance.

The manner in which a Court should approach the issue of apportionment in cases of psychiatric injury was buttressed in that it was accepted to by multifactorial and fact specific, in the Judgment of **BAE Systems (Operations) Ltd v Konczak** [2017] EWCA Civ 1188[296].

[296] **BAE Systems (Operations) Ltd v Konczak** [2017] EWCA Civ 1188

The claim involved an employee who had made a number of allegations of sexual harassment against some of her colleagues which in turn, caused her to be moved to a new role at a different site. Sadly, she was unhappy there and her line manager suggested that she should return to her previous team.

Understandably bearing in mind the facts of the claim, she decided to decline this proposal as it would inevitably require her to work with the same people whom she had experienced issues with culminating in her move initially. Following this, her manager appears to have made a sexist comment about her perceived inability to "*move on*" regarding the conflict on the 26th April 2006 in a meeting. The Judgement notes that there was no malice in the comment but none the less, the comment had a detrimental impact to the Claimant who was diagnosed with work related stress as a result and signed off work. She was sadly dismissed on the 23rd July 2007 on the basis that there were no roles for her to return to with her old employer that were suitable.

The Claimant brought a claim in the Employment Tribunals, which was successful on the basis of sex discrimination arising from this comment referred to above. When dealing with the issue of damages, there were a number of complicated features in the claim, since there were a number of factors and events all of which could be said to contribute to her injury. Of note, the Claimant was said to have not sought to mitigate her loss by taking psychotropic medication July 2010. The issue was, what level of damages should the Defendant be liable for? The Court of Appeal in dealing with apportionment highlighted at paragraphs 71 – 72 of the Judgment that "*In other words, the question is whether the tribunal can identify, however broadly, a particular part of the suffering which is due to the wrong; not whether it can assess the degree to which the wrong caused the harm.*

That distinction is easy enough to apply in the case of a straightforward physical injury. A broken leg is "indivisible": if it was suffered as a result of two torts, each tortfeasor is liable for the whole. It is less easy in the case of psychiatric harm. The message of ***Hatton*** *is that such harm may well be* *divisible. In **Rahman** the exercise was made easier by the fact... that the medical evidence distinguished between different elements in the Claimant's overall condition, and their causes, though even there it must be recognised that the attributions were both partial and approximate. In many, I suspect most, cases the tribunal will not have that degree of assistance. But it does not follow that no apportionment will be possible. It may, for example, be possible to conclude that a pre-existing illness, for which the employer is not responsible, has been materially aggravated by the wrong (in terms of severity of symptoms and/or duration), and to award compensation reflecting the extent of the aggravation. The most difficult type of case is that posited by Smith LJ in her article, and which she indeed treats, rightly or wrongly, as the most typical: that is where "the Claimant will have cracked up quite suddenly, tipped over from being under stress into being ill". On my understanding of **Rahman** and **Hatton**, even in that case the tribunal should seek to find a rational basis for distinguishing between a part of the illness which is due to the employer's wrong and a part which is due to other causes; but whether that is possible will depend on the facts and the evidence. If there is no such basis, then the injury will indeed be, in Hale LJ's words, "truly indivisible", and principle requires that the Claimant is compensated for the whole of the injury – though, importantly, if (as Smith LJ says will be typically the case) the Claimant has a vulnerable personality, a discount may be required in accordance with proposition".*

In summary, the Court of appeal highlighted that the correct approach to dealing with the issue of apportionment in a case of psychiatric injury was to consider two propositions as set out in **Barber v Somerset CC** [2002] EWCA Civ 76[297].

a. Firstly, that where a psychiatric harm complained had more than one cause, then a Defendant should only pay for that proportion attributable to his wrongdoing, unless the harm was truly indivisible;

[297] **Barber v Somerset CC [2002] EWCA Civ 76**

b. Secondly, any Court should when dealing with an assessment of damages bear in mind of any pre-existing disorder or vulnerability, and of the chance that the Claimant would have succumbed to a psychiatric injury (in this case a stress disorder) in any event.

In practise, the first point applies to cases where the injury complained of has multiple causes, one or more of which can be (on the facts) attributable to a Defendant's conduct, but one or more cannot be. The second position applies applied in cases where a Claimant suffers from a pre-existing vulnerability which is not in and of itself, injury related but could well go onto give rise to an injury even if the acts complained off did not occur. There was a conflict identified legally between the case of **Barber**[298] and **Dickens**[299],. In cases where there were multiple extrinsic causes of any injury, then a Court had to make "*sensible attempt*" to apportion the harm.

Practically, when carrying out such an exercise, the question was whether to identify, albeit broadly, if a particular part of the suffering which was due to the wrong; not whether it could assess the degree to which the wrong caused the harm (see **Thaine v London School of Economics** [2010] I.C.R. 1422[300]). In short and in practise it is highly fact specific, and often expert led. Whilst in practise the basic rule of a Defendant must take his victim as they find him stands true, the level of damage does remain it appears open for challenge.

298 **Barber v Somerset CC [2002] EWCA Civ 76**

299 **Dickins v O2 plc** [2008] EWCA Civ 1144

300 **Thaine v London School of Economics** [2010] I.C.R. 1422

CHAPTER SIXTEEN

THE EQUALITY ACT 2010 IN STRESS CLAIMS

This text must consider claims in the Employment Tribunal for psychiatric injury. However, the scope and volume of material that needs to be considered is vast and complex. It is covered in texts that are dedicated in their entirety to the area and practices are advised to consider these texts in addition to this one, which intends to provide a practical overview.

What can the Employment Tribunal award?

The principle that Employment Tribunals have jurisdiction to award compensation for personal injury caused by unlawful discrimination, whether physical or psychiatric, was confirmed by the Court of Appeal in **Sheriff v Klyne Tugs (Lowestoft) Ltd** 1999 ICR 1170, CA[301].

Following this and helpfully, a Claimant can seek to present claims damages relating to psychological (or physical) injury for discrimination as a separate head of loss in its own right. The key point to remember is that this must flow from the act of Discrimination complained of medical evidence on this point is going to be required, and focus on the causative aspects of the injury's manifestation will need to be set out, and supported. It may well be the case that due to how discrimination is assessed in the Employment Tribunal that a Claimant has a more straightforward cause of action that seeking to rely on the difficulty and multifaceted approach the Courts are required to adopt.

301 **Sheriff v Klyne Tugs (Lowestoft) Ltd** 1999 ICR 1170, C

The Court of Appeal also made it clear in **Sheriff**[302]. that a Claimant who has suffered a personal injury as a result of discrimination must ensure that they expressly claim for personal injury in the discrimination proceedings.

A failure to do this can, and often will create the risk that they will lose the chance to litigate the point later in any later proceedings for damages based on brought in the Courts due to the doctrines of "*res judicata*", issue estoppel or the rule in **Henderson v Henderson** 1843-60 All ER Rep 378, Ch D[303].

As a further safeguard, it is not possible to claim twice in respect of the same injury under two different heads of loss, however, as this amounts to double recovery so Employment Tribunals must be clear about what is being compensated as injury to feelings and what amounts to personal injury. Where separate awards are made, the Employment Tribunal must be cautious in creating a situation where there is effectively double recovery.

Practically, this often results in a real difficulty where there is a genuine overlap between an award for pain, suffering and loss of amenity arising from psychiatric injury and an award for injury to feelings resulting from discrimination. Quite often an Employment Tribunal may feel that they must err on the side of caution which can cause no small amount of frustration of individual Claimants, and Respondents alike when they are considering offers of settlement.

The EAT in **HM Prison Service v Salmon** [2001] IRLR 425, EAT[304] addressed the issue and accepted that, although the two heads of loss and award are distinct in principle, they are not easy to delineate as its challenging to identify when the distress and humiliation suffered as a

---

302 **Sheriff v Klyne Tugs (Lowestoft) Ltd** 1999 ICR 1170, C

303 **Henderson v Henderson** 1843-60 All ER Rep 378, Ch D

304 **HM Prison Service v Salmon** [2001] IRLR 425, EAT

result of unlawful discrimination manifested into a recognised psychiatric illness, and where the balance of the harm and upset truly rests. The EAT rightly expressed that practically, there was no criticism of an Employment Tribunal treating the personal injury as having been compensated for under the heading of injury to feelings, as long as the Employment Tribunal identifies which aspects of Claimant's consequential psychiatric injury the award is intended to cover.

The Vento guidelines

In cases where the Employment Tribunal finds that discrimination has occurred can make an award for injury to feelings under the **Vento** Guidelines ranges. From the 6th April 2024 the Vento bands were be increased to the following

a. Lower band acts of Discrimination that are normally awarded in cases involving one-off incidences of discrimination such as a single discriminatory insult or slur £1,200 to £11,700);

b. Middle band acts of Discrimination that are normally awarded cover serious cases, which could include a serious one-off incident, where an award in the upper band is not appropriate £11,700 to £35,20);

c. Upper band acts of Discrimination that are normally are reserved for the most serious offences such as discriminatory campaigns in the workplace which result in a profound impact on the victim such as causing depression, anxiety or extreme distress (£35,200 to £58,700)

Practitioners should always remember that a Tribunal has a wide range of discretion when it comes to quantum of an award. They do not need to make an award in the brackets set out above, and they can be higher or lower. It is possible for no award to be made. When considering if an award would be appropriate the Employment Tribunal needs to consider all of the facts of the claim including things such as the vulnerability of the Claimant, the seriousness of the treatment and the impact the discriminatory treatment had on the employee.

The overlap between the Vento award and General Damages

The Court of Appeal in **Vento v Chief Constable of West Yorkshire Police (No.2)** 2003 ICR 318, CA[305], reinforced that Employment Tribunal should take due account of any overlap between individual heads of damage to prevent double compensation.

In **Cuerden v Yorkshire Housing** [2010] 7 WLUK 502[306] the Claimant suffered an exacerbation of an existing depressive disorder as a result of the employer's failure to make reasonable adjustments. The Employment Tribunal found that the exacerbation of her condition would have lasted for about two years and made an award of £7,500 for psychiatric injury. It also awarded £9,000 for injury to feelings, but stressed that it took great care to ensure that there was no double recovery.

Stress as a disability

In most circumstances involving stress at work claims, an employee suffering from stress related symptoms will be suffering from a disability within the meaning of the Equality Act 2010. Section 6 Equality Act 2010 provides that an individual qualifies as having a disability if they have a physical or mental impairment, and this impairment has a substantial or long-term adverse effect on their ability to carry out their normal day to day activities.

Schedule 1 of the Equality Act 2010 provides at part 2 (1) (a – c) that the effect will be long term if it has lasted for at least 12 months, is likely to last for at least 12 months or is likely to last for the remainder of the

[305] **Vento v Chief Constable of West Yorkshire Police (No.2)** 2003 ICR 318, CA

[306] **Cuerden v Yorkshire Housing** [2010] 7 WLUK 502

affected individuals life. Further, under part 2 (2), if any impairment ceases to have a substantial adverse effect on a person's ability to carry out normal day-to-day activities, it is still to be treated as continuing to have that effect if it is likely to recur.

These broad parameters benefit Claimants in stress at work claims for a number of reasons. Firstly, while a Claimant's condition may be satisfactorily controlled by medication, it does not remove it from the definition as cessation of medication may result in a recurrence of such symptoms.

Secondly, psychiatric issues can lie dormant and are often not deemed to have resolved or dissipated.

Thirdly, if an employee has suffered from a condition but has recovered, they may still be disabled if the condition it is likely to recur.

Therefore, in a case where a Claimant who has had a period of "*mental impairment*" as a result of stress (even if relatively brief), employers should be advised that it is safer to assume that the impairment remains as present for the purposes of the Equality Act 2010, at least until they are presented with medical evidence upon which they can firmly rely to rebut this presumption.

The duty to make reasonable adjustments

Following an employee suffering from a stress related illness, and disclosing this fact to their employer, it is logical for them both to be concerned as to how they will continue in employment. Once an employer is notified of an employee's disability, an employee should expect them to seek to make reasonable adjustments. This is set out in section 20 Equality Act 2010, with the requirement being broken down into three criteria.

Firstly (section 20 (3) Equality Act 2010) dictates that there needs to be a "*provision, criterion or practice of A's puts a disabled person at a substantial disadvantage in relation to a relevant matter in comparison with persons who are not disabled, to take such steps as it is reasonable to have to take to avoid the disadvantage*".

Secondly (section 20 (4) Equality Act 2010), requires that "*a physical feature [must] put a disabled person at a substantial disadvantage in relation to a relevant matter in comparison with persons who are not disabled, to take such steps as it is reasonable to have to take to avoid the disadvantage*"

Finally, (section 20 (5) Equality Act 2010) requires that "*a disabled person would, but for the provision of an auxiliary aid, be put at a substantial disadvantage in relation to a relevant matter in comparison with persons who are not disabled, to take such steps as it is reasonable to have to take to provide the auxiliary aid*".

Whilst it is unlikely that section 20 (4) Equality Act 2010 will apply in stress claims, section 20 (3) and (5) Equality Act 2010 have a clear application and failure by an employer to make such adjustments will invariably be met with a claim for disability discrimination by virtue of section 21 Equality Act 2010.

But when should reasonable adjustments be made?

It is a settled proposition that where ill health arises because of an employee's work or working environment, employers may be acting unreasonably if they do not take reasonable steps to remove the cause. Within the stress at work context the case of **Thanet District Council v Websper** [2002] 10 WLUK 813[307] provides a useful example. In **Thanet**[308] the EAT upheld an employment tribunal's decision that, in refusing to transfer Mr Websper to an alternative role to alleviate stress caused by his work, the Council had breached an implied term that it

[307] **Thanet District Council v Websper** [2002] 10 WLUK 813

[308] **Thanet District Council v Websper** [2002] 10 WLUK 813

should provide a safe place to work. This led to a finding of unfair constructive dismissal following Mr Websper's prompt resignation.

Further, in **Royal Bank of Scotland v McAdie** [2008] I.C.R. 1087[309] the Court of Appeal accepted that where an employee's illness has been caused by stress at work, it may be necessary for the employer (as said by Wall LJ,) to "*go the extra mile*" (paragraph 37 of the Judgment) and seek for example to, "*find [the employee]... alternative employment for such an employee, or to put up with a longer period of sickness absence than would otherwise be reasonable*" (paragraph 37 of the Judgment).

In cases where stress related symptoms surface in a clear and unambiguous manner, such as an employee making a complaint or bursting into tears, a certain level of initiative is to be expected from an employer. In **Cosgrove v Caesar & Howie** [2001] IRLR 653[310], the EAT stated that "*there will no doubt be cases where the evidence ......will establish a total unavailability of reasonable and effective adjustments. But it does not seem to follow that because a former secretary, long absent from the firm and clinically depressed to the point of disability, and her general practitioner could postulate no useful adjustment, that the duty ... should without more be taken to have been satisfied*".

Employers would also be well advised to consider that a reasonable adjustment might actually require the transferring of an employee to a wholly different job within the organisation (**Electronic Data Systems Ltd v Travis** 4th Mar 2004, EAT[311]).

Other adjustments could include placing the Claimant on sick leave and instituting a gradual return to work, starting with part-time work or an adjustment to working hours to enable the employee to better cope with any condition they are suffering. This does not provide Claimants with

---

309 **Royal Bank of Scotland v McAdie** [2008] I.C.R. 1087

310 **Cosgrove v Caesar & Howie** [2001] IRLR 653

311 **Electronic Data Systems Ltd v Travis** 4th Mar 2004, EAT

a unilateral right, however. Employers who do all they can to assist a Claimant who, despite their attempts at prevention, still suffers from a psychiatric disorder will be treated favourably by Courts (**Olulana v Southwark LBC** [2014] EWHC 2707 (QB)[312]. The question is one of fact in relation to any adjustments put in place.

No option but to go?

Employees should also be confident that in the event they raise concerns regarding their health as a result of occupational stress but feel that they are being managed out, their roles are being diminished in some way or their concerns ignored, that they may have strong claims in constructive dismissal.

Considering this point, **Greenhof v Barnsley MBC** [2006] IRLR 98[313] is a tale of caution for employers. Mr Greenhof, a former employee of the Barnsley MBC, appealed against the decision of an employment tribunal which dismissed his complaint of unfair dismissal but upheld his complaint of disability discrimination. Mr Greenhof had suffered from clinical depression and had been asked by Barnsley MBC to take a lesser role on his return to work after a period of illness, which in response to he resigned. The matter went to the EAT who upheld the employee's appeal on the grounds that the failure to make reasonable adjustments itself constituted a fundamental breach entitling him to leave his employment.

Further support for employees can be found in **Chief Constable of Avon and Somerset v Dolan** [2008] 4 WLUK 566[314]. In this matter Mr Dolan had complained to his employer of stress related symptoms in 2004 and early 2005, and was found to have been suffering from "*mental health symptoms*". He was placed on sick leave and upon his return to work he

312 **Olulana v Southwark LBC** [2014] EWHC 2707 (QB).

313 **Greenhof v Barnsley MBC** [2006] IRLR 98

314 **Chief Constable of Avon and Somerset v Dolan** [2008] 4 WLUK 566

was assessed a further seven times, and his condition described as "*non-medical*". His employer also decided that after the "*adjustments*" had been made, there was no reason why he could not perform his work as an inspector. Mr Dolan accepted a supernumerary CID role on the basis of an unequivocal promise that his pay would not be reduced, yet he had received a letter in August 2006 threatening to place him on half pay.

In response to this he resigned and brought claims of failure to make reasonable adjustments, disability discrimination and constructive dismissal. While an appeal to the EAT was successful in part, the finding of constructive dismissal was, on the evidence, upheld due to the employer's failings. It was in essence, the combination of his Employer's failure to make reasonable adjustments and the proven acts of disability-related discrimination had led Mr Dolan to conclude that he had lost trust in his employer, and that such loss of trust was the reason for his resignation.

Is it stress, or just unhappiness?

Cases where employers face claims predicated on stress at work naturally bear certain similarities. One trait, which seems to permeate in a number of cases is that of an employee who having taken umbrage with a decision or act carried on the behalf of their employer becomes so entrenched in their opposition to such a decision, that their reaction begins to develop into a recognised psychiatric disorder, or to affect their health in other ways. It's a difficult position for any employer to be placed in. On one hand, an employer is entitled to pursue its genuine commercial interests but at the same time, must balance this against its duty of care owed to its employees. This is particularly true in cases where employees suffering from significant stress react emotionally, perhaps even obstructively to genuinely commercially motivated decisions. In these cases, a crossroads is reached where an employer has to decide on how to proceed – do they accommodate the obstructive employee, or push on fearing the threat of legal action for the greater good of their operation?

On this point the recent decision of **Herry v Dudley Metropolitan Council and Governing Body of Hillcrest School** [2019] 6 WLUK 767[315] is of assistance and highlights the distinction between the infliction of a recognisable psychiatric injury and "*stress*" as a broader concept. Despite **Herry**[316] reaffirming the principles established in **J v DLA Piper UK LLP** [2010] ICR 1052[317] the decision has reignited the debate as to the level of the duty of care owed to an employee when dealing with issues of stress at work.

With the current framework set out, it's clear that the obligations placed on an employer are very wide, and that each case is highly fact specific. **Herry**[318] provides but one factual example of the commonly encountered workplace situation set out above. Mr Herry was employed by the Respondent as a design and technology teacher and part-time youth worker. From May 2010 Mr Herry lodged many sickness certificates and the Employment Judge found that he had been continuously away on sick leave from June 2011. From May 2010 until April 2013 the certificates in the main referred to physical injuries, but from October 2013 onwards, they ceased to refer to any physical problem and instead gave the description of "*stress at work*", "*work related stress*", "*stress*", or "*stress and anxiety*". Mr Herry alleged in part that his employer had discriminated against him on grounds of his disabilities, which he claimed were dyslexia, as well as stress and depression. His employer did not accept that Mr Herry had a disability during this period, a point agreed upon by Employment Judge Goodier in the Employment

315 **Herry v Dudley Metropolitan Council and Governing Body of Hillcrest School** [2019] 6 WLUK 767

316 **Herry v Dudley Metropolitan Council and Governing Body of Hillcrest School** [2019] 6 WLUK 767

317 **J v DLA Piper UK LLP** [2010] ICR 1052

318 **Herry v Dudley Metropolitan Council and Governing Body of Hillcrest School** [2019] 6 WLUK 767

Tribunals Judgment of the 27th April 2015 where Mr Herry was found to not have been disabled at the relevant times.

Of note, the Judgment reflected on there being a "*dearth of information*" in the medical documents as to the nature of the "*work related stress*". For example, Mr Herry took no medication for stress, he was mentally and physically fit enough to perform his role and from a medical point of view, he could return to work as soon as possible. It was recorded however that there were "*still outstanding management (non-medical) issues at the workplace which are causing stress*" and it appears these were the root cause of the issues between him and his employer.

Employment Judge Goodier found that with regards to stress, the stresses Mr Herry complained of found their origin "*largely a result of his unhappiness about what he perceives to have been unfair treatment of him, and to that extent is clearly a reaction to life events*". Effectively, factual causation was paramount but so was the necessity of establishing medical causation. He could not point to a recognisable psychiatric disorder, but rather only the wider concept of "*stress*" in support his disability claim.

On appeal the EAT dismissed Mr Herry's disability discrimination claims. The EAT ruled that on the facts of the case, stress caused by being unhappy with a decision or colleague was not a mental impairment and in this sense, Mr Herry was not disabled. This is a decision that should be welcomed by practitioners as it seeks to draw a line in the sand by which parties can identify when and where liability and disability could, and can crystallise. HHJ Richardson at paragraph 56 of the Judgment concluded that "*although reactions to adverse circumstances are indeed not normally long-lived, experience shows that there is a class of case where a reaction to circumstances perceived as adverse can become entrenched; where the person concerned will not give way or compromise over an issue at work, and refuses to return to work, yet in other respects suffers no or little apparent adverse effect on normal day-to-day activities… Unhappiness with a decision or a colleague, a tendency to nurse grievances, or a refusal to compromise are not of themselves mental impairments: they may simply reflect a person's character or personality.... in the end the question whether there is a mental impairment is one for the Employment Tribunal to assess*".

Effectively, a Claimant cannot simply complain of ill feelings or dissatisfaction with their employer's decisions and expect the Equality Act 2010 to automatically step in.

Establishing disability for the purposes of the Equality Act 2010 remains a relatively low bar for Claimants. The decision in **Herry**[319] may have been different had Mr Herry provided more detailed medical evidence, particularly as to the likelihood of the presence of a recognisable psychiatric illness and how this would have had an adverse effect on his day-to-day activities. Employers should always therefore take a cautious approach and treat longstanding complaints of stress as being indicative of a potential disability and worthy of proper investigation.

Herry[320] in many respects provides a tableau of a commonly faced issue in the workplace, that of a disgruntled employee on long term sick leave who complains of stress based symptoms being caused by decisions and events they perceive as being unfair. It is not difficult to imagine where the cost of trying to accommodate such an employee could be detrimental to a business commercially, or where the capitulation on certain points may well encourage future demands from an employee. There is then the further concern that an employer may feel that as soon as it accepts that an employee has suffered from a disability caused through stress, that they are adding "*fuel to the fire*" of any future litigation in the County or High Court.

Whilst there is a distinction between an employee who suffers from a recognisable psychiatric injury caused as a result of stress and one who is

---

319 **Herry v Dudley Metropolitan Council and Governing Body of Hillcrest School** [2019] 6 WLUK 767

320 **Herry v Dudley Metropolitan Council and Governing Body of Hillcrest School** [2019] 6 WLUK 767

simply unhappy at work, employers should take the investigation of such issues seriously as opposed to brushing them off. A potential concern posed by **Herry**[321] is that employers may see the decision as encouraging a less proactive and sympathetic stance on their part in dealing with cases of workplace stress. Ironically, this could lead to situations where employees may well suffer serious and foreseeable psychiatric injuries due to an employer labelling the root cause of such an illness as not being their working practices, but rather that an employee is simply disgruntled and unhappy. In such a case, it is straightforward to imagine how an employee who regularly complained about such issues could far more easily establish that such injuries were not only foreseeable but that the refusal to investigate and intervene was negligent on the part of their employer.

Whilst it is a difficult tightrope to balance on, early advice and, if necessary, intervention can provide the essential safety net that both employees and employers require.

321 **Herry v Dudley Metropolitan Council and Governing Body of Hillcrest School** [2019] 6 WLUK 767

CHAPTER SEVENTEEN

OTHER TORTIOUS ACTS

Whilst the bulk of this work has been concerned with concept of negligence and dealing with the aftermath of accidents, what happens in the rare few cases where the acts complained of are not accident but intentional? This work does not intend to discuss the issues arising from the Criminal Injury Compensation Scheme with this being covered in further works, but rather to identify how such claims can be brought in the County Courts. Claims for psychiatric injury, arising from intentional acts largely arise from 4 distinct tortious acts:

a. Assault

b. Battery

c. The intentional infliction of harm

d. Harassment

This chapter does not intend to cover criminal offences other than to say that in the case of a violent assault or sexual abuse, a Claimant is entitled where there is a conviction by a Court to rely on the facts of that conviction to bring a claim in the County or High Court for personal injury (section 11 Civil Evidence Act 1968). More often than not, this can create a watertight case as to liability, since the facts of an indictment will in the case of conviction have either been proved or accepted.

Vicarious liability and tortious conduct

A Defendant employer may well seek to argue that they own no vicarious liability for the actions of their employee who is engaged in the commission of intentional torts. Simply put, vicarious liability means that one person takes the place of another as far as liability is concerned and has been a consistent feature of the development of the law of negligence for the last century.

This work does not intend to consider this point beyond the practical implications for cases of psychiatric injury which this chapter envisages (the scope of such matters being outside of this work and worthy of books of their own). Practitioners seeking a more detailed consideration of the point would do well to consider what to my mind are the seminal texts on the matter, Charlesworth and Percy and Clerk and Lindsell. Generally speaking, and employer will be vicariously liable for the actions of any of its employees, carried out in the performance of their employment.

An individual is liable not only for their own torts, but also, classically, for those torts they have authorised. Lord Phillips set out in **Various Claimants v Catholic Child Welfare Society** [2012] UKSC 56[322], the question of if an employee can be held liable for the torts of its employee, servant or agent involves a two-stage test.

a. Stage one is concerned with the relationship between the Defendant and the tortfeasor. The test is whether the relationship between them was one of employment or akin to employment (the relationship test).

b. Stage two is concerned with the link between the stage one relationship and the commission of the tort. The test is whether the wrongful conduct was so closely connected with acts that the tortfeasor was authorised to do that it can fairly and properly be regarded as done by the tortfeasor while acting in the course of their employment or quasi-employment (the "close connection" test).

322 **JSC in Various Claimants v Catholic Child Welfare Society** [2012] UKSC 56

The relationship test

The first stage entails considering "*the relationship of between the parties to see whether it is one that is capable of giving rise to vicarious liability*". Vicarious liability can be imposed where there is a relationship that is "*akin to that between an employer and an employee*". The question of if it is it is fair, just and reasonable to impose such liability and the public policy reasons that need to be factored in are set out by Lord Phillips at paragraph 35 of the Judgment, and are that

a. "*The employer is more likely to have the means to compensate the victim than the employee and can be expected to have insured against that liability;*

b. *The tort will have been committed as a result of activity being taken by the employee on behalf of the employer;*

c. *The employee's activity is likely to be part of the business activity of the employer;*

d. *The employer, by employing the employee to carry on the activity will have created the risk of the tort committed by the employee;*

e. *The employee will, to a greater or lesser degree, have been under the control of the employer.*"

The close connection test

The second stage of the test requires there to be a sufficient "connection that links the relationship between the Defendants and the act or omission which occurs, and can (according to paragraphs 49 of the Judgment in **Various Claimants**[323], be answered by the Court, but considering if the tortfeasor can be said to be "*working on behalf of an*

[323] **JSC in Various Claimants v Catholic Child Welfare Society** [2012] UKSC 56

enterprise or on his own behalf and, if the former, how central the workman's activities were to the enterprise and whether these activities were integrated into the organisational structure of the enterprise"

The second limb of the test originates from the jurisprudence of the Canadian Supreme Court, and in particular its decision in **Bazley v Curry** [1999] 2 SCR 534[324], arising from sexual abuse of children in a residential care facility. The reasoning can be summarised as follows;

a. The imposition of vicarious liability is justified by a connection between the risk of wrongful conduct created by an enterprise and the commission of such conduct;

b. The mere fact that the employment provided an opportunity to commit a tort is insufficient to justify the imposition of vicarious liability: "*Incidental connections to the employment enterprise, like time and place (without more) will not suffice*". The fact that the tort was committed during working hours or at a place of work "*may not, standing alone, be of much importance*".

Therefore, the employment "*must materially enhance the risk*". There must be a "*significant connection between the creation or enhancement of a risk and the wrong that accrues therefrom*": Some factors determining the sufficiency of the connection were said to be:

a. The opportunity that the enterprise afforded the employee to abuse his or her power;

b. The extent to which the wrongful act may have furthered the employer's aims (and hence be more likely to have been committed by the employee);

---

[324] **Bazley v Curry** [1999] 2 SCR 534

c. The extent to which the wrongful act was related to friction, confrontation or intimacy inherent in the employer's enterprise;

d. The extent of power conferred on the employee in relation to the victim

e. The vulnerability of potential victims to wrongful exercise of the employee's power.

Recent Developments

The law on vicarious liability continues to develop, and practitioners need to be aware of the Supreme Court in the decision of **WM Morrison Supermarkets plc v Various Claimants** [2020] UKSC 12[325] which in cases where psychiatric injury is caused by an intentional act, is likely to determine if the case succeeds or fails. The case involved a disgruntled employee of Morrison's, a Mr Skelton who uploaded a file containing the payroll details of the supermarket chain's entire workforce to a publicly accessible filesharing website. He then sent this file to various national newspapers, claiming to be a concerned member of the public who had found it online. He came into possession of this data months prior to this, and as part of his role on Morrisons' internal audit team, he had previously been responsible for sending the workforce payroll data to external auditors. For his own reasons, he chose to make the data public, and was subsequently prosecuted and sentenced to eight years' imprisonment.

Over 9,000 employees brought proceedings against Morrison's personally and on the basis of its vicarious liability for Mr Skeletons actions. By way of the Data Protection Act 1998, misuse of private information, and breach of confidence. Lord Reed giving the leading Judgment of the Supreme Court found that there was no vicarious liability on the part of Morrison's for the actions of Mr Skelton concluding that "*In the present case, it is abundantly clear that Skelton was*

[325] **WM Morrison Supermarkets plc v Various Claimants** [2020] UKSC 12

not engaged in furthering his employer's business when he committed the wrongdoing in question. On the contrary, he was pursuing a personal vendetta, seeking vengeance for the disciplinary proceedings some months earlier. In those circumstances, applying the test laid down by Lord Nicholls in ***Dubai Aluminium*** *in the light of the circumstances of the case and the relevant precedents, Skelton's wrongful conduct was not so closely connected with acts which he was authorised to do that, for the purposes of Morrison's' liability to third parties, it can fairly and properly be regarded as done by him while acting in the ordinary course of his employment*". The Judgment sets down as a 2 test to be applied and considered when considering if unauthorised acts by an employee could be said to give rise to vicarious liability. In doing so, a Court should consider

a. What functions or "*field of activities*" had been entrusted by the employer to the employee;

b. And then decide whether there was sufficient connection between the position in which the employee was employed and his wrongful conduct to make it right for the employer to be held liable.

Further, the Supreme Court in **Barry Congregation of Jehovah's Witnesses v BXB** [2023] UKSC 15[326] confirmed that the question of whether vicarious liability arises involves a two-stage test and when the Judgment is broken down, the individual steps that comprise each stage can be identified as follows;

a. Stage one – Was there is a relationship between the primary wrongdoer and the person alleged to be liable which is capable of giving rise to vicarious liability;

    i. It is established that some relationships can give rise to vicarious liability;

326 **Barry Congregation of Jehovah's Witnesses v BXB** [2023] UKSC 15

ii. Outside of the established categories, the test developed has been whether the relationship was sufficiently akin to employment for it to be just and fair to impose liability;

iii. There is no vicarious liability where the alleged wrongdoer is a true independent contractor in business on their own account.

b. Stage two – Is there a "sufficient connection";

i. Are the torts "*so closely connected with [the] employment that it would be fair and just to hold the employers vicariously liable*"

ii. That the "*the wrongful conduct*" must be so closely connected with acts the employee was authorised to do that, for the purpose of the liability, the wrongful conduct may fairly and properly be regarded as committed while acting in the ordinary course of the employee's employment.

Application to claims for psychiatric injuries

It is however helpful when considering cases of psychiatric injury to consider the earlier decisions which are of assistance and provide helpful illustrations of how vicarious liability may well manifest. In **Mohamud v WM Morrison Supermarkets plc** [2016] UKSC 11[327] a submission that the second stage of the test should be liberalised in favour of Claimants was rejected. The Claimant, a customer who was abused and then attacked by a petrol station attendant when he asked whether some documents could be printed, succeeded because the attendant's abusive response to his request was within the attendant's "*field of activities*" and

[327] **Mohamud v WM Morrison Supermarkets plc** [2016] UKSC 11

there was subsequently an "*unbroken sequence of events*" leading to the assault.

In this matter, Mr Mohamud went to a Morrisons' petrol station in Birmingham. He asked whether the garage could print off some images from a USB stick. A Mr Khan worked behind the counter and he responded to Mr Mohamud's request with foul and abusive language. Mr Mohamud protested at being spoken to in this manner, which led to another barrage of abuse from Mr Khan, who ordered Mr Mohamud to leave. Matters then spiralled out of control. Mr Mohamud went to his car, but was followed by Mr Khan. Mr Khan opened the passenger door and told him in a threatening manner never to come back. When Mr Mohamud asked him to shut the door, he was punched by Mr Khan. Mr Mohamud got out of the car to close the passenger door. Mr Khan punched him to the ground and severely assaulted him, despite his supervisor telling him to stop.

At trial of first instance, and when the matter was referred to the Court of Appeal, it had been held that Morrisons were not vicariously liable for Mr Khan's actions. Although his job involved some interaction with customers, it involved nothing more than serving and helping them. There was not a sufficiently close connection between what he was employed to do and assaulting a customer. Mr Mohamud had died before the case went to the Supreme Court, but his family continued with the action and argued that the test of "*close connection*" was outdated. They sought a new, broader test of "*representative capacity*". This raised the issue of "*was Mr Khan acting in the capacity of a representative of the employer at the time of the assault*"? Alternatively, was Mr Khan was acting within the "*field of activities*" assigned to him in dealing with Mr Mohamud?

The Supreme Court allowed the appeal, holding **Morrisons** vicariously liable for Mr Khan's actions. They considered the development of vicarious liability and placed appropriate and correct emphasis on the need for a close connection between the acts of Mr Khan, and the operation of Morrisons. On the facts before the Supreme Court;

a. Mr Khan's job was to attend to customers and respond to their inquiries;

b. His foul-mouthed response and ordering Mr Mohamud to leave was inexcusable but within the "*field of activities*" assigned to him.;

c. There was no break in the chain by Mr Khan then following Mr Mohamud to his car;

d. "*It was a seamless episode*" leading to the tragic events as described above;

e. When he opened the passenger door, Mr Khan he ordered Mr Mohamud to keep away from his employer's premises, which was reinforced by the assault.

The Supreme Court held the fact that it was a gross abuse of his position was irrelevant, as was Mr Khan's true motive. Morrisons had entrusted him to deal with members of the public and it was just that they should be responsible for his abuse of this trust.

Likewise, managing director who chooses to assert his authority over a subordinate by using violence after a Christmas party may also be acting within the field of his activities as shown in **Bellman v Northampton Recruitment Ltd** [2018] EWCA Civ 2214, [2019] ICR 459[328]. In this matter Mr Bellman was a sales manager for the Respondent recruitment firm. Mr Major was the firm's managing director. A Christmas party was organised. At its end, Mr Major arranged taxis to transport staff to a hotel where they continued drinking, with drinks mainly paid for by the company. After a couple of hours, an argument broke out about a new employee's placement and terms. Mr Major got cross and summoned staff to give them a long lecture on his authority. When Mr Bellman

[328] **Bellman v Northampton Recruitment Ltd** [2018] EWCA Civ 2214, [2019] ICR 459

questioned Mr Major's decisions, Mr Major punched him Mr Bellman, causing brain damage. The Court was asked to decide whether the company was vicariously liable for Mr Major's actions. The Judge at first instance held not, but the Court of Appeal disagreed. Two key matters needed to be considered;

a. The nature of the employee's job was to be construed broadly and objectively; and

b. If there was sufficient connection between his job and the wrongful conduct to render vicarious liability appropriate.

Mr Major owned the company, was its most senior employee and directing mind, and had full control over how he conducted his role. When he lectured his staff at the afterparty, he was wearing his metaphorical Managing Director's hat and establishing his authority in that role. Additionally, that party was not a purely social event happening to involve colleagues but a follow-on from an organised work event attended by most of the company's employees, where the company paid for taxis and drinks. In those circumstances, there was a sufficient connection between Mr Major's wrongful conduct and his role, and accordingly the company was vicariously liable for his actions.

It has been recognised that the presence or absence of an employment contract is not decisive and there are other relationships, akin to employment, where it is just that vicarious liability should attach (**Various Claimants v Institute of the Brothers of the Christian Schools** [2012] UKSC 56; [2013] 2 A.C. 1[329] and **Armes v Nottinghamshire CC** [2017] UKSC 60[330]). When dealing with vicarious liability the Supreme Court as recently as last month in **Armes**[331]. In dealing with the issue of

[329] **Various Claimants v Institute of the Brothers of the Christian Schools** [2012] UKSC 56; [2013] 2 A.C. 1

[330] **Armes v Nottinghamshire CC** [2017] UKSC 60

[331] **Armes v Nottinghamshire CC** [2017] UKSC 60

vicarious liability Lord Reed referred to the case of **Cox v Ministry of Justice** [2016] UKSC 10[332] and the two questions posed when dealing with the issue of the imposition of vicarious liability, namely;

a. What sort of relationship has to exist between an individual and a Defendant before the Defendant can be made vicariously liable in tort for the conduct of that individual?

b. In what manner does the conduct of that individual have to be related to that relationship in order for vicarious liability to be imposed?

Assault

It's entirely understandable that most people, when they hear the tort "*assault*", will consider these to mean a violent attack, saying that they have been "*assaulted*". However, legally assault is distinct and is comprised of two components. Firstly, there must be an act carried out towards a Claimant and secondly, that act must have caused the Claimant to apprehend the infliction of immediate and unlawful violence. Sheer words and abuse are unlikely to reach the threshold required of assault within the civil context.

The act must also be capable of constituting a battery of the victim. For example, a hand moving to touch a person's shoulder is hardly likely to constitute an assault, whereas a fist being drawn back for a punch, would be (**Thomas v NUM** [1986] Ch 20[333]).

When a Claimant is considering a claim predicated on the assault of tort, one of the first steps to take practically has be considering the evidence available at this point in time if the conduct complained of can be classed objectively as sufficiently threatening to found the tort of assault. Whilst there is a substantial body of case law on the point, a central thread

[332] **Cox v Ministry of Justice** [2016] UKSC 10

[333] **Thomas v NUM** [1986] Ch 20

running between the cases is that of the requirement for immediacy of the perceived threat. Running towards someone and stopping immediately before them within striking distance can constitute an assault (**Stephens v Myers** (1830) 4 C & P 349[334]) on the basis of a reasonable apprehension of battery, whilst the case of a person standing passively in front of someone, blocking their way, is unlikely to amount to an assault.

Battery

Battery is a common tort, and one that most practitioners will be familiar with. Its components are that there must be direct physical contact between the Claimant and Defendant. Interestingly, the concept of "direct" require that the touching between the Claimant and Defendant is physical, and objects used, or thrown can constitute direct contact for example the throwing of a bucket of water over someone (**R v Cotesworth** (1704) 6 Mod 172[335]) or even holding onto someone's arm to talk to them (**Collins v Wilcock** [1984] 1 WLR 1172[336]).

Not all physical contact however will constitute a legal battery. Lord Goff in **F v West Berkshire Health Authority** [1990] 2 AC 1[337] summarised the point with: "*I start with the fundamental principle, now long established, that every person's body is inviolate. ... the effect of this principle is that everybody is protected not only against physical injury but against any form of physical molestation.*

Of course, as a general rule physical interference with another person's body is lawful if he consents to it; though in certain limited circumstances the public interest may require that his consent is not capable of rendering the act lawful. There are also specific cases where physical interference without

---

334 **Stephens v Myers** (1830) 4 C & P 349

335 **R v Cotesworth** (1704) 6 Mod 172

336 **Collins v Wilcock** [1984] 1 WLR 1172

337 **F v West Berkshire Health Authority** [1990] 2 AC 1

consent may not be unlawful – chastisement of children, lawful arrest, self-defence, the prevention of crime, and so on… a broader exception has been created to allow for the exigencies of everyday life – jostling in a street or some other crowded place, social contact at parties, and such like. This exception has been said to be founded on implied consent, since those who go about in public places, or go to parties, may be taken to have impliedly consented to bodily contact of this kind".

Practically, the level of contact required to be established to form the tort of battery is actually quite loose. The two points which need to be established are that:

a. The contact was deliberate; and

b. The contact was in excess of what was "generally acceptable in everyday life".

One point to note is that civil battery does not require a component of intent on the part of the tortfeasor to cause any harm. As stated by Lord Goff, an overzealous slap on the back or a prank gone wrong can step outside of the bounds of being socially acceptable, and into the realm of tortious liability. Generally, a victim doesn't need to be injured or physically injured for a battery to have occurred (these types of circumstances being covered and deterred by Criminal Law as well) and as long as an offensive contact is involved the Tort will be founded. One useful and practical example is that of spitting. The individuals involved are not physically injured, but the act would constitute offensive contact capable of constituting a battery. In assessing if the contact is to be considered offensive it will be decided on the concept of the "*ordinary person*".

Intentional infliction of harm

When considering the everyday passage of life, and the almost infinite circumstances which can come to be between individuals there is a smaller tort, that of the intentional infliction of harm. The essence of this tort is that a Defendant intends through their action to cause harm, and that some harm occurs. Practically, approaching the events on which the tort is based, four points need to be identified:

a. That the Defendant acted intentionally or recklessly.

b. That the Defendant's conduct was "*extreme and outrageous*".

c. That the Defendant's act was the cause of the distress.

d. That the Claimant suffered severe emotional distress as a result of Defendant's conduct.

Whilst an old case, the case of **Wilkinson v Downton** [1897] 2 QB 57[338] is not only the bedrock from which the tort springs, but provides a practical example of how the tort can manifest in day to day to day life. In the case of **Wilksinson**[339], Mrs Wilkinson went to a race-meeting, and on the evening of the same day the Defendant came to her home and represented to her that her husband, while returning in a wagonette with some friends from the races, had met with an accident and had both his legs broken. He told her that he was lying at a public-house, and had asked him to go to his home, and ask the Claimant to take a cab, along with some pillows and bring him home. Fortunately, all these statements, were false.

They were intended by the Defendant to be believed to be true, and the Claimant did. As a result, she became seriously ill due to nervous shock.

Wright J held that the Defendant was liable to the Claimant since his actions had been wilfully performed, and also calculated to cause harm. This tort is distinct from a tort based on negligence, but in certain circumstances, will be made out. The act which causes harm must be

[338] **Wilkinson v Downton** [1897] 2 QB 57

[339] **Wilkinson v Downton** [1897] 2 QB 57

either intentional in its causation, or reckless as to it (**Wainwright v Home Office** [2001] EWCA Civ 2081[340]).

The current test

The test was recently revised in case of **Rhodes v OPO** [2015] UKSC 32[341] where the supreme Court held the tort was comprised of three limbs. Firstly, that the act complained of had to be done with the aim of intentionally causing physical or psychological harm (or wilfully infringing the right to personal safety). This would require words or conduct directed towards the Claimant for which there was no justification or reasonable excuse.

Secondly, there was a required mental element on the part of the tortfeasor, namely that there was an intention to cause physical harm or severe mental or emotional distress. Mere recklessness would not suffice, which represented the departure from the previous decision of **Wilkinson**[342].

Thirdly, physical or psychiatric harm would have to flow as a consequence of these actions, mere upset or grief would not be enough.

Let's consider for a moment, this historic tort in a modern context. whilst it may well seem extreme, the tort has been used in cases where a teacher had encouraged a vulnerable child to send him indecent photographs of herself (**C v WH** [2015] EWHC 2687 (QB)[343]). There seems to be natural tangent for the tort to be applied in cases of "*revenge porn*". There are as yet, no such reported cases but sadly, it is unlikely to be long until such a case emerges. Further, with the proliferation of mobile recording devices, it does not seem impossible to consider how an individual could

340 **Wainwright v Home Office** [2001] EWCA Civ 2081

341 **Rhodes v OPO** [2015] UKSC 32

342 **Wilkinson v Downton** [1897] 2 QB 57

343 **C v WH** [2015] EWHC 2687 (QB)

be shown images which are known by the potential tortfeasor, to be likely to cause that person severe emotional stress, for example, footage of an execution. A more practical example is likely to be something analogous with **Wilkinson**[344] but the tort is likely to be revisited in the future.

One of the more interesting aspects of the use of this tort is how it would interplay with a claim for stress at work arising from bullying. In these case **Daniel v Secretary of State for the Home Department** [2014] EWHC 2578 (QB)[345] provides that bullying should be classed as cases where "*conduct must be genuinely offensive and unacceptable, examples of which may be intimidating, malicious or insulting behaviour intended to undermine, humiliate or denigrate*".

When you consider an intentional aspect of seeking to cause harm there is no clear reason why bullying claims if the facts allow should also be articulated in this manner.

Harassment

Claimants will sometimes find they are capable of relying on the Protection from Harassment Act 1997. Whilst originally designed to deal with cases of stalking, it has become a piece of legislation which has been applied to cases of Animal Protestors, workplace bullies, private publications and internet based campaigns.

Section 1 (1) of the Protection from Harassment Act 1997 (herein in this chapter refeed to as the Act) creates a statutory tort prohibiting a person from pursuing a course of conduct:

a. Which amounts to harassment of another, and

---

344 **Wilkinson v Downton** [1897] 2 QB 57

345 **Daniel v Secretary of State for the Home Department** [2014] EWHC 2578 (QB)

   b. which he knows or ought to know amounts to harassment of the other.

Section 1A of the act deals with largely cases of intimidation rendering it an offence for a person to harass 2 or more persons in circumstances in;

   a. Which he knows or ought to know involves harassment of those persons, and

   b. By which he intends to persuade any person (whether or not one of those mentioned above)

      i. Not to do something that he is entitled or required to do, or

      ii. To do something that he is not under any obligation to do.

In short, it is an effective statutory instrument to stop and bring to an end unwanted activity. Any person who is a victim of harassment needs to look no further than section 3 of the Act to find that they are entitled to a raft of remedies, but most notable at section 3 (2) of the Act that "*On such a claim, damages may be awarded for (among other things) any anxiety caused by the harassment and any financial loss resulting from the harassment*".

What is harassment?

Section 4 of the Act provides that "*(1) A person whose course of conduct causes another to fear, on at least two occasions, that violence will be used against him is guilty of an offence if he knows or ought to know that his course of conduct will cause the other so to fear on each of those occasions.*

Section 7 (2) of the Protection from Harassment Act 1997 provides in addition that "*(2) References to harassing a person include alarming the person or causing the person distress.*"

It is necessary to consider the full spectrum into which this behaviour can fall. The Courts ultimately have the last word in defining whether or not they believe that the behaviour complained of crosses the relevant threshold. This position was summed up well in **Majrowski v Guy's and St. Thomas' NHS Trust** [2006] UKHL 34[346] by Baroness Hale (paragraph 66) as the decision ultimately being "*Left to the wisdom of the Courts to draw sensible lines between the ordinary banter and badinage of life and genuinely offensive and unacceptable behaviour.*"

In the case of **Majrowski**[347] the Claimant alleged that he had been subjected to bullying and intimidation by his departmental manager. She had humiliated him in front of other staff, imposed unrealistic performance targets (backed by threat of disciplinary action), been excessively critical of his time-keeping and work and had, at times, refused to talk to him. It was suggested that this behaviour was due to homophobia. Although the Trust had responded to a formal complaint in 1998, the Claimant, who was dismissed in 1999 for reasons unrelated to the case, brought an action some four years later for damages under section 3 Protection from Harassment Act 1997 for distress, anxiety and consequential losses.

In case of **Veakins v Kier Islington Ltd** [2009] EWCA Civ 1288[348], the Court of Appeal held that the Claimant had in the context of her employment been harassed by virtue of the act. The nature of the conduct complained of in question was a very generalised set of allegations made by the Claimant, namely that her supervisor did not like her and picked on her. Her claim was unsuccessful in the lower Courts but the Court of Appeal allowed the Claimant's appeal. Giving the Judgment of the Court Maurice Kay LJ noted that the primary test to be drawn from

[346] **Majrowski v Guy's and St. Thomas' NHS Trust** [2006] UKHL 34

[347] **Majrowski v Guy's and St. Thomas' NHS Trust** [2006] UKHL 34

[348] **Veakins v Kier Islington Ltd** [2009] EWCA Civ 1288

Majrowski[349] was whether or not the conduct was "*oppressive and unacceptable*" *although* the Court would need to bear in mind that the conduct must be "*of an order which would sustain criminal liability*".

In the case of **Rayment v Ministry of Defence High Court** [2010] EWHC 218 (QB)[350] the Claimant, Ms Rayment was a volunteer member of the Territorial Army from 1987 to 2003. During her time with the TA, she received driver training which qualified her to drive vehicles ranging from cars to HGVs. In 2003 she got a job working at the Honourable Artillery Company in City Road, London and in early 2004 won promotion and became the driver for the Commanding Officer of the HAC. For various reasons Ms Rayment did not get on well in this job. She fell ill and took time off work. Correctly or otherwise, she came to believe there was a real sense of hostility directed towards her by those who worked at the HAC. She complained to her CO that; "*I have been discriminated and harassed in my working environment with varying degrees of verbal and non-verbal abuse, resulting in feelings of isolation and anxiety*"

She was eventually discharged and then brought an action for damages in the High Court alleging breach of the Protection from Harassment Act 1997 and/or negligence and claimed she had been subjected to bullying, victimisation and harassment in the form of persistent, offensive, abusive, intimidating, bullying, humiliating and insulting behaviour. Davis J found that to establish liability under the Protection from Harassment Act 1997 there must be;

a. Conduct which occurs on at least two occasions;

b. Which is targeted at the Claimant;

349 **Majrowski v Guy's and St. Thomas' NHS Trust** [2006] UKHL 34

350 **Rayment v Ministry of Defence High Court** [2010] EWHC 218 (QB)

c. Which is calculated in an objective sense to cause alarm or distress; and

d. Which is objectively judged to be oppressive and unreasonable.

The Court found that, from a long catalogue of allegations, there were three incidents which satisfied the "*oppressive and unreasonable*" test. The incidents had exacerbated Ms Raiment's recurrent depression from a mild to a moderate degree and so she won part of her claim. As an aside it is noteworthy that, while the Claimant only recovered £5,500.00 in general damages and £1,060.00 in special damages, the Judgement is silent as to costs. However the Independent newspaper, on the 18th February 2010 *reported on the matter in an article titled "Harassed' female soldier wins damages award"* that Ms Rayment had rejected an offer to settle out of Court made before the trial by the Ministry of Defence of £60,000.00 plus £125,000.00 costs. There may well have been obvious consequences.

Tactical flexibility

there are practically, four main broad areas where a claim under the Act confers tactical, and practical advantages on a Claimant.

Firstly there is no requirement that the harm suffered be foreseeable. Once a Claimant has made out the harassment, then they are capable of pursuing a claim for compensation. Placing this into a common context, a practitioner may find some assistance form the Court of Appeal decision in **Jones v Ruth** [2011] EWCA Civ 804[351]. In this case the Claimants brought an action against their neighbours, the Defendants, arising from extensive building work undertaken by the Defendants which began in May 2002. It should have been completed that year but sadly continued for 4 years, causing them loss of amenity and restricting their enjoyment of their property due to the constant noise and nature of the works. Whilst this was found to be a nuisance there was another

351 **Jones v Ruth** [2011] EWCA Civ 804

aspect of the claim which was a lot more sinister. The Defendants erected scaffolding on the Claimants' land, and threw rubbish into the Claimants' garden. Sadly, because of these events, the Claimant went on to developed back pain, depression and subsequently lost her job.

Following a successful claim at first instance, the Claimants appealed to the Court of Appeal seeking to recover damages for personal injuries and consequential losses flowing from the harassment, the claim in harassment having been dismissed as the injuries were not deemed foreseeable. Patten LJ in allowing the appeal remarked;

"*I am not persuaded that foreseeability of the injury or loss sustained by a Claimant in a case of harassment is an essential element in the cause of action. The obvious starting point is the 1997 Act itself. Conduct of the kind described in section 1(1) is actionable under section 3 in respect of anxiety or injury caused by the harassment and any financial loss resulting from the harassment. There is nothing in the statutory language to import an additional requirement of foreseeability. Nor is the foreseeability of damage the gist of the tort. Section 1(1) is concerned with deliberate conduct of a kind which the Defendant knows or ought to know will amount to harassment of the Claimant. Once that is proved the Defendant is responsible in damages for the injury and loss which flow from that conduct. There is nothing in the nature of the cause of action which calls for further qualification in order to give effect to the obvious policy objectives of the statute*".

Secondly, there is no need, unlike in an action in negligence for a Claimant to show they have suffered from a recognisable psychiatric injury, damages can be awarded solely for anxiety, and financial losses flowing from this. In many respects, this acknowledges that in cases where conduct is designed to scare, intimidate or unsettle, a Claimant can be compensated without the requirement for a specific psychiatric injury to be identified. Of Course, medical evidence can still be produced.

Thirdly, and often of most practical application in a workplace environment where bullying is occurring, it is not a defence to a

Defendant who is vicariously liable for the actions of an employee, to seek to argue that they had in place a system to prevent harassment. The commission of the offense is often enough to found liability (See **Majrowski v Guys and St Thomas NHS Trust** [2007] 1 AC 224[352]).

Finally, section 6 of the Act a Claimant has a limitation period of 6 years, as opposed to the usual 3 for personal injury claims as envisaged by section 11 of the Limitation Act 1980.

Collateral victims

The law has expanded to acknowledge this, and notably, bystanders to traumatic events may now seek damages for psychiatric injuries suffered as secondary victims (**Alcock v Chief Constable of South Yorkshire Police** [1992] 1 AC 310[353]). Employees can seek compensation for stress at work caused by a variety of reasons, notably overworking (**Hatton v Sutherland** [2002] P.I.Q.R P241 C.A[354]). Furthermore, with the increasing reach of social media, and the ability of individuals to readily and freely communicate in a variety of media, it was only a matter of time until the law of harassment was required to expand in order to deal with individuals who use these recently developed tools for improper means. It is notable that under Section 3 (2) Protection from Harassment Act 1997 the civil remedy a Court may impose includes damages (among other things) for any anxiety caused by the harassment and any financial loss resulting from the harassment. The potential scope of what damages may well be recoverable is incredibly broad and is reflective of the flexibility a Court has, and in many respects needs when dealing with the issue of damages arising from such conduct.

However, the issue of how secondary victims, or "*collateral victims*" who fall outside of the intended scope of such harassment should be dealt with

352 **Majrowski v Guys and St Thomas NHS Trust** [2007] 1 AC 224

353 **Alcock v Chief Constable of South Yorkshire Police** [1992] 1 AC 310

354 **Hatton v Sutherland** [2002] EWCA Civ 76

has been a complex issue, with the individual concerned often unable to or struggling to find protection under the Protection from Harassment Act 1997.

With this point in mind, the case of **Levi and Levi v Bates, Leeds United, Football Club Limited and Yorkshire Radio Limited** [2015] EWCA Civ 206[355] is an exciting legal development in that it provides a strong indication from the Court of Appeal that (circumstances and facts permitting) the Courts are entitled to find that an individual who causes another psychiatric injury through an untargeted act of harassment can be liable for damage to secondary, or "*collateral victims*" who were not the target of their course of conduct.

The facts of the claim itself are lengthy and protracted but can be summarised as follows. Mr Levi and Mr Bates had fallen out in quite a dramatic manner regarding the running of Leeds United FC. This in turn had resulted in years of animosity and litigation between the two. Mr Bates had published articles in the Leeds United FC match-day programmes and broadcasted via Yorkshire Radio his version of his feud with Mr Levi arising out of their mutual business dealings, which manifested itself in an ugly course of conduct spanning 2005 – 2011. By the time of trial, ten publications were capable of being highlighted as offending articles against Mr Levi, and Mr Levi had already successfully sued Mr Bates previously for libel in respect of three of these publications.

In two of these publications Mr Bates had had insinuated that fans of Leeds United FC should contact Mr Levi at his home address to air any grievances they may have with the running of the club. The article was entitled "The *Enemy within*" in which Mr Bates wrote that Mr Levi's father must be "*turning in his grave at his antics*". Mr Bates wrote that the actions of Mr Levi were "*little short of blackmail*" and that his behaviour was "*totally scurrilous*". Mr Bates suggested that readers should put

[355] **Levi and Levi v Bates, Leeds United, Football Club Limited and Yorkshire Radio Limited** [2015] EWCA Civ 206

questions to Mr Levi to justify his behaviour and published Mr Levi's home address where he lived with Mrs Levi.

The second article was entitled "*Why Mr Levi Why?*" in which Mr Bates accused Mr Levi of trying to frighten off would-be investors and trying to blackmail him personally into paying Mr Levi money. Mr Bates wrote "*Thanks Melvyn. By the way, you do know that your phone number is in the book don't you*". Mr Levis phone number appears to have then been printed, and although the last sentence was blacked out in most programmes, it could still be read clearly from both the front and behind the page. Evidently the phone number that referred to was clearly that of both Mr and Mrs Levi.

At first instance, HHJ Gosnell sitting at Leeds County Court found Mrs Levi's claim of harassment failed, whilst Mr Levi's claims succeeded on the basis that the publications were not targeted against her, but at Mr Levi.

Firstly, HHJ Gosnell found that as the above cited allegations of harassment were not targeted against Mrs Levi, they could therefore not constitute or contribute towards the two acts required to give rise to a course of conduct capable of being constructed as harassment against her (as per section 7 (3) Protection from Harassment Act 1997). Of interest with regards to the latter article, Mr Bates was asked in cross-examination why he did not give more consideration to the Second Claimant's feelings and health. He replied that she did not come into his calculations at all.

Secondly there was a finding that while the concept of "*targeting*", as a necessary element in the statutory tort of harassment was not to be found expressly set out anywhere in the Protection from Harassment Act 1997, it had emerged from judicial interpretation of the statutory definition of the tort.

In **Thomas v News Group Newspapers Limited** [2001] EWCA Civ 1233[356], in paragraph 30, Lord Phillips MR said that "*harassment*" is generally understood as describing conduct *"targeted at an individual*". However, nine years later this was reiterated slightly differently in **Dowson v Chief Constable of Northumbria Police** [2010] EWHC 2612 (QB)[357], where Simon J observed that it was essential for a claim in harassment to proceed, that it be proved (inter alia) that the relevant conduct "*is targeted at the Claimant*". Accordingly, there was a subtle shift from being targeted specifically at a person, to having to be targeted at the Claimant in the action. The acts were not found to be "*targeted*" at Mrs Levi and therefore her claim failed.

The Court of Appeal acknowledged in **Levi** that whilst in most harassment cases the distinction of whom was targeted would not arise, infrequently it could occur that a clear course of conduct and harassment, because it was targeted at C1, could cause just as much alarm and distress to C2, even though C2 was not the intended target of the perpetrator's misconduct, although it was foreseeably likely that C2 would be harmed by it.

Briggs LJ giving the leading Judgement of the Court of Appeal at paragraph 26 of the Judgment identified that the critical question was whether in transforming Lord Phillips' phrase in **Thomas**[358], of being "*targeted at an individual*" to Simon J's phrase in **Dowson**[359] of being "*targeted at the Claimant*", was a step too far.

356 **Thomas v News Group Newspapers Limited** [2001] EWCA Civ 1233

357 **Dowson v Chief Constable of Northumbria Police** [2010] EWHC 2612 (QB),

358 **Thomas v News Group Newspapers Limited** [2001] EWCA Civ 1233

359 **Dowson v Chief Constable of Northumbria Police** [2010] EWHC 2612 (QB),

Brigg's LJ found that it was, and stated in paragraphs 27 – 29 of the Judgment that,

"*there are two main reasons why I consider that it is not a requirement of the statutory tort of harassment that the Claimant be the (or even a) target of the perpetrator's conduct. The first is that I do not consider that Lord Philips had that question in mind. The purpose of the passage in his judgment in the* ***Thomas*** *case which I have cited was not designed to identify who may complain of harassment, but rather to draw out of the well-known word 'harassment' the concept that it is targeted behaviour, by which I mean behaviour aimed at someone, rather than behaviour which merely causes alarm or distress without being aimed at anyone.... My second reason for concluding that, provided that it is targeted at someone, the conduct complained of need not be targeted at the Claimant, if he or she is foreseeably likely to be directly alarmed or distressed by it, is that I cannot conceive why Parliament should by implication rather than express words (for there are none) have deliberately excluded from the protection of the Act persons who are foreseeably alarmed and distressed by a course of conduct of the targeted type contemplated by the word harassment*".

However, Briggs LJ stated in paragraph 33 of the Judgment that,

"*Alarm or distress suffered out of nothing more than sympathy for the targeted victim of harassment is insufficient to found a claim under the Act. The Claimant must be harassed by it, in the sense that the conduct complained of must have some direct effect upon the Claimant (in terms of causing foreseeable harm, usually, but not limited to, alarm and distress)*".

As a result of this analysis, on the facts of **Levi**[360] it was held that there was no reason to exclude Mrs Levi from a claim for harassment based on the above two articles. It was held that these articles constituted harassment of Mrs Levi not simply because they defamed her husband, but because they invited thousands of club supporters to intervene in a

360 **Levi and Levi v Bates, Leeds United, Football Club Limited and Yorkshire Radio Limited** [2015] EWCA Civ 206

hostile manner, at her home, about a business dispute between Mr Levi and Mr Bates. In answer to submission from Mr Bates that such a finding could be contrary to Mr Bates' Article 10 ECHR right to free speech, it was expressly stated at paragraph 37 that "*incitement of others to weigh in for the furtherance of a grudge about a private business dispute has nothing whatsoever to do with free speech, as the Judge rightly observed*".

It was held that the two publications taken in tandem amounted to a sufficient course of conduct. They were two separate publications, each pursuing the same objective of incitement, focussed upon the Levi family home in different ways, the first by direct visit (or perhaps letter) and the second by telephone. They shared the same essential characteristics they were closely connected. Briggs LJ found on this basis, the tort of harassment be made out against Mrs Levi, and awarded her damages in the sum of £6,000.00.

Apart from the useful clarification of the application of the Protection from Harassment Act 1997 to what may be best termed "*collateral victims*", there is an immediate and obvious application to a number of potential types of claim which practitioners need to be, and should be aware of.

Firstly, as in the case of **Levi**[361], actions founded either in defamation and/or the Protection from Harassment Act 1997 will inevitably attract a certain degree of animosity and ill will between the parties that can foreseeably lead to a similar situation as in *Levi*. It is also foreseeable that such actions could well expand to encompass multiple persons in a Claimant's life. Considering the ongoing enquiries into the mobile telephone hacking by certain media groups (as recently demonstrated by **Gulati v MGN Ltd** [2015] EWHC 1482 (Ch)[362]), it is not impossible that in phone hacking claims which are in part often based on the

361 **Levi and Levi v Bates, Leeds United, Football Club Limited and Yorkshire Radio Limited** [2015] EWCA Civ 206

362 **Gulati v MGN Ltd** [2015] EWHC 1482 (Ch

Protection from Harassment Act 1997, that a Claimant may seek to bring in "*collateral victims*" as additional Claimants in certain circumstances. As the reach and accessibility of the media (both regular and social) continues to grow, there is the ambit for such claims to be considered potentially on a more regular basis.

Secondly, in property disputes which are often ferociously fought with a certain degree of acrimony, and will often contain express pleaded allegations of harassment, it is not difficult to envisage for example, in a boundary dispute case, visitors to a certain address, or members of a family being exposed to untargeted harassment as in **Levi**[363]. These individuals could seek remedies under the Protection from Harassment Act 1997 due to the conduct of a Defendant for a myriad of reasons despite never being the intended target of such a Defendant's conduct.

Thirdly, within the context of Stress at Work claims, particularly in cases where an action is based on bullying and harassment by a Defendant's employees, it is easy to envisage situations where "*collateral victims*" could bring claims pursuant to the Protection from Harassment Act 1997 on the basis of the ratio of **Levi** in circumstances where the oppressive and unreasonable conduct complained of by a Defendant's employees reached a Claimant's home, for example, the sending of hate mail or other offensive messages.

The impact of the **Levi**[364] decision is yet to be seen, but it should in any event be seen as an indication from the Court that "*collateral victims*" are able to seek remedies in damages for the harassing actions of a Defendant. They can do so safe in the knowledge that the Courts will seek to view the circumstances in which the course of conduct was perpetrated as a whole, and will look more to the result of the conduct complained of,

[363] **Levi and Levi v Bates, Leeds United, Football Club Limited and Yorkshire Radio Limited** [2015] EWCA Civ 206

[364] **Levi and Levi v Bates, Leeds United, Football Club Limited and Yorkshire Radio Limited** [2015] EWCA Civ 206

rather than the intent of the perpetrator. Much like how the Court may approach the civil liability of a person who carelessly throws a rock into a crowd of people aiming for a single individual and striking another, a similar approach appears to now be likely to be taken where it is conduct, rather than stones which are hurled at individuals and their families.

CHAPTER EIGHTEEN

QUANTUM AND EVIDENCE

The first reaction of any Claimant in a personal injury action is generally one of despair and frustration – despair and frustration that for no fault of their own they have been injured. Courts regularly hear the words "*I don't care about the money; I just wish this had never happened*". In dealing with damages, no more can be done than to attempt to place the Claimant in the same position they would have been had the accident never occurred. In reality this is a sad impossibility.

All that can be done is to ensure that the Claimant is placed in the same position financially as they were before the accident and in this, perhaps cynically, the job of the practitioner is to help a Claimant "*break even*". In cases of psychiatric injury this is far more complex than first imagined since, in cases of a persistent injury and its consequences, the impact can be far reaching, difficult to articulate and in some cases even predict.

Types of Damages

There are two separate heads of damage in personal injury claims, these are:

a. General Damages

b. Special Damages

General Damages

General damages can be defined as a level of quantum assessed by a Court, or agreed between the parties for injuries suffered to a person physically or psychiatrically, that additionally include compensation for pain, suffering and loss of amenity. Whilst this is arguably an oversimplification, for the purpose of practise it is a valid and useful method of dealing with the head of loss.

The first port of call in dealing with general damages is simple. The Claimant must prove it.

Experts

It is all very well and good a Claimant complaining of suffering from psychiatric injury, disability and loss of amenity as a result of an event, but without independent expert evidence on the matter this will not, and cannot get the Claimant any further than a complaint which a Court will generally, and quite justly be forced to disregard in the assessment of damages due to an absence of evidence.

It is important that an expert, when selected, is an appropriate expert to deal with the issues put before them. This will almost always be either a psychologist or a psychiatrist. There would for example be little point in sending an individual complaining of shooting pains in his chest and blackouts to see a dentist and the same is true in the case of psychiatric injuries.

In high value claims it is advisable to remember that where causation of injury is in dispute the ability, and also the experience of an expert to stand up for, and support their opinion in not only joint discussion and at trial is a factor to consider. Many experts may well be brilliant on paper, and have impressive C.V.'s but appearing in front of a Court to explain, justify, support and sustain an opinion under cross examination is a very different skill than those developed in the consulting room and lecture hall.

A common criticism in cases of low value psychiatric injury arising from Road Traffic Accidents is where a Claimant attends on General Practitioner with a serious psychiatric complaint with a view to them producing the part 35 CPR medical report on which they will base their case. In this case it is clear that a General Practitioner would not have been the correct expert to employ to deal with evidencing a Claimant's injury and that a more specialised and experienced psychiatrist's opinion should have been sought.

Secondly, where this is not done a Claimant's case may well be left open to criticism when considering the experts reliability, or potentially a robust evidential challenge if the Defendant obtains their own report of a psychiatrist.

Part 35 CPR provides a vehicle whereby the Claimant can secure a medical report to support such a contention and the contents of this element of the CPR are self-descriptive.

Clarification of a report pre-service

Before a party serves a report, it is always sensible to consider if there any areas that a practitioner disagrees with, or wants clarification on. Once a report is served it very much takes on a life of its own. If a practitioner has fears as to an expert's competency, they shouldn't be afraid to ask if the issues before them are outside of their field of expertise, and if so, which discipline of expert they should instead approach. Obviously, the evidence must be indecent but in the gathering of evidence pre-service, it is the obligation of the practitioner to ensure that the report is ready to be served. Don't be afraid once a draft report is received to consider the possibility of a conference with Counsel to clarify any issues.

Questions to the expert

Of note, if a practitioner seeks "*clarification*" of a point in a report which has been served (or often in reality does not agree with a conclusion of a report), part 35.6 CPR provides the mechanism whereby the practitioner can put written questions to the expert. This should always be used as failure to do so will result in criticism. A party has 28 days to do so from service of the report and can only do so once, so it must be made to count. Whilst it is uncommon for a party to seek to argue that questions raised in this manner are effectively cross examination as opposed to clarification, it's always sensible to reflect on the questions, and do one's level best to ensure they can be seen, and justified to be points of clarification, rather than out and out disagreement. Failure to do otherwise can lead to costly applications before a Court.

Parties can always remember that they are allowed to apply to a Court to seek permission for their own expert evidence if necessary, and it is fair to say that in claims allocated to the multi-track, this will rarely be objected to by a Court, although the concept of proportionality, the claim's value and tracking can sometimes limit the scope of this option, or more importantly, a Court's willingness to allow it.

The use of questions and also, seeking to clarify any issues with a report pre its service is an important point in practice since it provides a mechanism whereby if there are discrepancies between the evidence of a Claimant and a medical expert which are overlooked, they can effectively be remedied and additional points supported, namely what the expert can comment on and deal with. The following points are highlighted:

Tactical points of questions

Once a claim has been served, and direction provided by a Court it is common for a direction to allow and permit not only the Defendant leave to obtain their own evidence, but also for a Claimant to serve an updated report. In cases of dual experts, a joint report will almost always be ordered and this point in the trial lifespan can be a critical phase since the medical evidence at this point, and the opinion and prognosis will be crystallised, the point of contention and the reasons for them entrenched.

Practically, questions to an expert can be used for a variety of means by way of clarification, for example:

a. If a Claimant's symptoms are continuing or worsening, putting questions can be a useful way to have an expert state if a re-examination is required.

b. If a Claimant's symptoms would benefit from further treatment (i.e. CBT) an expert can recommend this and give a notion as to the cost of such.

c. If a Claimant's symptoms have increased in severity due to intervening acts, how this affects the overall prognosis and the potential for recoverability (**Wincanton Logistics Ltd** [2009] EWCA Civ 1404[365]).

d. If a Claimant in trying to recover, has paid for treatments, were these reasonable and assisted their recovery?

e. Whether a Claimant requires care and assistance.

f. The Claimant's ability to work, and if they should be classed as disadvantaged on the open labour market.

g. Effectively plugging any holes which emerge during the litigation.

Witness evidence

When dealing with issues of quantum in witness evidence, there are a number of pitfalls. The most obvious one is more often than not encountered in lower value psychiatric injury claims, where a statement is short, and points are not outlined. Furthermore, as set out at the onset of this chapter, the onus is on a Claimant to prove their injuries.

Always ensure that at any trial involving psychiatric injury (be it a liability trial or assessment of damages as opposed to a paper-based disposal hearing) that the Claimant is in attendance otherwise, unless the Court orders otherwise, that statement cannot be relied upon (part 32.5 (1) (b) CPR).

365 **Wincanton Logistics Ltd** [2009] EWCA Civ 1404

In preparing a witness statement it is always wise to consider and make sure that the following points are addressed:

a. Prepare detailed witness evidence from the Claimant and if appropriate, from friends and family to deal with the impact of any psychiatric injury on the Claimant. Where causation is disputed, never underestimate the evidential weight of witnesses being able to speak first hand of the change they have seen in a Claimant;

b. Always try and have the Claimant in attendance to deal with discrepancies and have them prepared as of what to expect.

c. Where there is a claim predicated on a loss of earnings, be it past or future (including a Smith and Manchester award) explain why there is a restriction or disability, and how work life is affected by the Claimant's injuries.

d. Ensure that where claims for consequential losses are made for care and assistance (care, DIY etc.), that a full history of, and the reasons for, the claims is prepared and set out.

e. Emphasise any loss of amenity including sports, hobbies and leisure activities, quoting prior membership to clubs and organisations, showing proof as to commitment for example, photographs of equipment.

f. In cases of an inability to engage in leisure activities, set out in the statement how the loss of time caused by the accident has impacted on leisure.

g. Spoilt enjoyment of a holiday must be dealt with in depth.

h. Spoilt enjoyment of social events, such as birthday parties should be particularised.

i. Additional stress caused through occasions such as exams, caring for a young infant etc should be expanded upon.

j. The presence and interplay of a psychiatric injury with other physical symptoms should be explained so that a complete and holistic picture of the Claimant's condition is given to the Court.

k. Where appropriate, in the case of psychiatric injury, powerful evidence can be gathered through explaining the impact such an injury has had on a Claimant's relationships.

Points of attack

Witness evidence is a statement of case, and one that is signed with a statement of truth. Whilst the importance of that statement is never lost on practitioners, some Claimants can be unaware of its reach and potential consequences. Of note, parties should be aware that section 57 Criminal and Courts Act 2015 provides that in a personal injury claim (being the primary claim) where any compensation is awarded, but on the balance of probabilities a Claimant is found to have been fundamentally dishonest in relation to the primary claim (or a related claim, such as a claim for loss of earnings predicated on a disability), then the Court must dismiss the claim. There are also the costs consequences of such a finding on a Claimant personally, but also the offence of Contempt of Court which is an imprisonable offence.

Points to be aware of and points Defendants are advised to consider attacking a Claimant on are:

a. In cases where a Claimant has a pre-existing condition which has been accelerated or aggravated, ensure that the point is dealt with within the witness evidence (**Smithurst v Sealant Construction**

Services Ltd [2011] EWCA Civ 1277[366] and **Kenth v Heimdale Hotel Investments Limited** [2001] EWCA Civ 1283[367]).

b. Be aware that people who know a Claimant, such as work colleagues, may well give very different versions of the impact of a psychiatric injury on a Claimant.

c. Be aware that in cases where a Claimant alleges that they cannot work, or makes positive assertions in a witness statement, that video surveillance could well be used to establish dishonesty, malingering or exaggeration.

d. Emphasise what the Claimant can do and the activities he or she has been able to return to.

e. Establish that the pain and suffering element of the injury was reduced to a low level relatively promptly.

f. Be able to point to discrepancies in medical evidence, written evidence and oral evidence to destroy Claimant's credibility.

JSC Guidelines

The first port of call in assessing general damages should always be the JSC guidelines. While these are not definitive and in some cases Claimant's injuries may well fall within brackets where at first blush, they should not be they need to be considered.

Comparable cases

In assisting in how to understand and argue where levels of quantum for injuries should fall, there are numerous comparable cases, available in Kemp and Kemp and on the online services of westlaw.com and

---

366 **Smithurst v Sealant Construction Services Ltd** [2011] EWCA Civ 1277

367 **Kenth v Heimdale Hotel Investments Limited** [2001] EWCA Civ 1283

lawtel.com. These are similar cases which give a description of the level of damages awarded for specific examples of injuries.

These can be criticised in the sense that there is nearly always a comparable to support an extreme submission on general damages at either end of the spectrum of general damages, but their application and its usefulness cannot be denied. While they are not binding on a Court, they are illuminative and nearly always appreciated by a Court. As a practice point, always remember to update the value of the award to the relevant index rate.

Live Witness Evidence and the general damages

A Court will also consider a Claimant's witness statement of course, and additionally any oral evidence in assessing quantum for general damages. In general, the presence of a Claimant providing live evidence will add to general damages for the simple reason that Judges do not like to tell injured people they are not worthy of an award that they ask for and argue for.

If the symptoms of the injury persist for longer than the period expected in the medical report, if this is dealt with in the witness statement, and the Claimant is available at trial to be challenged on the point, Courts do have the power and ability to extend the prognosis period contained within the medical report to reflect the symptoms reported by the Claimant to a conservative level, but do not expect a Court to ever stray significantly from the contents of a medical report.

There is a danger that a practitioner opens him or herself up to criticism in the form of questioning of the expert, namely why Part 35 CPR questions were put to the expert, or why the Claimant was not sent to different medical expert for a second opinion.

In a contested Court hearing the following are key points of concern for the Court, and therefore, in dealing with general damages in personal injury claims, they should also be yours. There is no harm, and a great deal of gain to be taken from ensuring that a Claimant is able to deal with the following points:

a. If the Claimant was not re-examined to be able to deal with why they were not re-examined.

b. If a Claimant did not complete a course of medical treatment to be able to explain why.

c. The age of a Claimant (more particularly where permanent symptoms, nuisance or otherwise are present, as this will depend on how long the Claimant must endure the symptoms).

d. Particular skills of the individual and the interference caused by the injury with hobbies and recreational activities.

e. Pre-existing disabilities of the Claimant. This factor is usually used by Defendants to limit damages available and if a Claimant can deal with this, then a Defendant's attempts will face problems.

f. In cases of interference with a holiday or a special event the Claimant must be realistic as to the impact this had.

Discrete sites of injuries

The most important and immediately effective manner in which a Claimant can greatly increase their general damages is to be able to argue for discrete awards for the injury suffered. This is relevant in case of physical and psychiatric injury. Where a Claimant has suffered with more than one injury, but there is an overlap between those injuries, there will always be a significant discount in the level of damages awarded.

It is not simply a case of adding all the relevant levels of quantum together by compensating the Claimant for the injury suffered globally. As a practise point it can be beneficial to assess each site of injury individually and then apply an overlap yourself to understand how a Court would approach the Claimant's case.

There is an exception to this point in cases where it is it arguable that the Claimant has suffered "discrete sites of injury" which did not overlap such as a whiplash injury to the neck, and a knee injury. If so, general damages should be, and generally will be calculated for each of the injuries sustained without discount, or no significant discount (**George v Stagecoach South East London & Kent Bus Co. Ltd** [2003] EWCH 2042[368]). This point is a little trickier in cases of psychiatric injury which, by their nature, may seem immediately intangible.

Pain, suffering and loss of amenity

It is also worthwhile to consider the below points. They will not apply to each and every case a practitioner sees but where they are relevant, they should be addressed.

[368] **George v Stagecoach South East London & Kent Bus Co. Ltd** [2003] EWCH 2042

CHAPTER NINETEEN

GENERAL DAMAGES

Psychiatric injuries in general

When dealing with the issue of general damages, Chapter 4 (A) JSC guidelines is the first port of call. The range is really quite broad, but in specific terms the following bands of injury are identified. The sums cited below include the **Hone v Castle** uplift.

In all cases, the Court will consider;

a. The injured person's ability to cope with life, education, and work;

b. The effect on the injured person's relationships with family, friends, and those with whom he or she comes into contact;

c. The extent to which treatment would be successful;

d. Future vulnerability;

e. Prognosis;

f. Whether medical help has been sought.

Severe cases

In these cases the injured Claimant will sadly have a very poor prognosis for recovery if any, and experience serious restrictions in work, their social life and in relationships.

The JSC guidelines place a bracket of £66,920 to £141,240 (applying the **Hone v Castle** uplift) on an injury falling into this bracket.

Moderately Severe cases

In these cases, there will be significant problems socially, at work and in relationships, but there will be some hope of real improvement. Cases involving psychiatric injury following a negligent stillbirth or the traumatic birth of a child will often fall within this bracket as will cases of work-related stress resulting in a permanent or long-standing disability preventing a return to comparable employment would appear to come within this category.

The JSC guidelines place a range of £23,270 to £66,920 (applying the **Hone v Castle** uplift) as applying to this type of injury.

Moderate cases

These type of injuries are the sort where, whilst there has been a persistent and impact on a Claimant's personal wellbeing, the symptoms are not as pronounced as in the previous cases, and there is a good prognosis, and a marked improvement by the time of trial. Cases of work-related stress may fall within this category if symptoms are not prolonged.

The guidelines set a range of £7,150 to £23,270 (applying the **Hone v Castle** uplift).

Less Severe cases

In less severe cases, the real divining line is the length and intensity of the symptoms. The JSC guidelines set a range of £1,880 to £7,150 (applying the **Hone v Castle** uplift) for general damages.

Post-traumatic stress disorder

Practitioners will want to consider firstly at chapter 4 (B) JSC guidelines.

The guidelines reinforce that Cases within this category are exclusively those where there is a specific diagnosis of a reactive psychiatric disorder following an event which creates psychological trauma in response to actual or threatened death, serious injury, or sexual violation. The symptoms may include nightmares, flashbacks, sleep disturbance, avoidance, mood disorders, suicidal ideation, and hyper-arousal. Symptoms of hyper-arousal can affect basic functions such as breathing, pulse rate, and bowel and/or bladder control.

Severe cases

In the most severe cases a Claimant who suffers from serious and deep reaching symptoms which prevent the injured person from working at all or at least from functioning at anything approaching the pre-trauma level with aspects of their life badly affected, then a range of general damages of £73,050 to £122,850 (applying the **Hone v Castle** uplift) is suggested by the Judicial college as being the range of quantum for general damages.

Moderately severe cases

In moderately severe cases, there will be a better prognosis with the hope of some recovery with professional help. However, the effects are still likely to cause significant disability for the foreseeable future. The guidelines are useful in that they identify a broad bracket of £28,250 to £73,050 but stipulates that the majority of awards are between £35,100 and £45,300. (applying the **Hone v Castle** uplift).

Moderate cases

In these cases the injured Claimant is going to have largely recovered and the effects which persist are not going to be grossly disabling. A range, again applying the **Hone v Castle** uplift of £9,980 to £28,250 is suggested by the guidelines for the range of an award for general damages for injuries which fall into this bracket.

Less severe

Where a Claimant has a less severe form of the illness, and there has been a full recovery within one to two years and only minor symptoms will persist over any longer period, then a range of quantum of £4,820 to £9,980 (applying the **Hone v Castle** uplift) is likely to be awarded.

Practice points

The Courts assessment and award of damages has always appeared in contrast to the injury itself insufficient to properly compensate a Claimant. Who, after all can place a value on their ability to socialise, work and interact with others?

Where value is genuinely added in psychiatric injury cases is in the head of special damages dealing with past and future losses. A Claimant after all who due to their reaction to a traumatic event cannot work or is restricted from working in the same field is just as disadvantaged as a person who has suffered an orthopaedic injury.

Other conditions

Whilst it is very rare in practice, it is possible for a psychiatric injury to cause, or advance pre-existing conditions such as Somatisation, chronic pain or create a situation whereby substance misuse develops with a Claimant.

<u>Somatisation disorders</u>

Somatisation disorders are sinister and highly limiting in certain cases, with their symptoms largely being biologically unexplainable pain and discomfort. Emotional stress is known to cause or advance somatisation disorders, and such an injury would, depending on its severity, such an injury may fall into <u>chapter 9 (B) JSC guidelines</u> (absent a diagnosis of complex regional pain syndrome) and potentially attract general damages as high as £76,870 (applying the **Hone v Castle** uplift).

<u>Chronic pain</u>

Chronic pain is in many ways self-descriptive, but is a crippling and restrictive injury. Chronic pain is often defined as any pain lasting more than 12 weeks. Whilst pain from an injury is a normal and relatable reaction, chronic pain is distinct. Chronic pain persists often for months or even longer after the resolution of the organic reason for the pain.

It is easy to see how a case involving chronic pain may well rapidly grow to substantial size due to the injured party's ability to work. Practitioners should look to <u>chapter 9 (A)</u> and know that awards for general damages could reach as high anywhere between £64,070 to £102,520 (applying the **Hone v Castle** uplift).

When considering the injury, and dealing with evidence, the guidelines themselves ask that the Court considers:

a. The degree of pain experienced.

b. The overall impact of the symptoms.

c. The effect of the condition on the injured person's ability to work.

d. Any medication to control symptoms of pain and the effect of such medication on the person's ability to function in normal daily life.

e. The level of treatment required.

f. The sites of the body in which pain is present.

Overlap between multiple injuries

Where there is more than one site of injury (physical and psychiatric) always be alive to the fact that the Court will apply overlap between the two. There is no hard and fast formula to be applied, and it is a measure of Judgment rather than art, but it is possible to argue that a Claimant's psychiatric injury will restrict them in discrete and distinct ways from physical injuries and therefore work to reduce any overload to a minimum.

The forward to the current JSC Guidelines covers this point very well and I repeat it here that "*The assessment of general damages in multiple injury cases can give rise to special difficulty, in particular in determining the extent to which there is any overlap between injuries and how this should be reflected in the award. An illustration of such difficulties, and guidance as to the approach to be taken, can be found in the Court of Appeal decision in* ***Sadler v Filipiak*** *[2011] EWCA Civ 1728. We can do no better than quote in full paragraph 34 of the judgment of Pitchford LJ in that case:*

'"It is in my judgment always necessary to stand back from the compilation of individual figures, whether assistance has been derived from comparable cases or from the [Judicial College] guideline advice, to consider whether the award for pain, suffering and loss of amenity should be greater than the sum of the parts in order properly to reflect the combined effect of all the injuries upon the injured person's recovering quality of life or, on the contrary, should be smaller than the sum of the parts in order to remove an element of double counting. In some cases, no doubt a minority, no adjustment will be necessary because the total will properly reflect the overall pain, suffering and loss of amenity endured. In others, and probably the majority, an adjustment and occasionally a significant adjustment may be necessary."'"

Expanding on the concept of general damages

It is also worthwhile to consider the below points. They will not apply to each and every case a practitioner sees but where they are relevant, they should be addressed.

Loss of congenial employment

There is no closed category of work for which such damages can be claimed and has been defined by Edmund Davies LJ **in Morris v Johnson Mathey** [1967] 112 Sol Jo 32[369] that as "*the joy of a craftsman in his craft was beyond price*" any case where a Claimant takes a genuine sense of accomplishment from his work, could be compensated. Such awards are

369 **Morris v Johnson Mathey** [1967] 112 Sol Jo 32

not common, and traditionally were reserved for the "*uniformed professions*" although there are cases where carpenters and chefs have received a similar award. A conventional award is one of between £2,500.00 and £5,000.00. Medical evidence will be required to identify the restrictions in work, but also witness evidence stressing the passion for, and fulfilment derived from a particular role.

In order to prove such a loss the following evidence as far as check list goes can assist:

a. Medical evidence as to limitation (part 35 CPR compliant)

b. Clear, cogent and persuasive witness evidence on the effect of any restrictions;

c. The standard of the worker's work. This can be shown through awards/certificates/training;

d. Length of service or the time committed to the trade.

e. Social standing and comradeship enjoyed through the profession.

f. The social value of the work carried out.

g. Whether there was an outdoor or enjoyable working environment which the Claimant has been deprived of.

Loss of leisure time

A Claimant may recover an award to reflect loss of leisure time caused by a need to work longer hours to earn the same income per Mustill J **Tindale v Dowsett Engineering Construction Ltd** [1981] C.L.Y. 598[370]. This can be a particularly complex calculation, but it is always

---

370 **Dowsett Engineering Construction Ltd** [1981] C.L.Y. 598

recommended that if an application for such an award is to be made then it must be supported by medical evidence.

Smith and Manchester Awards

Occasionally and in rather serious personal injury claims, a Claimant despite suffering injury may have been able to return to gainful employment either at the same rate of remuneration as at the date of the injury, or at a lower rate but while continuing to suffer from residual disability that they will carry for the rest of their life.

It is recognised that in such a case, if that employment were to end for any reason the Claimant would suffer a loss in the sense of being thrown onto the labour market and thereby in competition with other able-bodied persons for work. The current practice is to meet this loss with a lump sum award named after the decision in **Smith v Manchester Corporation** (1974) 17 K.I.R. 1 CA[371].

The factors usually taken into account in assessing the size of the award are the degree of residual disability and the risk of the Claimant being forced onto the labour market. A Court must bear in mind the risk of overlap between damages for future loss of earnings and damages for loss of earning capacity or handicap on the labour market.

The Claimant must demonstrate a substantial risk of being forced onto the labour market as opposed to a negligible risk. The starting point usually bears some relation to the Claimant's annual net earnings and quite often, a figure of between ½ – 5 years' salary is applied. Medical evidence will be required to expressly state that the Claimant is disadvantaged on the open labour market before such an award can be properly considered.

The most typical situation is that of the employee continuing to work after the injury for the same employer at the same rate of pay, as in **Smith**

---

371 **Smith v Manchester Corporation** (1974) 17 K.I.R. 1 CA

v **Manchester**[372]. In this matter the Claimant was a domestic worker in one of Manchester Corporation's old people's homes and the Corporation had undertaken to continue with her services at the same wage as long as they could properly do so, but there was "*a real risk*" that she would lose her job. There are, however, well recognised permutations of this concept.

What if there is a pay cut due to injury?

A Claimant at the date of trial may be working for the same employer at a lower wage, which was the position in **Nicholls v National Coal Board** [1976] I.C.R. 266 CA[373] where the pitman coal cutter had been kept on in a lighter job with his wages cut.

In these circumstances there will be a claim in respect of the reduced earnings as well as for the handicap in the labour market. Furthermore, in **Clarke v Rotax Aircraft** [1975] 1 W.L.R. 1570 CA[374] it was remarked that there was a need to avoid any overlap between the awards for loss of earnings and for loss of earning capacity. They are two very distinct claims and overlap will always result in significant under compensation.

What if the Claimant is self-employed?

However, what occurs where the Claimant is self-employed? Do the same principals still apply? In short, yes. In **Tait v Pearson** [1996] P.I.Q.R. Q92 CA[375] a Claimant, who was working at a new job on an oil rig, was even making more than before the injury, but the work was intermittent and was not work that the Claimant would be able to continue doing

372 **Smith v Manchester Corporation** (1974) 17 K.I.R. 1 CA

373 **Nicholls v National Coal Board** [1976] I.C.R. 266 CA

374 **Clarke v Rotax Aircraft** [1975] 1 W.L.R. 1570 CA

375 **Tait v Pearson** [1996] P.I.Q.R. Q92 CA

indefinitely, so the Claimant was found to be capable of advancing a Smith and Manchester claim.

What if the Claimant is unemployed?

Interestingly, and in stress claims, quite importantly, as set out in **Cook v Consolidated Fisheries** [1977] I.C.R. 635 CA[376] the Court of Appeal made it clear that the Claimant being in employment at trial was not a prerequisite of an award. In **Cook** a deckhand on a trawler decided that in the future he would drive lorries but was not driving at the time of the trial as he had not yet gained the necessary qualifications. He had a residual disability and in these circumstances, it was appropriate for a **Smith and Manchester**[377] award to be considered.

Assessment of such an award

The Courts have spoken of the problem of arriving at an appropriate figure on a number of instances when dealing with Smith and Manchester awards. Famously Auld L.J. referred in **Dhaliwal v Hunt** [1995] P.I.Q.R. Q56[378] to a remark of Megaw L.J. in an unreported case that the assessment of damages under this head usually involves "*nothing but a guess*" while in **Moeliker v Reyrolle & Co** [1977] 1 W.L.R. 132 CA[379] Browne L.J. said "*It is impossible to suggest any formula for solving the extremely difficult problems involved in … the assessment. A judge must look at all the factors which are relevant in a particular case and do the best he can.*"

However, in quite a number of cases the Court has taken a number of years of the Claimant's pre-injury earnings as the basis for the calculation. Thus in **Foster v Tyne and Wear County Council** [1986] 1 All E.R. 567

376 **Cook v Consolidated Fisheries** [1977] I.C.R. 635 CA

377 **Smith v Manchester Corporation** (1974) 17 K.I.R. 1 CA

378 **Dhaliwal v Hunt** [1995] P.I.Q.R. Q56

379 **Moeliker v Reyrolle & Co** [1977] 1 W.L.R. 132 CA

CA[380] the trial judge awarded five times the Claimant's annual salary, an award which was upheld by the Court of Appeal though said to be on the high side. Of some note, generally when this method has been used the number of years taken has been lower, even as low as half a year as in **Moeliker**[381].

In **Moeliker**[382] the Court of Appeal emphasised the need to show a substantial, rather than a negligible, risk of the Claimant being thrown on the labour market. This need has since been stressed again in **Frost v Palmer** [1993] P.I.Q.R. Q14 CA[383] and **Robson v Liverpool City Council** [1993] P.I.Q.R. Q78 CA[384] but that the requirement that there be a real risk of future unemployment is not to be interpreted too strictly is also evidenced by both of these cases.

Smith and Manchester award checklist

The following are always useful to consider when going about the task of evidence gathering with seeking to substantiate such a claim, and whilst not a complete checklist, it is hoped that this can help in practical terms;

a. There needs to be clear evidence (medical and lay) that the Claimant will, and does in fact suffer from a disadvantage on the open labour market that can be classed as causing the Claimant to be "*disadvantaged on the open market place*";

b. In gathering evidence to support this point it is recommended the following points are considered;

380 **Foster v Tyne and Wear County Council** [1986] 1 All E.R. 567 CA

381 **Moeliker v Reyrolle & Co** [1977] 1 W.L.R. 132 CA

382 **Moeliker v Reyrolle & Co** [1977] 1 W.L.R. 132 CA

383 **Frost v Palmer** [1993] P.I.Q.R. Q14 CA

384 **Robson v Liverpool City Council** [1993] P.I.Q.R. Q78 CA

   i. The nature and prospects of the Claimant's employers' business to establish the position was there, and that the Claimant may have had the opportunity of advancement;

   ii. Undertakings from the Claimant's employers as to Claimant's future employment with them;

   iii. The Claimant's qualifications and net salary at the date of injury;

   iv. The Claimant's length of service with his current employer;

   v. The Claimant's remaining years of working life through which his handicap will persist;

   vi. The effect of the Claimant's symptoms on his ability to work and to gain work;

c. There must be a substantial risk that at some point in the Claimant's future working life they will find themselves on the open labour market;

d. If so, the Claimant's disability must place him/her at a disadvantage in finding new employment;;

e. Apply the **Moeliker**[385] guidance in dealing with witness evidence, namely;

   i. The degree of risk that the Claimant will lose his current job before the end of his working life?

   ii. When that risk is likely to materialise?

[385] **Moeliker v Reyrolle & Co** [1977] 1 W.L.R. 132 CA

iii. How far the Claimant would be handicapped by his/her disability if thrown onto the open labour market – i.e. what are his chances of getting a similarly paid job?

The Courts have not laid down specific guidelines as to how to calculate such an award but it is rare for an award to be outside of 3 months – 3 years depending on the facts of a case. Awards of 2 – 3 years are not uncommon in cases of young Claimants facing significant disabilities. It really is a matter for judgment. However, as a starting point, there needs to be a real and powerful argument to consider pleading in excess of 3 years' loss of earnings by way of such an award. If there are good, and clear arguments on the issue, then the point can be pushed, but it is a point that can rapidly inflate a claim beyond a realistic value if applied in a cavalier fashion.

Blamire awards

A **Smith v Manchester**[386] award should not be confused with a **Blamire**[387] award, although in reality, they often are. A Blamire award (arising from the case of **Blamire v South Cumbria Health Authority** [1993] PIQR Q1[388] is appropriate where there is a continuing loss of earnings, but the evidence is too uncertain to approach the assessment thereof on a conventional multiplier/multiplicand basis, whereas a Smith v Manchester award is contingent future loss dependent on the Claimant losing his current employment and finding himself at a disadvantage in the labour market. Effectively, a **Blamire**[389] award should be seen as the even more "*rough and ready*" version of a Smith and Manchester award. The two may be combined but they are conceptually distinct.

386 **Smith v Manchester Corporation** (1974) 17 K.I.R. 1 CA

387 **Blamire v South Cumbria Health Authority** [1993] PIQR Q1

388 **Blamire v South Cumbria Health Authority** [1993] PIQR Q1

389 **Blamire v South Cumbria Health Authority** [1993] PIQR Q1

Ward v Allies [2012] EWCA Civ 1287

The Judgment of the Court of Appeal in **Ward v Allies and Morrison Architects** [2012] EWCA Civ 1287[390] provides a good example of how such awards work. In this matter the appellant was a graduate with a first-class honours degree in model making and she hoped to develop a career as a model maker in the performing arts. While on a work experience placement with the respondent firm of architects she was injured in an accident involving an unguarded circular saw. Her left (non-dominant) index finger was amputated and the middle finger was dislocated, although she made a considerable recovery.

She maintained her ambition to work in theatre but brought a claim for future loss of earnings on the basis that she would be hampered in her efforts because of the ongoing effects of her injury. The trial Judge heard evidence from the appellant and a former tutor of hers but concluded that he was unable to predict what the appellant's potential was: he did not have sufficient evidence as to what the appellant had lost or what she was likely to earn in the future. He was therefore "*driven*" to award loss of future earnings on the basis of the "*broad-brush*" Blamire principle rather than adopting the conventional multiplicand/multiplier approach, using the Ogden tables. The appellant had sought an award of £176,633.46 in compensation for her future loss of earnings. The judge awarded £30,000. The Court of Appeal upheld the trial Judges decision emphasising that for a Court to calculate future loss using a multiplier and multiplicand, a Claimant must establish a likely pattern of future earnings if s/he had not been injured and a likely pattern of future earnings given the fact of an injury. In **Ward**[391], the case presented to the trial Judge contained "*too many imponderables*" and he was, indeed,

[390] **Ward v Allies and Morrison Architects** [2012] EWCA Civ 1287

[391] **Ward v Allies and Morrison Architects** [2012] EWCA Civ 1287

"*driven*" to apply **Blamire**[392] and award a great deal less in compensation than the Ogden tables would have provided for.

Evidence to consider in cases of a Blamire award

Evidence to consider in the case of the Blamire awards realistically I wide, and broad, but the following points, if considered and evidenced, should provide the practitioner with the bulk of what they need to make out their claim:

a. Track record of earnings;

b. Is there an established/predictable career at all?

c. Frequent job changes?

d. Forensic financial history?

e. Cases where the Claimant was stressed/struggling pre-accident;

f. Medical history;

g. What is C's partner earning, or doing?

h. Plans to start a family, for mainly young ladies.

392 **Blamire v South Cumbria Health Authority** [1993] PIQR Q1

CHAPTER TWENTY

SPECIAL DAMAGES

Special damages are essentially any monetary losses that flow as a result of the injuries suffered by a Claimant.

Whilst the concepts of a **Smith and Manchester**[393] award and **Blamire**[394] award have been discussed in general damages, special damages are always set out by way of a schedule of loss. It is useful in any event to include these two separate heads of general damages in any schedule.

The concept of damages and the heads of loss are discussed at great length in other works and this guide is meant to give an overview of the types of heads of loss that can be considered. It is not intended to be conclusive, rather to provide guidance as a starting point when considering a claim for special damages. It is right to identify that texts focus in their entirety on this single issue.

Early evidence gathering

The simplest way to establish such claims is to ensure that all items lost, or on which monies were spent can be accounted for by way of evidence. The keeping or receipts for travel, medical expenses (including any treatment costs) and wage slips showing a loss of earnings need to be kept and collated.

A framework?

It may be helpful to set out a framework when approaching the issues of special damages. However each approach will be individual to any

393 **Smith v Manchester Corporation** (1974) 17 K.I.R. 1 CA

394 **Blamire v South Cumbria Health Authority** [1993] PIQR Q1

practice and developed over the course of their life. However, it may help as a starting potin to consider the following;

a. Firstly, identify what the injury stops a Claimant from doing and how this causes loss;

b. Secondly assess what assistance or treatment they can receive to mitigate this impact;

c. Thirdly, assess at what point in time in the future the Claimant's condition will reach a pre-accident level of plateau

d. Fourthly, assess how and where the Claimant's losses flow from up to this point of resolution or plateau, taking into account how and if improvement should be reflected;

e. Fifthly, assess how and the Claimant's losses flow from this point of resolution or plateau into the future;

f. Finally do not lose sight of the fact a schedule of loss should reflect where the Claimant would find themselves financially, but for their injury. It is compensatory and not designed to produce a windfall.

Past and future losses

It is also necessary to break down the claims into two separate areas;

a. Past loses (up to the date of anticipated trial); and

b. Future losses (after the date of anticipated trial).

When approaching schedules of future loss, future losses Practitioners are directed to the recent 8th edition of the Ogden tables and the helpful guidance there which will assist them in assessing what multipliers for what periods should be applied.

Loss of earnings

Loss of earnings are in nearly all cases arising from serious psychiatric injury often significant and one of the main sources of quantum when the claim is considered in the round.

When considering such claims, medical evidence will be required to identify that due to an injury a Claimant either cannot work, or cannot work at the same level as before. Once this is established the next question is will this be permanent, and if not, when and what improvement is likely.

Past loss of earnings in this context are straightforward. It is a case of establishing what losses flow up to the date of anticipated trial due to the psychiatric injury complained of. There is no reason for the Ogden tables to be applied to this period.

Calculations for future loss of earnings are a bit more complicated, and involve a certain amount of assumption and judgment, but also a proper application of the Ogden tables. With the change in the discount rate in the Ogden tables to -0.25 from the 15th July 2019, this is ever more important since a seriously psychiatrically injured individual who is unable to work due to their injuries, now can present a claim of significantly more value than before.

When one considers a claim for loss of earnings, there are two apparent methods which can be applied;

a. Full loss of earnings;

b. Loss of earning capacity

When considering a claim for a full loss of earnings, a practitioner will be dealing with a seriously injured Claimant. Medical evidence will required which supports that a return to paid employment will not be possible. Once this evidence is obtained the process is straightforward. The Ogden tables then applied to the period after the anticipated date of trial and a conclusion arrived at with appropriate discounts provided.

In cases where the where there is of significant loss of earnings or earning capacity, the question is more complex. For example, is the Claimant as a result of the accident disabled? Can they do any work? Are there specific areas of work to which their experience applied that are now closed to them? It is also practical to consider how the following factors (not definitive) interplay with the any loss of earning capacity;

a. The result of missing out on education, failing of exams etc;

b. The result of the delay in starting of employment and missing out on promotion;

c. The result of the likely restriction on the ability to be promoted due to an injury.

Expert evidence from a recruitment or employment consultant should be considered. After all, a Claimant must prove their case. However, issues of proportionality may well impact on this in many claims, but there will be claims (in excess of £200,000) where such evidence is warranted.

Pension claims

There are two types of pension;

a. Money purchase/defined contribution schemes; and

b. Final salary/defined benefits schemes.

Often in cases of significant psychiatric injury, a Claimant may well have on losing their employment lost their ability to pay into their pension, and in turn lost the benefit of its growth. The 8th edition Ogden tables are very helpful in addressing such calculations. However and practically, in cases where such a claim arises, practitioner are advised to consider obtaining an expert report from a pension expert.

In a case where a pension benefit is linked to promotion, and the Claimant had a reasonable expectation of promotion, such claims can quickly grow to be significant, and the failure to investigate them properly detrimental to a Claimant.

Future Loss of Chance

As has been stated above, where there are considerable uncertainties as to what the Claimant would have gone on to do but for the accident (for example where dealing with a teenager), it would appear that the loss of earnings claim will be akin to a loss of chance claim. However, in **Herring v MoD** [2004] 1 All ER 44[395] the Court of Appeal, impressed by a career model advanced at trial and adopted by the Trial Judge, held it to be neither necessary nor appropriate to adopt the "percentage chance" approach in respect of the possibility that the particular career path identified would not have been followed at all. A discount of 25% for contingencies by the trial Judge was reduced to 10%. Whilst such cases are always hard to pursue, they can be and often are meritorious in cases of serious injury and shouldn't be discounted in their entirety.

The past loss of a chance to pursue a business opportunity

This is a particularly complex point to pursue. Multiple aspects of evidence will be required to identify that this is no mere "loss of chance claim", but is always something to consider.

Treatment costs

One the most important aspects of a psychiatric injury claim is ensuring a Claimant receives treatment so that they may not only manage their recovery to the best possible outcome but also mitigate their loss. The costs of treatments, on the assumption that an expert approves the treatment will, subject to any arguments on cost, often be recoverable. It

395 **Herring v MoD** [2004] 1 All ER 44

is therefore advisable that invoices of all treatments are retained, and estimates for future costs secured.

In cases of psychiatric injury this will most commonly take the form of CBT or EMDR therapies. Where the Claimant suffers from somatisation for example, it is not uncommon to see treatment costs extending to pain management. Expert evidence on these points will guide and assist a practitioner.

It is also not unheard of for ill Claimants to seek to fund their own treatments by way of for example counselling. While there may well be arguments over its reasonableness and recoverability, the receipts and costs should always be retained.

Practically, Claimants can also approach Defendants at an early stage and seek an interim payment towards the costs of any such treatment which will in turn mitigate the Claimant's injuries in the future. Whilst such payments may well be made with no admission to liability, it is safe to say that psychologically, it can change the tone of any negotiations, once some monies have passed hands to assist the Claimant.

Care and assistance

Gratuitous care

In many medium and small value cases there is often the potential for a claim for compensation in respect of the care provided to the Claimant by family members or friends free of charge. In cases of more serious and pronounced injury, this Claimant may well need substantial care, and on occasion on a professional level.

It is now settled law that the Claimant is entitled to recover damages in respect of the fair and reasonable value of such care and domestic assistance (**Cunningham v Harrison** [1973] QB 942[396] and **Donnelly v**

[396] **Donnelly v Joyce** [1974] QB 454

Joyce [1974] QB 454[397]). Usually, the issues in dispute concern the number of hours and the hourly rates claimed in respect of gratuitous care. Many Defendants seek to rely on **Mills v British Rail engineering** [1992] PIQR Q130 to try and reduce damages recoverable in respect of gratuitous care.

However, the Court of Appeal in **Giambrone v Sunworld Holidays** [2004] 2 AER 891[398] rejected the proposition that **Mills v British Rail Engineering** [1992] PIQR Q130[399] was binding authority for the proposition that awards for gratuitous care were reserved for "*very serious cases*".

The cases of **Housecroft v Burnett** [1986] 1 AER 322[400] and **Evans v Pontypridd Roofing** [2002] PIQR Q5[401] assist in establishing this point and the latter establishing that the correct reduction on any amount of money paid is one of 25% to reflect the fact that the recipient would not have to pay tax or national insurance contributions on the monies received.

There are various recognised commercial care rates found in a number of sources, but of most assistance are practically those found in the annually published and already referred to Facts and Figures. In order to maximise the value of the claim for gratuitous care, the schedule of loss and any supporting witness statements (Claimant and carers) should set out clearly the type of care provided, when and by whom the care was provided and, if appropriate, the pre-accident norm to highlight the need for the care. A detailed list of the care and domestic tasks undertaken can be of great assistance (consider outlining a typical day or introducing

397 **Donnelly v Joyce** [1974] QB 454

398 **Giambrone v Sunworld Holidays** [2004] 2 AER 891

399 **Giambrone v Sunworld Holidays** [2004] 2 AER 891

400 **Giambrone v Sunworld Holidays** [2004] 2 AER 891

401 **Giambrone v Sunworld Holidays** [2004] 2 AER 891

diary or video evidence if available). Remember to stipulate increases in rates over time. Note that, where, by reason of his/her injuries, the Claimant has suffered a restriction upon their ability to care for a third party (such as a relative living in the same household) this loss of ability to care for a third party is a loss capable of recovery (see **Lowe v Guise** [2002] QB 1369[402]).

Hospital visits by family and friends, if they aid in recovery, can be recoverable as in **Owen v Brown** [2002] EWHC [2002] EWHC 1135 (QB)[403] in which Silber J allowed 12 hours of gratuitous care per day even though C was in hospital. There is of note, no discount for gratuitous care where no uplift for care provided during evenings, weekends and unsociable hours as per **Newman v Folkes** [2002] EWCA Civ 591[404]. Whilst this may make calculations hard, the fact of this is a strong bargaining tool.

Reasons for agency care

There are no clear-cut reasons as why care cannot be recovered from agency workers, if the care is required in order to give main carers a break. Furthermore, in cases of extreme injury, a Claimant who does not have any close family to assist them, the only option. There are additional arguments that can be made for care to be carried out in cases where pets or animals need to be cared for.

Arguments commonly raised by Defendants as to care

The following arguments are commonly raised by Defendants regarding care claims:

402 **Lowe v Guise** [2002] QB 1369

403 **Owen v Brown** [2002] EWHC [2002] EWHC 1135 (QB)

404 **Newman v Folkes** [2002] EWCA Civ 591

a. Gratuitous care must go "*distinctly beyond the ordinary regime of family life*" (**Evans v Pontypridd Roofing** [2001] EWCA Civ 1657[405]);

b. Was the carer in receipt of Carer's Allowance (**Dorrington v Lawrence** [2001] All ER (D) 145[406];

c. Would care have been required in any event?

d. The effect of old age, particularly with regard to the need for assistance with domestic chores;

e. Are the hours claimed appropriate?

f. Were the tasks claimed to have been undertaken in reality undertaken?

Past and future Travel expenses

A Claimant will almost certainly have some small expenses in this this head of loss from travelling to see their appointment medical expert, but it can soon rise if there are multiple visits to a distant treatment centre. Courts will generally award mileage at a rate of 0.45p a mile, or assess damages based on the production of taxi receipts, or public transport tickets.

Interest

Often overlooked or dealt with as an afterthought, the accurate calculation of interest is an effective way of increasing the level of damages in medium and small value claims.

---

405 **Evans v Pontypridd Roofing** [2001] EWCA Civ 1657

406 **Dorrington v Lawrence** [2001] All ER (D) 145

The power to award interest is set out in Section 35A of the Supreme Court Act 1981 in relation to the High Court and (of more relevance in lower value cases) section 69 of the County Courts Act 1984 in relation to the County Court. The power is discretionary and subject to the provisions of the CPR.

A claim for interest must be included in the Particulars of Claim (rule 16.4(1) (b) and (2) CPR)).

Interest on damages for pain, suffering and loss of amenities is awarded at 2% per annum from the date of service of the Claim Form to the date of trial (**Wells v Wells** [1999] 1 AC 345[407]).

The rate of continuing losses (such as loss of earnings or care costs, including gratuitous care attracts interest from the commencement of the period of loss (usually the date of the accident) to the date of trial at half the applicable Special Account Rate per annum (**Roberts v Johnstone** [1989] 1QB 878[408] and **Jefford v Gee** [1970] 2 QB 130[409]).

Single items of loss or expenditure (such as the purchase of special equipment) attract interest from the date of loss or expenditure to the date of trial/disposal at the whole applicable Special Account Rate(s) per annum. It is advisable to plead the facts relied upon when departing from the conventional approach and seeking interest at the full rate (**Dexter v Courtaulds Ltd** [19841 WLR 372[410]).

No interest is awarded in respect of future losses (**Clarke v Rotex Aircraft Equipment Ltd** [1975] 1 WLR 1570[411]).

---

407 **Wells v Wells** [1999] 1 AC 345

408 **Roberts v Johnstone** [1989] 1QB 878

Jefford v Gee [1970] 2 QB 130

410 **Dexter v Courtaulds Ltd** [19841 WLR 372

411 **Clarke v Rotex Aircraft Equipment Ltd** [1975] 1 WLR 1570

CHAPTER TWENTY-ONE

TRIAGE CHECKLIST

When first considering if a claim for psychiatric injury is capable of being pursued, let alone if it has a positive and reasonable prospect of success, it's very rare that any practitioner will have all the evidence they need to be able reach a final and conclusive opinion. After all, a claim can, and often will look very differently evidentially at trial, to how it first appears on initial investigation.

This checklist is intended to be a document which can be applied to any claim for psychiatric injury. It will then direct the practitioner to the relevant parts of this text.

A practical framework

Practically it is useful, if not necessary to approach such claims with a fairly rigid framework in place when initially assessing such claims. Practitioners need to be able to identify into which category of psychiatric injury claim it falls quickly, and with confidence. This will in turn enable a proportionate and focused evidence gathering and reviewed exercise to be undertaken, with the legal criteria required by each type of claim being broadly understood and set out.

Experience shows that it always far better that problems in claims are identified as quickly, and as efficiently as possible. Whilst this can result in intensive periods of work at the start of a claim, it almost always saves wasted effort and missteps in the future.

Whilst all practitioners will draw up and develop their own individual methods and mechanisms over time for establishing how they approach claims, it is suggested that the following framework can be applied, and is a good starting point;

Medical evidence

a. Firstly, in every case the Claimant must have suffered a recognised psychiatric disorder. Mere anger, grief or anxiety is not enough;

   i. Has the Claimant suffered physical or psychiatric injury? If so, what? Where no injury has been caused or is alleged to have been caused there is no claim;

   ii. If available, does a part 35 CPR compliant medical report identify that the symptoms of which the Claimant complains are capable of classification as a recognisable psychiatric disorder?

   iii. If not, have questions been raised of the expert to clarify any issues in the report?

   iv. If not available, do the Claimant's medical records evidence and support that the events complained of, have caused a recognisable psychiatric injury?

   v. If not available, is there any other evidence to support the allegation that the Claimant has suffered a recognisable psychiatric reaction as result of a breach;

   vi. What symptoms does the Claimant describe experiencing and how do they intersect with the diagnostic frameworks of DMS-5 and ICD-11?

The type of Claimant

b. Is the Claimant a primary or secondary victim (where they placed in physical danger due to any act of negligence). This will determine how the law applies to the facts of the case.

The risk of physical harm

c. Where such an act takes place which carries with it the risk of physical injury to the Claimant, they may be classed as a primary victim, and can recover damages for psychiatric injury, if the act or omission causes him psychiatric injury, even if the infliction of psychiatric injury wasn't reasonably foreseeable (**Page v Smith** [1996] A.C. 155). Consider;

Rescuers

d. In cases of rescuers (Claimants expose themselves to danger in an objective sense, or reasonably believe that they have exposed themselves to danger when seeking to protect others), they can recover damages whether the psychiatric injury is caused by fear for their own safety or horror at what they see and experience (**Frost v Chief Constable of South Yorkshire Police** [1999] 2 AC 455);

Involuntary participants

e. Where a negligent act or omission of the Defendant has put a Claimant in the position of being, or thinking that he is about to be, or has been, the involuntary cause of another's death or injury, and psychiatric injury flows from the shock of this to the Claimant, the Claimant can recover damages;

Secondary victims

f. Claimants who suffer psychiatric injury as a result of witnessing death or injury of another, or who perceive the risk of death or injury to another can claim damages as secondary victims, but only if they satisfy the **Alcock** control mechanisms (**Alcock v Chief Constable of South Yorkshire Police** [1992] 1 A.C. 310).

Occupational stress

g. In occupational stress claims, first decide if the psychiatric injury has been caused by exposure to stress or nervous shock? If it's the later, refer to primary and secondary victims. If it is stress realted, **Hatton v Sutherland** [2002] EWCA Civ 76).

The duty

h. What duty is said to the owed to the Claimant by the Defendant?

    i. Is it an employer and employee relationship, or something distinct?

    ii. If so, what can it be said to extend to?

    iii. How does this duty relate to what has caused them to become unwell?

    iv. What evidence is there available to evidence the existence of this duty?

Breach of duty and causation

i. Can the Claimant evidence that their psychiatric injury has been caused by an actionable wrong;

    i. What is the nature of the act complained of and what sources of evidence are there available?

    ii. Does it fall into one of the exceptions that are non-actionable for reason of public policy?

    iii. What other are owed by the Defendant to the Claimant?

    iv. What has actually, when the evidence is really interrogated, show caused the Claimant to develop an injury?

MORE BOOKS BY LAW BRIEF PUBLISHING

A selection of our other titles available now:-

'A Practical Guide to Probation Breaches and Other Applications' by Mark Thomas
'A Practical Guide to Remarriage and Divorce' by Cordelia Williams & Claire Howard
'A Practical Guide to Privacy, Transparency, Reporting Restrictions and Closed Proceedings in the Court of Protection' by Laura Mannering
'Beaumont on Barristers – A Guide to Defending Disciplinary Proceedings (Second Edition)' by Marc Beaumont
'A Practical Guide to Payments for Environmental Services' by Ben Sharples
'A Practical Guide to the Law of Pregnancy and Maternity at Work' by Rebecca Thomas
'A Practical Guide to Redundancy – Second Edition' by Philip Hyland & Collette Moore
'A Practical Guide to International Issues for Scottish Family Lawyers' by Susie Mountain, Donna McKay, Ken MacDonald
'A Practical Guide to the Law on Deprivation of Liberty' by Ben Troke
'A Practical Guide to Rights over Airspace and Subsoil – Second Edition' by Daniel Gatty
'A Practical Guide to the Law in Relation to Inquests' by Ramya Nagesh
'A Practical Guide to the Construction and Rectification of Wills and Trust Instruments (Second Edition)' by Edward Hewitt
'A Practical Guide to Data Protection in Social Housing' by Clare Paterson
'A Practical Guide to Spousal Maintenance – Second Edition' by Liz Cowell
'A Practical Guide to International Parental Child Abduction Law (England and Wales)' by Dr Onyója Momoh
'A Practical Guide to Deprivation of British Citizenship' by Sean Ell
'A Practical Guide to Commercial Property Service Charges' by Rachel Garton
'A Practical Guide to Clinical Negligence – Third Edition' by Geoffrey Simpson-Scott (Geoff)
'A Practical Guide to the Rights of Grandparents in Children Proceedings – Second Edition' by Stuart Barlow

'The Electronic Communications Code: A Practical Guide – Second Edition' by Kerry Bretherton KC, James Castle, Mark Loveday
'A Practical Guide to the Independent School Standards – September 2023 Edition' by Sarah McKimm
'A Practical Guide to Estate Administration and Crypto Assets' by Richard Marshall
'A Practical Guide to Parental Alienation in Private and Public Law Children Cases' by Sam King QC & Frankie Shama
'Contested Heritage – Removing Art from Land and Historic Buildings' by Richard Harwood QC, Catherine Dobson, David Sawtell
'The Limits of Separate Legal Personality: When Those Running a Company Can Be Held Personally Liable for Losses Caused to Third Parties Outside of the Company' by Dr Mike Wilkinson
'A Practical Guide to Transgender Law' by Robin Moira White & Nicola Newbegin
'A Practical Guide to 'Stranded Spouses' in Family Law' by Mani Singh Basi
'A Practical Guide to Residential Freehold Conveyancing' by Lorraine Richardson
'A Practical Guide to Pensions on Divorce for Lawyers' by Bryan Scant
'A Practical Guide to Challenging Sham Marriage Allegations in Immigration Law' by Priya Solanki
'A Practical Guide to Digital Communications Evidence in Criminal Law' by Sam Willis
'A Practical Guide to Legal Rights in Scotland' by Sarah-Jane Macdonald
'A Practical Guide to New Build Conveyancing' by Paul Sams & Rebecca East
'A Practical Guide to Inherited Wealth on Divorce' by Hayley Trim
'A Practical Guide to Practice Direction 12J and Domestic Abuse in Private Law Children Proceedings' by Rebecca Cross & Malvika Jaganmohan
'A Practical Guide to Confiscation and Restraint' by Narita Bahra QC, John Carl Townsend, David Winch
'A Practical Guide to the Law of Forests in Scotland' by Philip Buchan
'A Practical Guide to Health and Medical Cases in Immigration Law' by Rebecca Chapman & Miranda Butler
'A Practical Guide to Bad Character Evidence for Criminal Practitioners by Aparna Rao
'A Practical Guide to Extradition Law post-Brexit' by Myles Grandison et al
'A Practical Guide to Hoarding and Mental Health for Housing Lawyers' by Rachel Coyle

'Stephens on Contractual Indemnities' by Richard Stephens
'A Practical Guide to the EU Succession Regulation' by Richard Frimston
'A Practical Guide to Solicitor and Client Costs – Second Edition' by Robin Dunne
'Constructive Dismissal – Practice Pointers and Principles' by Benjimin Burgher
'A Practical Guide to Religion and Belief Discrimination Claims in the Workplace' by Kashif Ali
'A Practical Guide to the Law of Medical Treatment Decisions' by Ben Troke
'Fundamental Dishonesty and QOCS in Personal Injury Proceedings: Law and Practice' by Jake Rowley
'A Practical Guide to the Law in Relation to School Exclusions' by Charlotte Hadfield & Alice de Coverley
'A Practical Guide to Divorce for the Silver Separators' by Karin Walker
'The Right to be Forgotten – The Law and Practical Issues' by Melissa Stock
'A Practical Guide to Planning Law and Rights of Way in National Parks, the Broads and AONBs' by James Maurici QC, James Neill et al
'A Practical Guide to Election Law' by Tom Tabori
'A Practical Guide to the Law in Relation to Surrogacy' by Andrew Powell
'A Practical Guide to Claims Arising from Fatal Accidents – Second Edition' by James Patience
'A Practical Guide to Asbestos Claims' by Jonathan Owen & Gareth McAloon
'A Practical Guide to Stamp Duty Land Tax in England and Northern Ireland' by Suzanne O'Hara
'A Practical Guide to the Law of Farming Partnerships' by Philip Whitcomb
'A Practical Guide to the Law of Unlawful Eviction and Harassment – Second Edition' by Stephanie Lovegrove
'A Practical Guide to Costs in Personal Injury Claims – Second Edition' by Matthew Hoe
'A Practical Guide to the General Data Protection Regulation (GDPR) – Second Edition' by Keith Markham
'A Practical Guide to Working with Litigants in Person and McKenzie Friends in Family Cases' by Stuart Barlow
'Protecting Unregistered Brands: A Practical Guide to the Law of Passing Off' by Lorna Brazell
'A Practical Guide to Secondary Liability and Joint Enterprise Post-Jogee' by Joanne Cecil & James Mehigan

'A Practical Guide to the Pre-Action RTA Claims Protocol for Personal Injury Lawyers' by Antonia Ford

'A Practical Guide to Neighbour Disputes and the Law' by Alexander Walsh

'A Practical Guide to Coercive Control for Legal Practitioners and Victims' by Rachel Horman

'A Practical Guide to the Law of Driverless Cars – Second Edition'

by Alex Glassbrook, Emma Northey & Scarlett Milligan

'A Practical Guide to TOLATA Claims' by Greg Williams

'A Practical Guide to Elderly Law – Second Edition' by Justin Patten

'A Practical Guide to Responding to Housing Disrepair and Unfitness Claims' by Iain Wightwick

'A Practical Guide to the Law of Bullying and Harassment in the Workplace' by Philip Hyland

'How to Be a Freelance Solicitor: A Practical Guide to the SRA-Regulated Freelance Solicitor Model' by Paul Bennett

'A Practical Guide to Prison Injury Claims' by Malcolm Johnson

'A Practical Guide to Advising Clients at the Police Station' by Colin Stephen McKeown-Beaumont

'A Practical Guide to Antisocial Behaviour Injunctions – Second Edition' by Iain Wightwick

'Practical Mediation: A Guide for Mediators, Advocates, Advisers, Lawyers, and Students in Civil, Commercial, Business, Property, Workplace, and Employment Cases' by Jonathan Dingle with John Sephton

'The Mini-Pupillage Workbook' by David Boyle

'A Practical Guide to Crofting Law' by Brian Inkster

'A Practical Guide to the Law of Domain Names and Cybersquatting' by Andrew Clemson

'A Practical Guide to the Law of Gender Pay Gap Reporting' by Harini Iyengar

'NHS Whistleblowing and the Law' by Joseph England

'Employment Law and the Gig Economy' by Nigel Mackay & Annie Powell

'A Practical Guide to Noise Induced Hearing Loss (NIHL) Claims' by Andrew Mckie, Ian Skeate, Gareth McAloon

'An Introduction to Beauty Negligence Claims – A Practical Guide for the Personal Injury Practitioner' by Greg Almond

'Intercompany Agreements for Transfer Pricing Compliance' by Paul Sutton

'Zen and the Art of Mediation' by Martin Plowman

'A Practical Guide to Adoption for Family Lawyers' by Graham Pegg

www.ingramcontent.com/pod-product-compliance
Lightning Source LLC
LaVergne TN
LVHW052241200926
848481LV00002B/237